Growing All the Wiser

Growing All the Wiser

Wisdom Tips from the Book of Proverbs

Kyna Williams

Cover Design by Allison Cox

Elm Hill
A Division of
HarperCollins Christian Publishing
www.elmhillbooks.com

Growing All the Wiser
Wisdom Tips from the Book of Proverbs

Published in Nashville, Tennessee, by Elm Hill, an imprint of Thomas Nelson. Elm Hill and Thomas Nelson are registered trademarks of HarperCollins Christian Publishing, Inc.

Elm Hill titles may be purchased in bulk for educational, business, fund-raising, or sales promotional use. For information, please e-mail SpecialMarkets@ThomasNelson.com.

Library of Congress Cataloging-in-Publication Data

Library of Congress Control Number: 2019909403

ISBN 978-1-400326525 (Paperback)
ISBN 978-1-400326532 (eBook)

This book is dedicated to my father, Richarter Tolliver Jackson. The wisdom you expressed both in word and in deed has carried me throughout my life. To my children, Iman, Jayda, and Robert, may these written words guide you on your journey in becoming all that God has called you to be.

Table of Contents

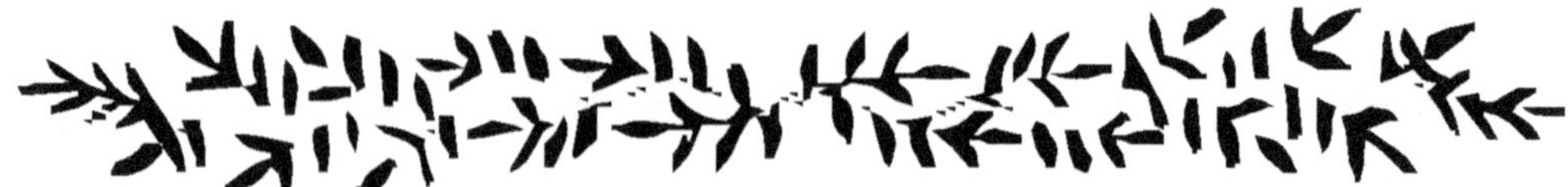

Introduction

> "Listen carefully to my wisdom; take to heart what I can teach you. You'll treasure its sweetness deep within; you'll give it bold expression in your speech. To make sure your foundation is trust in God, I'm laying it all out right now just for you. I'm giving you thirty sterling principles—tested guidelines to live by. Believe me—these are truths that work, and will keep you accountable to those who sent you."
>
> Proverbs 22:17–21 (THE MESSAGE)

It has been said that experience is the best teacher. I submit to you a new notion—wisdom is the best teacher. Accepting this new idea of "wisdom" as a teacher may require a bit of a paradigm shift. When wisdom is applied to your daily repertoire of decision-making and choice selection, you will experience the results of wisdom, not just for the moment but for the long haul. Selah, pause and think about that. Would you rather gain experience or gain the wisdom necessary to guarantee the result of your experience? If you intend to master money, then there is wisdom to instruct you on how to properly become a money master. If you intend to master relationships, then there is wisdom to instruct you on how to properly master your relationships. If you intend to master your health, again, wisdom exists to guide you on that journey as well. Regardless of the subject, wisdom is available to guide your daily decisions and choices toward the guaranteed experience that only comes when you apply wisdom to that area of your life. Making room in your life for the time-tested insights dispensed by wisdom will bring about the positive experiences you are desperately pursuing. I use the adjective desperate because many of you have made decisions that are directly opposed to your authentic self, and have not remained true to who you are and who you were created to be in an effort to arrive at a certain outcome. Was it really worth it? Your pursuit of wisdom, when applied, will change the tide of uncertainity and failure that plagues your mind, your actions, and the areas of your life vexed by foolish choices. Wisdom will set you on a course of life-long success. This book is meant to be a quick reference guide, not a substitute of your personal pursuit of wisdom. I have come to know that the greatest source of wisdom is the creator of wisdom, God Almighty, and my prayer is that you will come to experience and know Him as well.

What does wisdom consist of?

It is clearly communicated in the book of Proverbs that when wisdom enters your heart, she will bring companions of discretion and understanding with her (Proverbs 2:10–11).

> **"When wisdom enters your heart and knowledge is pleasant to your soul, Discretion will preserve you; Understanding will keep you. (NKJV)**
>
> **"Wisdom will control your mind, and you will be pleased with knowledge. Sound judgment and good sense will watch over you." (CEV)**

Wisdom is comprised of three main ingredients:

1. **The knowledge to discern.**
2. **Skill to judge: The ability to make keen decisions.**
3. **Activity to prosecute**

Knowledge to discern – Merriam Webster's dictionary defines discern as "to detect with the eyes" or "with the senses other than vision," to be able to recognize or identify.

How many times have you said to yourself, "If I knew then what I know now, I would have made a different choice" or "I would have acted differently." How about the popular phrases, "hindsight is 20/20" or "Monday morning quarterback"? A component of wisdom is the "knowledge to discern," the knowledge to see past what meets the human eye, the knowledge to detect or sense things that are not spoken or seen in order to arrive at the best course of action.

Skill to judge – Possessing the skill to judge is simply having the ability to make keen decisions. Wisdom gives you the discernment required to recognize, identify, and detect all the vital elements necessary to arrive at the best course of action.

Activity to prosecute – The basic definition of activity involves movement as derived from its root word, "act." The "activity to prosecute," or the "act" required to prosecute, is key to demonstrating a connection with wisdom. Prosecute in this context is defined as the ability to "participate in or pursue something to completion." Prosecute originates from the Latin word "*prosesutus*," meaning "follow after." Therefore, wisdom gives you the action steps required to see a desired outcome successfully completed.

Bringing all three components of wisdom together, we can best define wisdom as the ability to recognize, identify, and detect all the vital elements required to arrive at a decision that guides the action steps required to see a desired outcome successfully completed.

We can have a desired outcome for finances, for relationships, for career paths or business pursuits, for child rearing, or simply a desired outcome to tame an unruly mouth. According to our new definition, the pursuit of wisdom is the right place to start in order to see those desired outcomes as a completed work in our daily lives.

Now that we have a good definition of wisdom, let's explore the life of a person who pursued wisdom and received extraordinary results. His name is King Solomon and outside of Jesus Christ, he is said to be the wisest man to ever live. 2 Chronicles 1:7–12 (THE MESSAGE) conveys Solomon's first act of wisdom that set in motion a life characterized by an abundance of wisdom.

That night God appeared to Solomon. God said, "What do you want from me? Ask." Solomon answered, "You were extravagantly generous with David my father, and now you have made me king in his place. Establish, GOD, the words you spoke to my father, for you've given me a staggering task, ruling this mob of people. Yes, give me wisdom and knowledge as I come and go among this people—for who on his own is capable of leading these, your glorious people?" God answered Solomon, "This is what has come out of your heart: You didn't grasp for money, wealth, fame, and the doom of your enemies; you didn't even ask for a long life. You asked for wisdom and knowledge so you could govern well my people over whom I've made you king. Because of this, you get what you asked for—wisdom and knowledge. And I'm presenting you the rest as a bonus—money, wealth, and fame beyond anything the kings before or after you had or will have."

Solomon's first act of wisdom was to ask the Giver of Wisdom for wisdom. It is important to note that Solomon did not seek wisdom just for the sake of being known as a wise man, or a wise king. Solomon asked for wisdom and knowledge to fulfill the will of God for his life and the lives of God's people whom Solomon had been given the great task of leading.

King David, Solomon's father, wrote in Psalm 111:10 (NIV), "the fear of the LORD is the beginning of wisdom." Solomon later repeated this phrase in Proverbs 1:7, which identifies that Solomon had been taught by his father, David, to first and foremost reverence and seek after God; thus, the explanation for his initial prayer to God for wisdom.

It is also important to note that wisdom can be copied and wisdom can be mimicked, but true wisdom can only be found in those who have first reverenced the Giver of Wisdom, the Lord God Almighty. Solomon went on to say in Proverbs 1:7 (NIV) that "fools despise wisdom and instruction." Before we embark on the journey of discovering the wisdom tips outlined in the book of Proverbs, think back to all the times you have been a fool, done something foolish, or been made a fool of. Well, let's downscale that request to one particular occurrence, maybe even a recent occurrence. Did anyone in your life attempt to forewarn you? The majority of you will answer yes. Those individuals acted as "voices" of wisdom, but they are not the source of wisdom.

The ultimate goal is to get to know He who is the source of wisdom. Wisdom's principles can be applied with some success, but the power behind wisdom and the reality of a rock-solid life as a result of wisdom is not possible without "the fear of the Lord."

Let's further examine what transpired in Solomon's life as a result of his pursuit of wisdom.

> **God gave Solomon wisdom—the deepest of understanding and the largest of hearts. There was nothing beyond him, nothing he couldn't handle. Solomon's wisdom outclassed the vaunted wisdom of wise men of the East, outshone the famous wisdom of Egypt. He was wiser than anyone—wiser than Ethan the Ezrahite, wiser than Heman, wiser than Calcol and Darda the sons of Mahol. He became famous among all the surrounding nations. He created 3,000 proverbs; his songs added up to 1,005. He knew all about plants, from the huge cedar that grows in Lebanon to the tiny hyssop that grows in the cracks of a wall. He understood everything about animals and birds, reptiles and fish. Sent by kings from all over the earth who had heard of his reputation, people came from far and near to listen to the wisdom of Solomon.**
>
> **1 Kings 4:29–34 (THE MESSAGE)**

Solomon understood that wisdom is the source of all other acquisitions in life. The result of Solomon's wisdom was the composure of over 3,000 proverbs, let's just say he wrote 3,000 books and 1,005 songs. Although substantial, the intellectual property that resulted from Solomon's wisdom is not the sole result. The book of First Kings goes on to tell us that Solomon was also an authority on plants, animals, and fish, sounds like he held a doctoral degree in study of science. Additionally, Solomon became famous throughout the world. So much so, that other nations sent their leaders and ambassadors to work as interns under Solomon's tutelage. Solomon literally became a consultant to the nations. One of Solomon's most renowned consulting sessions was with the Queen of Sheba as recounted in 1 Kings 10:1–10 (THE MESSAGE):

> **The queen of Sheba heard about Solomon and his connection with the Name of God. She came to put his reputation to the test by asking tough questions. She made a grand and showy entrance into Jerusalem—camels loaded with spices, a huge amount of gold, and precious gems. She came to Solomon and**

talked about all the things that she cared about, emptying her heart to him. Solomon answered everything she put to him—nothing stumped him. When the queen of Sheba experienced for herself Solomon's wisdom and saw with her own eyes the palace he had built, the meals that were served, the impressive array of court officials and sharply dressed waiters, the lavish crystal, and the elaborate worship extravagant with Whole-Burnt-Offerings at the steps leading up to The Temple of God, it took her breath away. She said to the king, "It's all true! Your reputation for accomplishment and wisdom that reached all the way to my country is confirmed. I wouldn't have believed it if I hadn't seen it for myself; they didn't exaggerate! Such wisdom and elegance—far more than I could ever have imagined. Lucky the men and women who work for you, getting to be around you every day and hear your wise words firsthand! And blessed be God, your God, who took such a liking to you and made you king. Clearly, God's love for Israel is behind this, making you king to keep a just order and nurture a God-pleasing people." She then gave the king four and a half tons of gold, and also sack after sack of spices and expensive gems. There hasn't been a cargo of spices like that since that shipload the queen of Sheba brought to King Solomon.

Later in Solomon's life, he was esteemed with one of the greatest titles reserved only for the wisest elders in Judaism, "Teacher." The significance of the title "Teacher" is shown by order of its mention in Ecclesiastes 1:1 (NIV), "The words of the Teacher, a son of David, king in Jerusalem." The verse does not read the words of the king of Jerusalem, a son of David, the Teacher. The order of mention is, (1) the Teacher, (2) son of David, (3) king of Jerusalem, identifying the order of prominence or importance. In comparison, the honorable title of "Teacher" can be found on many occasions in reference to Jesus Christ. Solomon, the Teacher, shared great insights into the application of wisdom as he explained the unchanging nature of wisdom and its ability to be applied over the ages and throughout generations in order to achieve the same results of those who applied wisdom to their lives in times before. "What has been will be again, what has been done will be done again; there is nothing new under the sun. Is there anything of which one can say, 'Look! This is something new'? It was here already, long ago; it was here before our time" (Ecclesiastes 1: 9–11). Wisdom recycles itself and its' truths carry weight from one generation to the next.

Together, we will explore the wisdom bequeath by King Solomon in the Book of Proverbs. I had you, the reader, in mind when I was given the assignment of writing *Wisdom Tips* based on historically accurate and time-consistent words given by King Solomon that have the power to assist the lives of the young and old, foolish and wise, the underserved, and the privileged. Regardless of how you define yourself or what social standing you currently find yourself in, the proverbial wisdom dissected into wisdom tips in this book will provide you with immediate access to practical, yet relevant, biblical wisdom principles that can be readily applied to your life. These wisdom tips, if heeded, will transform you mindset, enhance your decision making and assist you along your personal path of growing all the wiser. You will soon find that wisdom in one area of life spills over to wisdom in other areas until, little by little, your life begins to reflect a compilation of victorious outcomes.

The Book of Proverbs begins by declaring loud and clear its purpose, "The proverbs of Solomon son of David, king of Israel: for gaining wisdom and instruction; for understanding words of insight; for receiving instruction in prudent behavior, doing what is right and just and fair" (Proverbs 1:1–3 NIV). I love that from the onset, the reader knows exactly what to expect from its contents. Proverbs also makes it resoundingly clear that this book of wisdom is for all people; it disregards age, gender, educational pedigree, and social status by stating, "for giving prudence to those who are simple, knowledge and discretion to the young—let the wise listen and add to their learning, and let the discerning get guidance" (Proverbs 1:4–6 NIV). In other words, no matter who you are and what status you currently find yourself in, prudent or simple, young or old, a seeker of knowledge or a tumbler of uncertainty, Proverbs has something for Y-O-U.

Proverbs goes on to give a simple disclaimer, "The fear of the LORD is the beginning of knowledge" (Proverbs 1:7 NIV). Before I go any further, before I divulge of the secrets to wisdom's success in life, there is one truth you must first understand. All of this information will profit your life, because the principles can be applied by anyone and will yield a measure of success, but the fullness of life cannot be found without knowing that the source of all knowledge is the Lord. James 1:5 (NIV) states, "If any of you lacks wisdom, you should ask God, who gives generously to all without finding fault, and it will be given to you." James gives us a breakdown of what wisdom steeped in truth looks like, "But the wisdom that comes from heaven is first of all pure; then peace-loving, considerate, submissive, full of mercy and good fruit, impartial and sincere" (James 3:17 NIV). Heavenly wisdom will be shown in your actions, heavenly wisdom is not just a matter of highly intelligent thoughts that are flaunted by adding titles to your signature block. James also tells us that those who have wisdom and understanding from God—true wisdom—will show forth this gift of wisdom by deeds done (action) in the humility that comes from wisdom.

While you are amongst the group of individuals who have pursued wisdom for living, it may surprise you that there is another group of individuals who have no desire to obtain and apply wisdom to their way of living. Solomon goes on to explain that the other group of individuals who will not benefit from proverbial wisdom are the "fools," those who no matter how you try to relay truth and wise instruction will shun and disregard, or in Solomon's words, "despise wisdom and instruction." This category of people will not receive wisdom or its tried and proven principles, so simply don't waste your time rattling off all the wisdom tips you will receive. This book has found its way into your life because you are amongst those who understand that you are in continual need of the wisdom required to arrive at a new playing field with new outcomes. Proverbs 3:13–18 (THE MESSAGE) best describes the rewards of adding wisdom to your portfolio:

You're blessed when you meet Lady Wisdom, when you make friends with Madame Insight. She's worth far more than money in the bank; her friendship is better than a big salary. Her value exceeds all the trappings of wealth; nothing you could wish for holds a candle to her. With one hand she gives long life, with the other she confers recognition. Her manner is beautiful, her life wonderfully complete. She's the very Tree of Life to those who embrace her. Hold her tight—and be blessed!

Growing All the Wiser

WISDOM TIP 1

Start strong by heeding the instructions of your elders.

> "Pay close attention, friend, to what your father tells you; never forget what you learned at your mother's knee."
>
> PROVERBS 1:8 (THE MESSAGE)

> "My child, listen when your father corrects you. Don't neglect your mother's instruction."
>
> PROVERBS 1:8 (NLT)

I'm a forty-ish mother of three, as such, when I say the word "child," I'm referring not just to the children I bore into the world, but any young person who comes to me for instruction or advice. Likewise, don't be thrown off by the word "child" in this wisdom tip. We are all children in one way or the other. When I go to an elder for advice in my forties, I'm still a child to a seventy-year-old. Here, the greater truth is that the course of your life is determined by your ability to humble yourself to heed the wise instruction of someone who has already been there and done that many times over. If you are blessed to have law-abiding, God-fearing parents, then do yourself a favor and listen to them. That includes all the little quirky sayings of your mother. If your wise counsel comes through a mentor or life coach, then heed their instructions. You will discover that old sayings often referred to as "wise tales" or "old wives' tales" have a staple of truth hidden behind the old-fashioned dialogue that translates across generational timelines. The wisdom of the Bible is an example of truth that never gets old and never changes. God's Word and the wisdom contained therein is TRUTH yesterday, today, and forever!

Reference:

Proverbs 4:1, 6:20, 23:22; Ephesians 6:1

WISDOM TIP 2

"Run" with the wrong crowd and you'll end up on a "dead-end" road.

> "Dear friend, if bad companions tempt you, don't go along with them. If they say— "Let's go out and raise some hell. Let's beat up some old man, mug some old woman. Let's pick them clean and get them ready for their funerals. We'll load up on top-quality loot. We'll haul it home by the truckload. Join us for the time of your life! With us, it's share and share alike!"—Oh, friend, don't give them a second look; don't listen to them for a minute. They're racing to a very bad end."
>
> Proverbs 1:10–16 (THE MESSAGE)

How many times have you been warned to stay away from a particular person because your mother, father, wise aunt or uncle, older sibling, or someone you trust and respect sensed that the person or group of people were up to no good? The old King James translation uses the word "sinners," meaning those who miss the mark or err habitually, knowingly, willfully, and maliciously. They are not content with doing their dirt on their own terms. In fact, those who belong to this group of individuals are happiest when they can persuade others to follow their example. Why? Because misery loves company. In this passage, Solomon is giving that same word of instruction to the readers of Proverbs. Stay away from bad characters, those who are enticing you toward the wrong path. The wrong path is not merely found in the most obvious behaviors such as criminal activity or drug abuse, but in many less obvious forms as well. The wrong path for you may be the friend who entices you to view pornography, participate in sexting or to cheat on your spouse because "everybody is doing it." For some, the bad companion may be the one who entices you to cheat on your taxes or hold hour-long gossip sessions. Whatever your personal vice may be, those who entice you to indulge in that vice should be avoided at all costs. As one translation of this passage states, "do not set foot on their paths" (NIV), "don't give them a second look, don't listen to them for a minute. They're racing to a very bad end."

Reference:

Proverbs 16:29, 13:20; Psalm 1:1, 119:101; Proverbs 4:14, 4:27, 24:1; Ephesians 5:11

WISDOM TIP 3

The "G-R-E-E-D" Eyed monster will destroy you.

"If a bird sees a trap being set, it knows to stay away. But these people set an ambush for themselves; they are trying to get themselves killed. Such is the fate of all who are greedy for money; it robs them of life."

PROVERBS 1:17–19 (NLT)

Here we find a warning against any and all attempts to get rich at "any" cost. The prison system and the graveyards are full of those who attempted to "get rich" or "die trying" regardless of the consequences. When the pursuit of money, possessions, fame, or even a career path causes you to cross over to "I got to have it at any cost," then greed for that "thing" has entered your heart. Greed is mostly referred to in terms of the possession of excess; however, the lustful influence that a possession exercises over a person is also grounds for greed. If we are truly honest with ourselves then we will admit that greed does not simply apply to money and possessions, but often to people as well. If you've "got to have" him or her so bad that you don't care if he or she is married or committed to someone else, then greed for that person has overtaken you. Or if you already have a Mr. Right or Mrs. Always Right and greedily want all of their time to the point of abusive jealousy and rage, the G-R-E-E-D Eyed Monster has a hold of you as well and the fate of that relationship could end fatally. Wisdom says, when you see the enticement of "greed" creeping into your heart, then be smarter than a bird and go the other way. No possession, no amount money, and no relationship is worth your life or the consequences of the life of another in your pursuit to get what you just "gotta" have. Losing all regard for the right path in the pursuit of what you desire will never end in your advantage. The greediness of gain, however applied, will cost you your life, literally. Imitate the birds and flee from the traps lured by the temptation of greed.

Reference:

Proverbs 28:16, 15:27; Isaiah 33:16; 1 Timothy 6:10

WISDOM TIP 4

Answer the phone when wisdom calls or she will stop calling! (Use it or lose it.)

"'Simpletons! How long will you wallow in ignorance? Cynics! How long will you feed your cynicism? Idiots! How long will you refuse to learn? About face! I can revise your life. Look, I'm ready to pour out my spirit on you; I'm ready to tell you all I know. As it is, I've called, but you've turned a deaf ear; I've reached out to you, but you've ignored me.

'Since you laugh at my counsel and make a joke of my advice, How can I take you seriously? I'll turn the tables and joke about *your* troubles! What if the roof falls in, and your whole life goes to pieces? What if catastrophe strikes and there's nothing to show for your life but rubble and ashes? You'll need me then. You'll call for me, but don't expect an answer. No matter how hard you look, you won't find me …

'Because you wouldn't take my advice and brushed aside all my offers to train you, well, you've made your bed—now lie in it; you wanted your own way—now, how do you like it? Don't you see what happens, you simpletons, you idiots? Carelessness kills; complacency is murder. First pay attention to me, and then relax. Now you can take it easy—you're in good hands."

Proverbs 1:23–31 (THE MESSAGE)

"Come and listen to my counsel. I'll share my heart with you and make you wise.

'I called you so often, but you wouldn't come. I reached out to you, but you paid no attention. You ignored my advice and rejected the correction I offered. So I will laugh when you are in trouble! I will mock you when disaster overtakes you—when calamity overtakes you like a storm, when disaster engulfs you like a cyclone, and anguish and distress overwhelm you.

'When they cry for help, I will not answer. Though they anxiously search for me, they will not find me. For they hated knowledge and chose not to fear the Lord. They rejected my advice and paid no attention when I corrected them. Therefore, they must eat the bitter fruit of living their own way, choking on their own schemes. For simpletons turn away from me—to death. Fools are destroyed by their own complacency."

Proverbs 1:23–32 (NLT)

My grandmother, like many of yours, had a saying that I'm sure is written somewhere in the hidden scrolls of wisdom, "You've made your bed hard, now lie in it!" Ouch, that hurts! That's exactly how most of us choose to learn, through the pain of experience. To a toddler, it is repeated over and over again, "do not touch the hot stove." What does the toddler do? Touch the hot stove. Moral of the story is this, receive wisdom when she presents herself to you or you will later regret turning a deaf ear to her loud cries for your attention. Sometimes wisdom attempts to get your attention through the words or advice of others. Other times wisdom will come directly to you through the Word of God, a thought, a premonition, or a knowing deep inside that cannot be explained. In whatever form wisdom has chosen to speak to you, pay attention and take heed!

The person in this proverb was so infatuated with doing things his own way to the point of ruin. The ruin that ultimately engulfed his life was not completely a result of rejecting wisdom, but also a result of doing things his own way. There is a way that seems right, but leads to death. When we follow wisdom, we are following God's right path. Ultimately, overindulgence in the wrong path is what leads to ruin. Turning a deaf ear to the voices of wisdom in your life, coupled with the continuous commitment to follow the wrong path, is a recipe for disaster. It may appear to you that it came about suddenly, but everyone else saw it coming from a mile away.

Think of it this way, if you keep talking to a friend who just will not hear you, will you continue to talk? Absolutely not! You still love your friend, but you have to sit on the sidelines and watch them make stupid choices until their choices show themselves to be stupid, then you can finally embrace them like a good friend and say, "Fool, I tried to warn you!"

Bottom line, following wisdom brings about unrelenting peace, security, and confidence for your present and your future that going your own way can never provide. Do yourself a favor and listen so you will not find yourself "eating the bitter fruit of living your own way, choking on your own schemes."

Reference:

Proverbs 5:22–23, 6:15, 8:36, 12:14, 15:10, 22:8, 29:11, 12:4; Ecclesiastes 8:12; Isaiah 65:2; Jeremiah 7:13; Psalm 66:18, 101:1; Job 4:8, 21:14, 35:12; Song of Solomon 5:6

WISDOM TIP 5

You can rest safely in the hands of wisdom.

"'But all who listen to me will live in peace, untroubled by fear of harm.'"

Proverbs 1:33 (NLT)

"'First pay attention to me, and then relax. Now you can take it easy—you're in good hands.'"

Proverbs 1:33 (THE MESSAGE)

Homeland Security consists of all the military branches combined with the police forces and other citizen-protecting agencies around this country. Yet, even with the mass shield of humans armed with weapons of mass destruction, most Americans do not have the peace that wisdom offers. Wisdom is making a promise to keep you safe without the mental fear of harm amidst all the dishevelment in the world, our country, and our local communities.

If you want to live a life free of fear and full of peace, then follow the light on the yellow brick road of wisdom.

When you listen to wisdom, one of the major benefits is the peace of knowing that you have chosen the right way, made the right decision, or followed a principle that in the end will prove to benefit your life most.

When my husband and I were members of a Lighthouse Christian Fellowship church in Anchorage, AK, these words were inscribed on a wall as you entered the sanctuary: "The end result of Kingdom Living is always increase." The end result of applying the principles of wisdom to your life is ALWAYS an increase of peace as you safely rest in the hands of wisdom.

Reference:

Psalm 25:12, Ecclesiastes 8:12, Proverbs 8:32–35, Isaiah 48:18

WISDOM TIP 6

Wisdom is a friend with benefits.

> "Good friend, take to heart what I'm telling you; collect my counsels and guard them with your life. Tune your ears to the world of Wisdom; set your heart on a life of Understanding. That's right—if you make Insight your priority, and won't take no for an answer, searching for it like a prospector panning for gold, like an adventurer on a treasure hunt, believe me, before you know it Fear-of-God will be yours; you'll have come upon the Knowledge of God."
>
> PROVERBS 2:1–5 (THE MESSAGE)

The attainment of wisdom should be at the top of your priority list. Here, you are urged to give your full attention to the pursuit of wisdom, meaning your emotions and intellect (mind) along with everything that makes you the person you are. Although the gift of wisdom is free, it does cost you the price of diligence and obedience. Why the price of both diligence and obedience? I'm glad you asked. To receive the great truths of wisdom without the obedient application of wisdom will simply make you a "wise fool," with nothing but a head full of knowledge that profits you none.

I'm reminded of the wealthy businessman who would hide money in different locations across America and send tweets and social media messages to people in that city, notifying them of where to search for the cash he had hidden. The national and local news reports showed droves of people out, searching desperately for envelopes of cash. Proverbs is compelling us to search for wisdom as if we are searching for hidden envelopes full of cash. As your search continues, you will soon discover that the true value of wisdom is not merely the external treasures it adds to your life, but the everyday relational divine interactions that increases your knowledge of God Himself.

Reference:

Proverbs 2:2–4, 4:10, 4:20, 7:1, 22:17, 8:17

WISDOM TIP 7

God Almighty is the personal benefactor of wisdom.

"God gives out Wisdom free, is plainspoken in Knowledge and Understanding. He's a rich mine of Common Sense for those who live well, a personal bodyguard to the candid and sincere. He keeps his eye on all who live honestly and pays special attention to his loyally committed ones."

PROVERBS 2:6–8 (THE MESSAGE)

"For the LORD grants wisdom! From his mouth come knowledge and understanding. He grants a treasure of common sense to the honest. He is a shield to those who walk with integrity. He guards the paths of the just and protects those who are faithful to him."

PROVERBS 2:6–8 (NLT)

The two fringe benefits of wisdom can best be described as knowledge and understanding. I once heard the difference between the two described this way, "knowledge is the mental capacity to know something and understanding is the ability to apply that mental capacity toward a concept in order to achieve success." The cousin to wisdom is common sense. There's a phrase that says, "common sense isn't so common." You know why? In order to truly function in the ultimate operation of your senses, you need the wisdom of God. After giving you the treasures of heaven in the form of sound wisdom and common sense, God promises to protect His investment in your life by guarding your course and protecting you along the way. I liken this plan to the FDIC insurance procured by banks that guarantee the currency you place in a bank up to $250,000. If anything were to occur to cause a financial upheaval, an FDIC insured institution is backed by the federal government up to $250,000 for each account holder. God is saying, "Hey, I am the personal guarantor of wisdom, I guarantee the principles of wisdom with understanding, knowledge, and success. On top of all of that, I will also shield you, guard you, and show you every good path for life." When you have God Almighty as your personal benefactor you can relax knowing that He gives success with no sorrow added!

Reference:

James 1:5; Job 32:8; Psalm 51:6, 66:9, 84:11, 97:10; Ecclesiastes 2:26; Exodus 31:3; Daniel 2:21; Proverbs 8:14; 14:8, 30:5; Colossians 2:3

WISDOM TIP 8

The guise of wisdom is more than meets the eye.

> "Wise choices will watch over you. Understanding will keep you safe. Wisdom will save you from evil people, from those whose words are twisted."
>
> Proverbs 2:11–12 (NLT)

> "Lady Wisdom will be your close friend, and Brother Knowledge your pleasant companion. Good Sense will scout ahead for danger, Insight will keep an eye out for you. They'll keep you from making wrong turns or following the bad directions of those who are lost themselves and can't tell a trail from a tumbleweed."
>
> Proverbs 2:11–12 (THE MESSAGE)

The benefits of wisdom are not limited to what they add to your life, but also the destruction it saves you from. If you want to be kept safe from the corruptions within your own heart that can lead you astray and the temptations that come in the form of distractions that misrepresent themselves as the easy way, then wisdom must become a constant companion to your way of life. Many times in life, "evil people with twisted words," aka "fake friends" or "haters," are not presented before you in that manner or you would immediately know to stay away from that person or group of people. The Bible gives reference to workers of evil appearing as angels of light (see 2 Corinthians 11:14–15). You are studying for a test and suddenly receive a Snapchat message from your "Boo" to have a private tutoring session. Wisdom warns you not to fall for the trap. Not only do you already know in your heart that the two of you will not study well together, you also know this "study group" distraction comes with the temptation of some close and personal contact that you are trying to avoid.

For my more mature readers, think back to that business proposition that appeared to be a great opportunity. However, after completing a detailed investigation into the matter, you continued to feel uneasy about the proposition; that's "wisdom saving you and understanding keeping you safe." Other times, an immediate internal sensor warned you that "something just ain't right" or "too good to be true," again, wisdom is operating in your life, guiding your actions and decisions in the way that is best for you. Wisdom gives you the ability to see to the heart of the matter and, in some cases, to the heart of the person speaking to you. Wisdom will allow you to discern when words are being twisted and when people presenting themselves as glittery diamonds are actually fake replicas. When you allow wisdom to guide you, you will not be a victim that falls prey to schemes, even when they come in the form of a nice neighbor, popular kid at school, or renowned public figure.

Reference:

Proverbs 6:22

WISDOM TIP 9

Wisdom stands guard against inappropriate relationships.

> "Wisdom will save you from the immoral woman, from the seductive words of the promiscuous woman. She has abandoned her husband and ignores the covenant she made before God. Entering her house leads to death; it is the road to the grave. The man who visits her is doomed. He will never reach the paths of life."
>
> Proverbs 2:16–19 (NLT)

Warning, DO NOT ENTER! From the beginning of time, men small and great have fallen prey to seductive women. Solomon in the Book of Ecclesiastes warns that there is nothing new under the sun. Wisdom will save you from adultery and from having unattached, uncommitted sex. While this verse addresses men, it also applies to women. Ladies, be on guard against the flattering words of a man who is not your husband, even you, single ladies. The path of LIFE is not found with the man who attempts to woe you from your husband or woe you into bed with no plans of ever becoming your husband. The great thing about this wisdom lesson is that the heart of the matter is revealed, the sexually immoral, seductive speaking, promiscuous person has ignored the covenant made before GOD! When marriage vows are broken in an adulterous relationship, you are breaking the covenant you made before God, it's not just about you and your spouse. It's so much bigger than that, it's about the covenant God has sealed in heaven pertaining to you and your spouse and the purpose He has planned for your union.

All my single ladies, the Bible clearly explains that your husband is "the Lord God your maker" (Isaiah 54:5). The path of death that follows inappropriate relationships are not always marked by a physical grave. Death can come in the form of the death of your marriage; the death of your reputation; the death of your future plans because of an untimely sexual relationship; and let's not discount the death of a generational legacy. Heed the words of wisdom and run the other way when you sense the immoral person attempting to pursue you into an ungodly relationship. Matthew Henry's *Concise Commentary* sums up this wisdom lesson best: "If we are truly wise, we shall be careful to avoid all evil company and evil practices. When wisdom has dominion over us, then it not only fills the head, but enters into the heart, and will preserve, both against corruptions within and temptations without. The ways of sin are ways of darkness, uncomfortable and unsafe: what fools are those who leave the plain, pleasant, lightsome paths of uprightness, to walk in such ways!"

Reference:

Proverbs 5:3; 6:24, 7:5, 23:27; Ecclesiastes 7:26

WISDOM TIP 10

Be careful to follow the right leader.

"Follow the steps of good men instead, and stay on the paths of the righteous. For only the godly will live in the land, and those with integrity will remain in it."

PROVERBS 2:20–21 (NLT)

"So—join the company of good men and women, keep your feet on the tried-and-true paths. It's the men who walk straight who will settle this land, the women with integrity who will last here."

PROVERBS 2:20–21 (THE MESSAGE)

Does all of this wisdom business sound a bit intimidating? No need to reinvent the wheel, find someone who has consistently lived a life of integrity and goodness and follow their lead. I recommend starting with reading the Gospels to identify how Jesus lived while He was on this earth. Additionally, it is wonderful if you have personal access to someone such as a parent, teacher, pastor, older family member, or sibling. However, it is just as effective to follow someone from a distance. Meaning, read as much as possible about the life of a person you admire, observe them when you are in their presence, or schedule an interview with your chosen person and ask them to explain how they arrived at their current course in life. Most individuals will be thrilled to pass on the insight and wisdom they have gained over the years. Just remember that monetary success does not equate to a "good man" of integrity. Allow wisdom to guide you in your selection of a worthy candidate. Decide today whether you will share in the joys of those who have been there, done that, and perhaps sport both the gray hair and T-shirt that recounts the goodness of God in the land of the living.

Reference:

Hebrews 6:12, Proverbs 13:20, Psalm 119:63, 115

WISDOM TIP 11

Wisdom brings prosperity worth living for.

"Good friend, don't forget all I've taught you; take to heart my commands. They'll help you live a long, long time, a long life lived full and well."

PROVERBS 3:1–2 (THE MESSAGE)

The teachings and commandments of wisdom will (1) prolong your life, (2) give you peace as you live your long life, and (3) bring you prosperity as you enjoy your long peaceful existence. Don't limit the term of prosperity to financial success. While prosperity does in fact include financial success, money is just one portion of the prosperity portfolio. What does a prolonged life benefit one who has poor health? Prosperity in your health will prolong your life and the peace you enjoy as you live your life. Another question: How can a prolonged life benefit a person with poor familial relationships? Take it from King David, one of the most financially prosperous men of his time. Money and long life without peaceful and prosperous family relationships can lead to children who plan devious attempts to take your life! Think of prosperity in terms of a whole and full life with every area intact.

Reference:

Deuteronomy 30:15–18; Proverbs 3:16; 9:11, 16:31; Psalm 91:16 (THE MESSAGE)

WISDOM TIP 12

Earn a good reputation with love and loyalty.

> "Don't lose your grip on Love and Loyalty. Tie them around your neck; carve their initials on your heart. Earn a reputation for living well in God's eyes and the eyes of the people."
>
> PROVERBS 3:3–4 (THE MESSAGE)

> "Never let loyalty and kindness leave you! Tie them around your neck as a reminder. Write them deep within your heart. Then you will find favor with both God and people, and you will earn a good reputation."
>
> PROVERBS 3:3–4 (NLT)

Love and loyalty are two words to live by, as well as two character traits to pursue that are held in high regard by both God and mankind. When you observe the notable men and women who are highly respected in this generation and generations of the past, most of them have had one or a combination of the two traits strongly exhibited in their character and behavior. The benefits of having love (kindness) and loyalty are a favorable vantage point and a good name. I know many have gotten away from traditional values, but one principle that has stood the test of time is the value of a good name. A good name will get you a job, a loan, into the right school, and in the presence of a friend of a friend of a friend who is only helping you out this one time because such and such had good things to say about you. Now that's a wisdom nugget to grab hold on to tightly!

Even the Lord Jesus followed this wisdom principle while he walked the earth as a child growing into manhood. Luke 2:52 (NIV) tells us that Jesus, "grew in wisdom and stature, and in favor with God and man." His good reputation (favor) with God and man was directly correlated to his growth in wisdom. As a child, Jesus conversed with and asked questions of wise teachers in order to grow in wisdom, stature, and the benefits that follow such growth–favor with God and man.

I encourage you to identify wise teachers and advisors within your reach and seek to converse with them. Be wise about your choice by matching your selection against the biblical qualifications found in 1 Timothy 3:2–9: above reproach, faithful to his wife (or her husband), temperate, self-controlled, respectable, hospitable, able to teach, not given to drunkenness, not violent but gentle, not quarrelsome, not a lover of money, manages his (her) own family well, must not be a recent convert, he (she) must also have a good reputation with outsiders (those outside the church in the local community), be worthy of respect, sincere, not indulging in much wine, not pursuing dishonest gain, and must keep hold of the deep truths of the faith with a clear conscience. While this passage does address a man, verse eleven makes it very clear that the same qualifications apply to female mentors by clearly stating, "In the same way, the women are to be worthy of respect, not malicious talkers but temperate and trustworthy in everything" (1 Timothy 3:11 NIV).

Reference:

Psalm 85:10 (CEV and THE MESSAGE), Matthew 5:46, 2 Corinthians 8:21

WISDOM TIP 13

Trust in the Lord! Again, I say trust Him!

> "Trust God from the bottom of your heart; don't try to figure out everything on your own. Listen for God's voice in everything you do, everywhere you go; he's the one who will keep you on track."
>
> Proverbs 3: 5–6 (THE MESSAGE)

> "Trust in the Lord with all your heart; do not depend on your own understanding. Seek his will in all you do, and he will show you which path to take.
>
> Proverbs 3: 5–6 (NLT)

1. Trust in the Lord.
2. Do not give in to your own understanding, because your understanding is limited. Go back to #1.
3. Stop trying to figure out everything on your own. Close your eyes, get quiet and still, and listen to the direction that comes directly from God's Spirit. Go back to #1.
4. If you follow the instruction provided in steps 1, 2, and 3, then the benefits will be a path that is clear, full of zeal, and divinely carved just for you.
5. When in doubt, go back to #1.

John Gill's Exposition of the Bible offers profound insight and elaboration of this wisdom principle:

"Trust in the Lord with all thine heart, Not in a creature, the best, the holiest, and the highest; not in any creature enjoyment, as riches, strength, and wisdom; nor in any outward privilege, arising from natural descent and education;

not in a man's self, in his own heart, which is deceitful; nor in any works of righteousness done by him; not in a profession of religion, or the duties of it, ever so well performed; not in frames, nor in graces, and the exercise of them; no, not in faith or trust itself: but in the Lord, the object of all grace, and in him only; in Jehovah the Father, as the God of nature and providence, for all temporal blessings; and as the God of all grace, for all spiritual blessings, and all the needful supplies of grace; and for eternal happiness, which he has provided, promised, and freely gives. Trust in him at all times. Trust in Jehovah the Son; in his person for acceptance; in his righteousness for justification; in his blood for pardon; in his fullness for supply; in his power for protection and preservation; and in him alone for salvation and eternal life. Trust in Jehovah the Spirit, to carry on and finish the work of grace upon the heart; of which a saint may be confident that where it is begun it will be completed. And this trust in Father, Son, and Spirit, should be 'with all the heart,' cordial and sincere."

Reference:

Psalm 37:3–5, Proverbs 22:19 (AMPC, NLT, THE MESSAGE), Isaiah 30:21

WISDOM TIP 14

Wisdom does a body good.

"Don't be impressed with your own wisdom. Instead, fear the Lord and turn away from evil. Then you will have healing for your body and strength for your bones."

Proverbs 3:7–8 (NLT)

"Don't assume that you know it all. Run to God! Run from evil! Your body will glow with health, your very bones will vibrate with life!"

Proverbs 3:7–8 (THE MESSAGE)

The majority of mistakes we make are the result of the faulty perception that "we know what is best" for our lives. We believe we know what to do, how to do it, and when to do it. However, if we are proceeding with an action that is not steeped in the Word of God, it will most likely fail. Proverbs 14:12 (ESV) says, "There is a way that seems right to a man, but its end is the way to death." This message is so important that it was repeated again two chapters later in Proverbs 16:25. I think God is trying to tell us something. That something is, "learn to fear me, learn to follow my path of wisdom. I promise you that my way will lead you to life, but your way will lead to a path of death and destruction."

Do not allow the word fear to stammer you. This is a reverential fear of trust and respect that God wants us to have for him. Very similar to someone that you admire. If you are a basketball player and Michael Jordan gives you advice on the game of basketball, then you would fear his advice or reverence his advice as one of the greatest basketball players to ever grace the court. If you were to meet Oprah, most likely you would fear or reverence the advice that she would relay about all the things "she knows for sure."

Think of a person you have high admiration for, now add them to a list of individuals who have accomplished great achievements in this life. How much more should we reverence the wisdom of the Creator God who gave each of the previously mentioned individuals the very ideas and thoughts that have made them the people we have come to admire.

Just saying … if I were you, I would learn to fear the Lord and shun any attempt to be wise in your own eyes. The added benefit of God's wisdom is the protection of your physical body from snares, temptations, and habits that would ultimately destroy you both physically and spiritually. Milk may "do a body good," but it is not the best source of strength for your bones—wisdom is!

Reference:

Proverbs 4:22, Job 28:28

WISDOM TIP 15

Having money is not the best part, honoring God with your money is.

"Honor the Lord from your wealth and from the first of all your produce; so your barns will be filled with plenty and your vats will overflow with new wine."

Proverbs 3:9-10 (NASB)

"Honor the Lord with your wealth and with the first and best part of all your income. Then your barns will be full, and your vats will overflow with fresh wine."

Proverbs 3:9-10 (GW)

I personally do not know of a single person who would say they enjoy struggling financially. The key to financial freedom is to honor the Lord with the first and best part of ALL your income. Yes, that means tithe by giving the first ten percent of your income as a way of honoring God with your money. The previous wisdom tip just cautioned you to "not be wise in your own eyes." This is one subject that I would heed the voice of wisdom quickly and then seek to understand the whys later. I can only tell you from personal experience that, when you honor God with your money by following His instructions to present to Him the "first (ten percent) and best part of all your income" He will in turn give you more. When you give the first fruits (tithe – 10% of your income) back to His work so the Gospel of Jesus Christ may be preached in all the world and the lives of others can be enriched, He will bless the 90% you keep far above what you could ever imagine. Just try Him in this as He so graciously proposes in Malachi 3:10. The results will not be disappointing. Just as wisdom is the principal thing that leads to understanding, honoring God with the first 10% of all your income is the principal thing that leads to financial stability and enrichment. Verse 10 gives the result of following this basic financial principle, "so your barns will be filled with abundance, and your vats will burst open with new wine."

Most people today do not have barns that are filled with the harvest of agricultural labor, we have bank accounts. We go to work and are rewarded with a harvest of a salary deposited into our bank accounts. The result of honoring God is an abundant money harvest and instead of new wine, new opportunities to produce more money harvests until our accounts are brimming over. In this case, we are not hoarders, but we brim over with a money harvest in order to be a blessing to the lives of others. Our money has a mission, but you cannot give money a mission if you do not have any or if you don't know the rightful purpose behind having what you do have. Bottom line, every good gift comes from God, the job that brings you money so you can take care of yourself, or the parents with a job that brings them money to take care of you. When we honor God in the form of money, we are only giving back a portion of what he already owns, "The silver is mine, and the gold is mine, saith the Lord of hosts" (Haggai 2:8 KJV).

Reference:

Deuteronomy 26:2, 28:8; Malachi 3: 8–12

WISDOM TIP 16

Proper discipline produces maturity.

"Do not reject the discipline of the Lord, my son, and do not resent his warning, because the Lord warns the one he loves, even as a father warns a son with whom he is pleased."

Proverbs 3:11–12 (GW)

> "My child, don't reject the LORD's discipline, and don't be upset when he corrects you. For the LORD corrects those he loves, just as a father corrects a child in whom he delights."
>
> PROVERBS 3:11–12 (NLT)

Most parents understand the depth of this verse. Correction must take place in order to raise healthy, productive, and sound minded children. Likewise, we are God's children. Like any other children known to man we sometimes miss the mark. When this occurs, how do you receive correction? When I say receive, I'm speaking in terms of rejecting or accepting the correction like a package you may "receive" in the mail. My personal experience is that God will warn me with gentle whispers of correction at first. These whispers may be in the form of another person speaking indirectly to me through television, an overheard conversation, or my pastor on Sunday morning teaching a lesson on kindness and patience when I just told myself that I have a "right" to be mad because of what "they" did to me.

If we make the choice to disregard the gentle whispers, then the knocks will come. Someone close to you may request to have a face-to-face, so they can tell you "about yourself" by speaking the truth in tough love. However, if you get an attitude and refuse to listen to the warning knock, then you are setting yourself up for what I call the "B-O-O-M" explosion correction. When "B-O-O-M" occurs, the gentle warnings turn into a set of circumstances that are physically uncomfortable and pierces like an arrow cutting into the red particles of a bull's eye. Circumstances you cannot deny or run from.

You've been shoplifting for months, ignoring the warnings, and "B-O-O-M," you are caught on camera and stopped by security as you attempt to leave the store. Explosion!

You've been cheating on your taxes for years by claiming other relative's children as your dependents. "B-O-O-M," you get an audit letter from the IRS. Explosion!

Having sex with your "bae" even after you attended Silver Ring Thing and decided to dedicate the temple of your body to the Lord, "B-O-O-M," untimely pregnancy. Explosion!

The scenarios are limitless and we all have an example or two about the consequences of ignoring correction when we are first confronted with poor choices or negative patterns of behavior. But check this, we receive the whispers of correction not because God wants to point out how flawed we are. We receive His warnings as an act of love because he desires what is best for our lives. The sooner you figure this part out, the more apt you are to "receive" the correction package that shows up on your doorstep in the form of gentle whispers before they turn into "B-O-O-M", Explosions! We must receive the warnings in whatever form they come with the same attitude of gratitude and humility in which we receive God's blessings. When God lovingly corrects us, His correction is designed to mature us, teach us, and mold us in His image so our lives will reflect His character and His original intent and purpose. God's correction also allows us to comprehend the magnitude of His glorious grace lavished upon our imperfect lives. Take a moment to reflect on Hebrews 12:5 (NLT), "And have you forgotten the encouraging words God spoke to you as His children? He said, 'My child, don't make light of the LORD's discipline, and don't give up when he corrects you.'" Shake the dust off your feet or, in this case, off your emotions and carry on with a new level of wisdom obtained by God's loving correction.

Reference:

Job 5:17, Psalm 94:12, Deuteronomy 8:5, Proverbs 13:24, Revelation 3:19

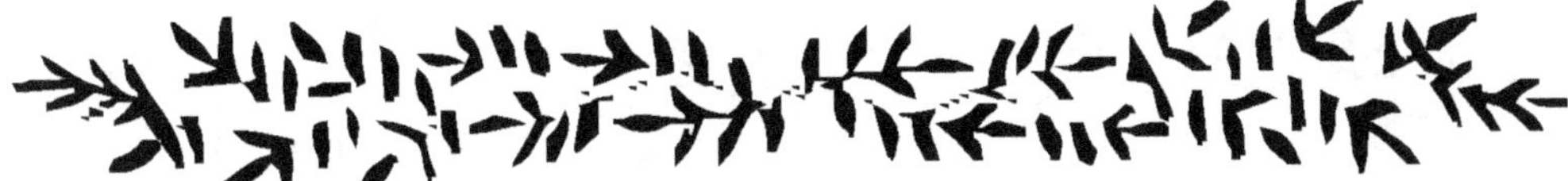

WISDOM TIP 17

Keep your feet out of the traps of life with wisdom.

"My child, don't lose sight of common sense and discernment. Hang on to them, for they will refresh your soul. They are like jewels on a necklace. They keep you safe on your way, and your feet will not stumble. You can go to bed without fear; you will lie down and sleep soundly. You need not be afraid of sudden disaster or the destruction that comes upon the wicked, for the LORD is your security. He will keep your foot from being caught in a trap."

PROVERBS 3:21–26 (NLT)

"My son, do not let wisdom and understanding out of your sight, preserve sound judgment and discretion; they will be life for you, an ornament to grace your neck. Then you will go on your way in safety, and your foot will not stumble. When you lie down, you will not be afraid; when you lie down, your sleep will be sweet. Have no fear of sudden disaster or of the ruin that overtakes the wicked, for the LORD will be at your side and will keep your foot from being snared."

PROVERBS 3:21–26 (NIV)

Wisdom is a safety measure that guards your life, causes you to sleep well, and keeps you from going down a path that will ultimately entrap you. In the era we are living in, danger lurks at every corner. However, we need not fall prey to the danger nor the fear that ultimately invites the danger into our lives. How is this accomplished? Through understanding, sound judgment, and discretion. Yes, these are all by-products of wisdom. When we keep our internal and external eye on wisdom, we are preserved from the pitfalls and stumbling blocks that create fear, guilt, and the gulf of shame that accompanies a guilty conscience. If you've ever dealt with these emotions, you know that they can keep you awake at night, play tricks with your mind, and cause you to make wrong choices that lead to unsafe territory on many different levels. Keeping your eye on wisdom creates an undisturbed composure within your mind that allows you to rest in God, His ability to guard you, His ability to protect you while keeping you safe from the exploits of this world. Your feet will literally be guarded from danger. Additionally, your life will be preserved from the traps of ruin discovered by those who make the choice to follow their own way in lieu of the way of wisdom.

Reference:

Psalm 91, Proverbs 1:33, 6:22, Psalm 112:7, Psalm 119:165

WISDOM TIP 18

Lend a helping hand when you can.

"Never walk away from someone who deserves help; your hand is *God's* hand for that person. Don't tell your neighbor "Maybe some other time" or "Try me tomorrow" when the money's right there in your pocket."

PROVERBS 3:27–28 (THE MESSAGE)

"Do not withhold good from those who deserve it when it's in your power to help them. If you can help your neighbor now, don't say, 'Come back tomorrow, and then I'll help you.'"

PROVERBS 3:27–28 (NLT)

Wisdom will lead you to a life of generosity. *Jamieson-Fausset-Brown Bible Commentary* brings clarity with its formal commanding language, "Promptly fulfil all obligations both of justice and charity." Simply put, do what is right at the very moment you are confronted with the opportunity. I love that the Jamieson-Fausset-Brown Bible Commentary does not limit us to acts of charity, but also encourages acts of justice as a form of charity. There are times when we must take a stand and justly act simply because it is the right thing to do. I am drawn to the people of the civil rights movement who stood for justice despite the discomfort and danger that accompanied their courageous deeds. Dr. Martin Luther King Jr. wisely stated, "History will have to record that the greatest tragedy of this period of social transition was not the strident clamor of the bad people, but the appalling silence of the good people." Another quote by Dr. King that adequately personifies the help we are called to give to those in need is, "The first question which the priest and the Levite asked was: 'If I stop to help this man, what will happen to me?' But … the good Samaritan reversed the question: 'If I do not stop to help this man, what will happen to him?'" Wisdom considers what will happen to another human being if "I" do not extend the help that is within my power to give. Wisdom also understands that what happens to your neighbor will also have some type of profound domino effect on your life. Wisdom prompts and even beckons us to impact the lives of others with generosity, benevolence, and justice when it is within our power to do so.

Reference:

Galatians 6:10, James 2:15–17, 1 Timothy 6:18–19

WISDOM TIP 19

Purpose in your heart to be trustworthy.

"Do not plan to do something wrong to your neighbor while he is sitting there with you and suspecting nothing. Do not quarrel with a person for no reason if he has not harmed you."

PROVERBS 3:29–30 (GW)

"Don't start none, won't be none!" is an old saying that dates back to my childhood. Don't start no mess, won't be no mess. Don't start no gossip, won't be no gossip. The principle behind "don't start none, won't be none" oddly aligns with the attribute of trustworthiness. Going behind someone's back to divulge of secrets told to you in confidence, setting "traps" for someone's downfall, frivolous litigation—these all fall under the category of deceit. I've heard this behavior described as "stirring up strife," "sowing discord," and "wreaking havoc" in places where it was nonexistent prior to your intentional actions. *John Gill's Exposition of the Bible* offers this advice, "Do not contrive and form schemes in thy mind and thoughts to do him any injury, in his name and character, in his person, property, or family: Wisdom seekers love peace."

Did you get that? Do not plan to hurt someone physically, but also do not assassinate the character of someone else, demolish their reputation, damage someone's property intentionally, or try to bring strife to their family unit. In my best Texas vernacular, this is deep y'all! Looks like the O'Jays were not the first to warn against "Backstabbers," wisdom was. Google the song if you have not heard of it.

To purposely try to hurt a friend is conniving on any level, but to do so when the person has no idea that you are a "hater" disguised as a friend is altogether "low-down"! You might as well crawl around on your belly and start hissing like a snake. If you've been guilty of this type of behavior in the past before you were introduced to Lady Wisdom, make an attempt to undo what you have done with an apology. Try to make peace with whoever you've hurt, understanding that trust will have to be rebuilt. The Bible tells us, as much as it depends on you, pursue peace with everyone (Romans 12:18). Let us start the peace process by increasing the character trait of trustworthiness in our daily interactions with others.

Reference:

Proverbs 6:16–18; 14:22, 25:9–10; Zechariah 8:17; Psalm 35:20 (NLT and THE MESSAGE)

WISDOM TIP 20

The "right path" is neither the easiest nor the shortest, but it is the most fulfilling.

"Don't envy violent people or copy their ways."
PROVERBS 3:31 (NLT)

"Don't try to be like those who shoulder their way through life. Why be a bully? 'Why not?' you say. Because GOD can't stand twisted souls."
PROVERBS 3:31–32 (THE MESSAGE)

The violent man represented in this scripture is the one who makes a living from ungodly and unlawful means. In our society, the man of violence looks like the drug dealer, the pimp/human trafficker, the extortioner, the white-collar money launderer, the identity theft crook, and in some cases, large corporations who exploit the poor abroad in poor conditioned, low-waged factory jobs. The examples you may see of these modern-day "violent" people may appear to be so glamorous that you are enticed to adopt their lifestyle over God's way of doing things. You may find your mind contemplating following in the path of the violent man with the hopes of duplicating the same wealth, notoriety, popularity, and power that he has. What does it profit a man to gain the world and lose his soul? Wisdom directs you to avoid such traps.

Unfortunately, our prison system is full of young and old people who were never taught this wisdom principle or perhaps choose to disregard this time and tested truth. It's a hard knocks life for those who choose experience as a teacher over wisdom. Our secular culture consistently displays examples of people who do the wrong thing and seemingly prosper. As a result, many of our young people have been plagued with examples of modern-day "violent" people, but not nearly as many examples of those who produce the results of the "right life" by following the wise path. To those young people who lack positive influences in their daily surroundings, I pray that the wisdom principles found in this book will come across your path, your eyes and your ears, and permeate your life. I pray that the powerful voice of wisdom will dissipate the negative influences you have witnessed and cause you to see with clear understanding the right path that God has chosen for your life.

Wisdom will guide you on the right path, it may not be the easiest path or the shortest path, but it will be the path that leads to a life of peace and fulfillment. Pursue your dreams along the right path and wisdom will take you further than you ever thought you would go. Let integrity guide you along the right path and longevity will trump deceit, eventually you will witness Proverbs 3:35(WBT), "The wise shall inherit glory: but shame [public contempt and humiliation] shall be the promotion of fools."

Reference:

Psalm 37:1–2, 7–9; Proverbs 24:1, 19–20

WISDOM TIP 21

Good advice will help straighten a crooked path.

> "Listen, friends, to some fatherly advice; sit up and take notice so you'll know how to live. I'm giving you good counsel; don't let it go in one ear and out the other."
>
> PROVERBS 4:1–2 (THE MESSAGE)

The purpose of advice is to receive guidance, good judgment, and correction from someone who has already walked the road you are currently traveling on or planning to travel in the near future. If you turn a deaf ear to advice, then you are essentially mocking the "good counsel" that was given by allowing it to travel no further than from ear to ear rather than the greater distance it takes to travel from ear to head, to heart, and ultimately to action. Your action creates the level of influence and the degree of impact you will have upon the lives of others. Life coaches are very popular these days, so consider this book your very own personal life coach taken straight from the Giver of Life and neatly compartmentalized for easy access when you need it most.

What exactly is good judgment? First let's take a look at a few synonyms for the word judgment: shrewdness, discernment, wisdom, prudence, intelligence, perceptiveness, acumen, good sense, or way of thinking. If you will listen or take heed to the advice—"good counsel" found in the Book of Proverbs—not only will you gain a heart of wisdom, but you will be empowered to apply the wisdom you have gained to operate in shrewdness, discernment, prudence, intelligence, perceptiveness, acumen, and good common sense in every area of your life.

If you have an area that requires correction, just listen and do what the Word of God is telling you to do, so that good judgment and good guidance may be added to that area of your life. Although instruction or correction may sometimes feel uncomfortable, we must welcome it into our lives in order to grow. I'm reminded of wisdom teeth, they are excruciatingly painful when attempting to pierce the gum line. The emergence of wisdom teeth is painful slightly because of all the other teeth that have taken root in your mouth that crowds the space where the wisdom teeth are attempting to occupy. Likewise, correction and instruction often feels uncomfortable because of all the other junk that has taken root in our lives that fights to crowd out the wisdom trying to push through and occupy the gum line of our lives. Go ahead and pull wisdom out so you can get some relief from the pain. Proverbs 4:10–15 in The Message translation explains why:

"Dear friend, take my advice; it will add years to your life. I'm writing out clear directions to Wisdom Way, I'm drawing a map to Righteous Road. I don't want you ending up in blind alleys, or wasting time making wrong turns. Hold tight to good advice; don't relax your grip. Guard it well—your life is at stake! Don't take Wicked Bypass; don't so much as set foot on that road. Stay clear of it; give it a wide berth. Make a detour and be on your way."

Reference:

Proverbs 8:33, 19:20, 22:17

WISDOM TIP 22

The "right path" and the "wrong path" will never coexist, so always proceed with wisdom.

"Don't set foot on the path of the wicked; don't proceed in the way of evil ones. Avoid it; don't travel on it. Turn away from it, and pass it by."

Proverbs 4:14–15 (HCSB)

Avoid looking at the appearance of what evildoers are getting away with or the appearance of having a good life filled with pleasures, for in the end they will search for those pleasures and will find none. Generally, a physical death will not be the consequences of wrong actions, but at times a physical death is exactly what will occur. Some forms of death that occur as a result of traveling down the path of the wicked are death of relationships, death of dreams when one must pay the consequences for actions, death of financial stability, death of health, death of trust, death of a family unit when divorce occurs. The list goes on and on.

Avoid the path of evil, not just a little bit here and there, but AVOID it with haste! *Matthew Henry's Concise Commentary* puts it this way, "The way of evil men may seem pleasant, and the nearest way to compass some end; but it is an evil way, and will end ill; if thou love thy God and thy soul, avoid it. It is not said, keep at a due distance, but at a great distance; never think you can get far enough from it."

Proverbs 4:19 goes on to give you the reason why you must get far away from evildoers. Their way is deep darkness that will eventually lead to a life full of stumbles, but they don't know when, where, or how the stumbles will come. The only guarantee is that stumbles will surely come!

Reference:

Psalm 1:1; Proverbs 1:15, 9:6, 13:20

WISDOM TIP 23

Shine light, shine bright, wisdom is the way and the might!

> "The ways of right-living people glow with light; the longer they live, the brighter they shine. But the road of wrongdoing gets darker and darker—travelers can't see a thing; they fall flat on their faces."
>
> PROVERBS 4:18–19 (THE MESSAGE)

Little by little, you grow from an egg in the womb into a full-blown adult. Think about that. You start out as a tiny egg about the size of a finger nail, and little by little you morph into the package of finesse you are currently working with. Two snaps and a head twist! The same is true for everything else that experiences a growth pattern. The longer you look intently at a light bulb, the brighter the light shines. The longer a person lives in a pattern of goodness, the brighter the light of their lives shine to others around them.

The same is true for darkness. If a person has a reputation for something negative, the tendency is for the negative reputation to expand and expand if nothing is done to deflect from the negativity. Before long, the person is no longer known as Saul the Zealot, but Saul the Christian Killer. How about this, Rahab the Harlot had light introduced to her path and she continued to shine until she became known as Rahab, the great grandmother of King David, and now forever known as Rahab, the woman listed in the direct genealogy of Jesus Christ, the Son of God. On the other hand, darkness only leads to more darkness, wrong leads to more wrong, sin leads to greater degrees of sin. When you lie, you have to cover up that lie with more lies; when you cheat, you have to cover up your cheating with lies so you can cheat more. When you steal, you form a habit of getting things quickly and with reckless abandon, so you steal even more. When you overeat, not only do you develop cravings that cause you to overeat more, but your stomach expands in the process, so what once filled you up no longer does and you require more food.

Darkness will lead you down a path that will cover up the right way with more darkness until you can no longer see your way back. The good news is that you have the ability to choose—light or darkness, bright future, or dark hazardous views. Open the brochure offered by Resort A-la-Wisdom; all of her accommodations are guaranteed to outshine the competition.

Reference:

Philippians 2:15, Psalm 97:11, Proverbs 13:9

WISDOM TIP 24

Protect the doors of your heart.

"Guard your heart above all else, for it determines the course of your life."

PROVERBS 4:23 (NLT)

Not only is your heart the center of life for your physical body, but it is also referred to as the center of life for your soul (mind, will, emotions, imagination, and intellect). Guarding your heart consists of guarding what you allow to come through the gates of your soul, which are your eyes and ears. What comes into your eye gates and ear gates enters your heart, forms your thoughts, and eventually comes out through your words and actions. Luke 6:45 tells us, "out of the abundance of the heart [the] mouth speaks." What's in your heart will eventually come out (Mark 7:21–23). Guard your heart, shield it, pour good things into it, and protect it at all costs because the condition of your heart is the source of everything you currently see in your life.

Reference:

Matthew 12:34–35, 15:18–19; Luke 6:45; Proverbs 23:19, 17:20

WISDOM TIP 25

Watch what you say.

"Don't talk out of both sides of your mouth; avoid careless banter, white lies, and gossip."

PROVERBS 4:24 (THE MESSAGE)

"Remove dishonesty from your mouth. Put deceptive speech far away from your lips."

PROVERBS 4:24 (GW)

Not only do you need to watch what you allow to come in, but what you allow to come out. Words of ill nature that contradict what you would like to see in your life or the lives of those whom you speak of should be eliminated from your speech. This, my friend, is easier said than done, but it is not impossible.

Gossip is a bad habit formed like any other habit—with practice over a period of time. You don't just fall into becoming a gossiper, backbiter, complainer, liar, or master of foul language. These skills take time to perfect. If you make a practice of avoiding them and people who operate in them, then you are "putting these things away" from you.

Don't confuse a slip of the tongue or a mistake here of there with who you are. Just make a concerted effort to avoid these things. Think of your words as being a part of who you are. Every time you speak a word, good or bad, it attaches itself to your being. The more bad you speak, the more gook is smeared all over your body. The more good you speak, the more beauty is reflected on your persona. This truth is echoed in 1 Peter 3:10 (NLT), "For the Scriptures say, 'If you want to enjoy life and see many happy days, keep your tongue from speaking evil and your lips from telling lies.'" Anyone who desires to live a life that is long and prosperous should practice keeping their tongue from speaking evil and their lips from telling lies! (Psalm 34:12–13).

Reference:

Proverbs 10:32, Ephesians 4:29–31

WISDOM TIP 26

Don't get sidetracked by distractions.

"Look straight ahead, and fix your eyes on what lies before you. Mark out a straight path for your feet; stay on the safe path. Don't get sidetracked; keep your feet from following evil."

Proverbs 4:25–27 (NLT)

"Keep your eyes straight ahead; ignore all sideshow distractions. Watch your step, and the road will stretch out smooth before you. Look neither right nor left; leave evil in the dust."

Proverbs 4:25–27 (THE MESSAGE)

Distractions come in all shapes and sizes. Isn't it funny that we are not distracted by things that we hold no interest in? When we are led astray, it's because something caught our attention that is of interest to us. Remember the importance of guarding your heart and the entrances to your heart being your eyes and ears. Wisdom cautions us to keep a fixed gaze on our path.

Stay focused and be alert. Focus allows you to keep your eyes steady along the path that is right and specifically chosen for you. Alertness and focus protects you from ravenous wolves who seek to devour your destiny. Imagine how much better off Little Red Riding Hood would have been if she would have ignored the distractions set by the Big Bad Wolf and never stopped to engage in a conversation with him. Don't allow destiny altering people, decisions, or distractions to enter your life. As the saying goes, "Stay woke!"

Reference:

Deuteronomy 5:33; Job 31:1; Psalm 119:37; Proverbs 16:17 (THE MESSAGE, NASB, CEV); Matthew 6:22; Ephesians 5:15–17, 5:15-17

WISDOM TIP 27

Train your life's palate to receive the acquired taste of wisdom.

> "Dear friend, pay close attention to this, my wisdom; listen very closely to the way I see it. Then you'll acquire a taste for good sense; what I tell you will keep you out of trouble."
>
> Proverbs 5:1–2 (THE MESSAGE)

> "My son, pay attention to my wisdom. Open your ears to my understanding so that you may act with foresight and speak with insight."
>
> Proverbs 5:1–2 (GW)

> "My son, pay attention to my wisdom; listen carefully to my wise counsel. Then you will show discernment, and your lips will express what you've learned."
>
> Proverbs 5:1–2 (NLT)

To acquire a taste for good sense tells me that you have the potential to be turned off from Lady Wisdom when you are first introduced to her. An acquired taste develops over time. For instance, the first time I had a sip of coffee, I wanted to spew it out my mouth. However, sometime in my mid-thirties, sleep-deprived with three kids and a demanding career, I decided to try the "energy booster" and over time coffee has become my morning drink of choice. I love the taste, the smell, and the pep it provides me at the start of my day. Likewise, you may want to spew wisdom out of your life because its ways appear to be too hard, too strong, and too limited. Over time, you will discover that wisdom has given you an advantage over your peers; you'll be the go to person for advice and counsel and the things that flow from your lips will be both wise and beneficial for you and others. You'll know how to get to the heart of issues that are brought before you without knowing the entire story, and you'll be able to easily know the best choice to make when presented with a litany of selections. It will sneak up on you and you will soon discover that you have "acquired" a taste for Lady Wisdom, her direction, and her rewards.

Reference:

Proverbs 10:21, 15:2, 16:23

WISDOM TIP 28

Beware of seduction!

> "The lips of a seductive woman are oh so sweet, her soft words are oh so smooth. But it won't be long before she's gravel in your mouth, a pain in your gut, a wound in your heart. She's dancing down the primrose path to Death; she's headed straight for Hell and taking you with her. She hasn't a clue about Real Life, about who she is or where she's going.
>
> "So, my friend, listen closely; don't treat my words casually. Keep your distance from such a woman; absolutely stay out of her neighborhood. You don't want to squander your wonderful life, to waste your precious life among the hardhearted. Why should you allow strangers to take advantage of you? Why be exploited by those who care nothing for you? You don't want to end your life full of regrets, nothing but skin and bones, Saying, 'Oh, why didn't I do what they told me? Why did I reject a disciplined life? Why didn't I listen to my mentors, or take my teachers seriously? My life is ruined. I haven't one blessed thing to show for my life!'"
>
> Proverbs 5: 3–14 (THE MESSAGE)

Warning ALERT! Warning ALERT! Now you can never say that no one told you what the outcome would be if you allow yourself to fall prey to the alluring words of a seducer. Proverbs has personified the seducer as a woman, but some of the best smooth talk known to the world has come from the lips of the male species. If you continue to read, then I must warn you that you will be held responsible for the information you receive. The ways of wisdom are not grievous or unreasonable. The ways of wisdom will literally save your life if you will take heed. Sex is one of those topics most people do not like to talk about openly. However, if you never have the opportunity to learn about the smooth lips of a person who will say anything to get you into bed, then you will not be prepared to combat the allure when it is staring you in the face: six feet tall, dark, and handsome. For my gentlemen: the perfect ten, body banging, hair flowing, and lips looking juicer than honey. Now is the time to come up with a predetermined response that will allow you to stay focused and alert.

There is nothing new under the sun, what is tempting now has been tempting since the beginning of mankind. The main seductions seem to linger along the lines of power, money, and sex. Allow this wisdom lesson to act as a warning alert to those who are currently involved in a sexual relationship outside of the confines of marriage. Sex may seem sweet at first, it may go down smooth at the moment, but sooner or later, it will be like gravel in your mouth. You will try to rid yourself of it, but the small particles and residue of the gravel will remain longer than you anticipated and do more damage than you ever thought both physically and emotionally. Notice that the path of the seductive woman (or man) leads to DEATH and HELL. No need to sugar coat this topic, truth is truth. Make a decision to get off that road today. Submit this area of your life to God, so He may endow you with the power you need to stay clear from the road of the seductress.

Reference:

Psalm 55:21; Proverbs 5:20, 6:24–26, 7:5, 22:14, 30:20; 2 Peter 2:14 (CEV and THE MESSAGE)

WISDOM TIP 29

Bloom where you are planted.

> "Drink water from your own well—share your love only with your wife. Why spill the water of your springs in the streets, having sex with just anyone? You should reserve it for yourselves. Never share it with strangers.
>
> "Let your wife be a fountain of blessing for you. Rejoice in the wife of your youth. She is a loving deer, a graceful doe. Let her breasts satisfy you always. May you always be captivated by her love. Why be captivated, my son, by an immoral woman, or fondle the breasts of a promiscuous woman?"
>
> Proverbs 5: 15–20 (NLT)

The grass is not greener on the other side, they just water their grass more often. In other words, if you make the commitment to cultivate your marriage and the spouse that you doted over during the dating and honeymoon stage, then you too will enjoy nice fertile springs that will nourish your garden of love. Love what belongs to you, cultivate what you have, bloom where you are planted. If you make the decision to be captivated by the breast of your covenant partner, your husband, or wife, you will be satisfied all the days of your life, both in loving and being loved. If you take this to heart, your marriage relationship will leave you so intoxicated with love and affection that there will be no room to desire the attention of another man or woman.

Reference:

Song of Solomon 4:12, Ecclesiastes 9:9, Malachi 2:14–15

WISDOM TIP 30

Secret sin will always be found out!

"Mark well that God doesn't miss a move you make; he's aware of every step you take. The shadow of your sin will overtake you; you'll find yourself stumbling all over yourself in the dark. Death is the reward of an undisciplined life; your foolish decisions trap you in a dead end."

Proverbs 5:21–23 (THE MESSAGE)

There is nothing hidden from God. Don't deceive yourself into thinking that you will get away with "IT," whatever the "IT" may be in your life. This is not meant to be a word of condemnation, but a gentle nudge that provokes you to get the "IT" out of your life so you can have a free conscience before God, within yourself, and before others. Sin is a killer, in fact, sin is the number one killer in our world today. The root of all societal woes is a sin problem. Apply wisdom to your life, so the foolishness of sin will not overtake you and alter the course of your life. You may be able to hide "IT" from me and everyone else, but the "eyes" of the Lord are everywhere. Ultimately, sin will expose you and its consequences will find you out.

Reference:

Hebrews 4:13; Proverbs 15:3, 1:31–32; Jeremiah 16:17; Numbers 32:23b

WISDOM TIP 31

Stay out of the affairs of others.

"My child, if you have put up security for a friend's debt or agreed to guarantee the debt of a stranger—if you have trapped yourself by your agreement and are caught by what you said—follow my advice and save yourself, for you have placed yourself at your friend's mercy. Now swallow your pride; go and beg to have your name erased. Don't put it off; do it now! Don't rest until you do."

Proverbs 6: 1–4 (NLT)

When you see a friend or loved one in a bind it is always tempting to rescue them, even at your own expense. The word of wisdom is very clear on this one, we must resist the urge to "put up security" for the debt of others. Putting up security may come in the form of cosigning for loans of others or agreeing to take on another person's responsibilities in an attempt to make their load a little easier. While we are given clear instructions to provide a helping hand when we see others in need, we are to act wisely and within our capacity to respond to the need. If you have to take out a loan to help someone, then you are not truly in a position to offer help to that person. If you are offering assistance at the expense of your own family or your own responsibilities, then you must pause and determine if this is really what you should be doing. If you find that you are already in this situation, it is not too late to reverse what you have done or agreed to. Swallow you pride and go quickly to have your name erased from that cosigned loan, or go quickly to your friend or loved one and explain why you can no longer handicap them with your assistance.

Often, God is trying to grow a person in the area of their trust and reliance being solely on HIM. When we step in to rescue without God's permission, we are interfering with the work He would like to do in the life of the person we are attempting to rescue. In addition, it creates a handicap by placing their reliance on you rather than the God who lives in them and has given them strength to do all thing through HIM (Jesus Christ). Pray for discernment to know when it is time to help and when it is time to step back and allow God to do the work He seeks to accomplish in their lives. Trust that the same God who began a good work in you will in fact complete that good work in the lives of those you care about when you take a back seat and stop rescuing them from the consequences of their decisions.

Reference:

Proverbs 11:15, 17:18, 22:26

WISDOM TIP 32

Model the wisdom of ants.

"Take a lesson from the ants, you lazybones. Learn from their ways and become wise! Though they have no prince or governor or ruler to make them work, they labor hard all summer, gathering food for the winter."

Proverbs 6:6–8 (NLT)

Think of how small and insignificant an ant is in comparison to the natural order of living beings. Despite the small and seemingly insignificant stature of an ant, it has been famous for centuries for its social habits, foresight, and industrious ways. Just as the proverb indicates, ants collect their food in the summer. It is reasonable to assume that we have all experienced an ant either outside or inside our homes in the summer. The food you may have witnessed them trailing off with in a systematic military straight line is prepared for winter by biting off the end of the grain to prevent it from germinating and lain in cells within the ant mound till needed. Each ant is said to work independently of the rest, though guided by a innate instinct to add to the common store. Now what is your excuse, Mr. Super Human, created with superior intelligence, abilities, and resources? Will you allow a being as tiny as a fingernail to put you to shame? If ants have enough fortitude to set a schedule, work when it is time to work, plan ahead, and function as a team for the common good, how much more should those of us created in the image of Allmighty God? Do not allow your potential to be wasted due to a failure to implement your dream. I once heard it put this way, "The dream is free, but the hustle is real." Meaning, your dreams may come from inspiration, but it takes work and proper planning to make your dreams transform into reality. Learn from the ant by putting your efforts toward the right type of work during the right season. There is a time for everything and a season for every activity under the heavens (Ecclesiastes 3:1). Go ahead and flex! Use your Super Human power to show the ant why you were given dominion over the earth. Wisely set your hand to the plow and work your plan until it metamorphoses into your reality.

Reference:

Proverbs 30:24–25, 19:15, 10:5

WISDOM TIP 33

Stop sleeping on opportunity.
(P-O-O-R – Passing on Opportunity Repeatedly)

"So how long are you going to laze around doing nothing? How long before you get out of bed? A nap here, a nap there, a day off here, a day off there, sit back, take it easy—do you know what comes next? Just this: You can look forward to a dirt-poor life, poverty your permanent houseguest!"

PROVERBS 6: 9–11 (THE MESSAGE)

> "But you, lazybones, how long will you sleep? When will you wake up? A little extra sleep, a little more slumber, a little folding of the hands to rest—then poverty will pounce on you like a bandit; scarcity will attack you like an armed robber."
>
> PROVERBS 6: 9–11 (NLT)

The previous wisdom tip provoked you to heed the work ethic of the ant. Now you are encouraged to rise and work. Procrastination is the demise of every genius with a brilliant idea. Yes, my friend, sleep and idleness are dream killers. An hour here and there turns into a day, a day here and there turns into a week, a week a month, a month a year. You get the idea. Literally and figuratively, within the blink of an eye you will have moved into your twenties, thirties, forties, fifties, and beyond without making any progress on your God-given idea or talent due to a poor work ethic. If that doesn't grab your attention, then maybe the poor financial state that seems to plague chronic procrastinators will get your attention. Sleepers wake up to find themselves unable to help themselves or anyone else because of their disregard and neglect of good old-fashioned hard work. In the words of Teddy Pendergrass, "Wake up everybody no more sleeping in bed, no more backward thinking, time for thinking ahead!" Arise and shine, your opportunity to display your greatness awaits you!

Reference:

Proverbs 6:9–11, 19:15, 20:13

WISDOM TIP 34

A scoundrel can be identified by his words, listen carefully.

> "A good-for-nothing scoundrel is a person who has a dishonest mouth. He winks his eye, makes a signal with his foot, and points with his fingers. He devises evil all the time with a twisted mind. He spreads conflict. That is why disaster will come on him suddenly. In a moment he will be crushed beyond recovery."
>
> PROVERBS 6:12–15 (GW)

A "good-for-nothing scoundrel" can be easily recognized by the words he speaks. A scoundrel cannot be judged by appearances. Scoundrels come in every shape, size, skin complexion, and social status known to man. Instead of "knowing one when you see one," you will definitely know one when you hear one. We've learned tons about the mouth of the wicked thus far, they spread conflict, gossip, fabrications, and intentionally slander the reputations of others. The "good-for-nothing scoundrel" will be heard from and heard of for miles away, all across campus, and all over town. Their reputation will precede them. The wink of his eye, the signal of his foot, or the point of his finger may all fly over your head at first, so pay close attention to his words. "Psst ... hey you, I want to let you in on a little something I heard," says the scoundrel. "I'm only telling you this because I like you," says the scoundrel. "I know you thought she was your friend, but this is what I overheard," says the scoundrel. "I promise I will keep this between the two of us," says the scoundrel ten minutes before the exaggerated version hits the rumor mill. When you hear of a person such as this, do not trust him. In fact, stay far away because, one day, his schemes will catch up to him and you do not want to be anywhere near his zip code when the sudden disaster brought on by his cunning schemes hits the fan.

Reference:

Proverbs 4:24, 10:32, 16:27

WISDOM TIP 35

Treasure wise parental guidance.

> "My son, obey your father's commands, and don't neglect your mother's instruction. Keep their words always in your heart. Tie them around your neck. When you walk, their counsel will lead you. When you sleep, they will protect you. When you wake up, they will advise you. For their command is a lamp and their instruction a light; their corrective discipline is the way to life."
>
> PROVERBS 6:20–23 (NLT)

If you have had the luxury of having wise parents, then you know that their words of wisdom are priceless. If you have heeded the words of wisdom your parents passed down to you, then you know firsthand that they saved you from much trouble, heart ache, and the consequences of misguided decisions. If you now have children of your own, you completely understand in hindsight exactly what your parents were trying to instill in your heart while you were young, and you most likely find yourself repeating the same commentary you once sneered at. The key in this passage is wise counsel. Some were not raised with such wise counsel so this idea of parental guidance seems foreign. I'm so happy that wisdom has no expiration date and no age limit; what you missed from wise parental guidance you can now gain from God's wisdom. The good news is that once you begin to operate in God's wisdom, He will accelerate your progress as if you've walked in the ways of wisdom your entire life. God's wisdom has a way of catching you up and making things right in your heart, so your decisions will guide you down a path of life that puts you in position to be the voice of wisdom for someone else.

Reference:

Ephesians 6:1; Proverbs 1:8, 7:1, 10:17; Ecclesiastes 7:5

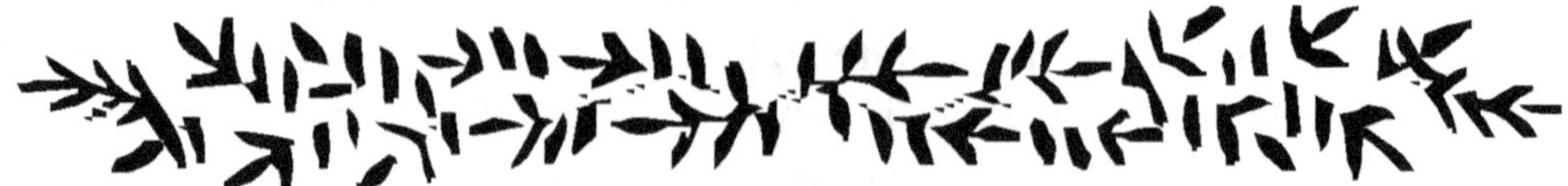

WISDOM TIP 36

Forbidden fruit will cost you; if you play with fire you are sure to get burned.

"Don't lust for her beauty. Don't let her coy glances seduce you. For a prostitute will bring you to poverty, but sleeping with another man's wife will cost you your life. Can a man scoop a flame into his lap and not have his clothes catch on fire? Can he walk on hot coals and not blister his feet? So it is with the man who sleeps with another man's wife. He who embraces her will not go unpunished."

PROVERBS 6:25–29 (NLT)

Just as fire destroys all that it touches, you can be sure that lust will singe your life in one way or another. Although the contents appear to be addressed to men, it bears truth for all people, men and women alike. You are warned to repress any lustful thoughts you may have for a beautiful woman who is married to another man or for a handsome, powerful man who is married to another woman. The warning is given to control your own internal lust because that's where the heart of the matter lies. If you can control yourself internally, chances are you will be able to conquer the temptation outwardly. Additionally, as with all other areas of wisdom, one word of wisdom can be applied to many areas of life. Take this warning to heart; if you play with fire, you are sure to get burned. Fire may be in the form of an alluring woman or man. Fire may be in the form of illegal business transactions, or fire may be in the form of alcohol or drugs. Whatever form your enticement toward lust may take on, be sure to not be enticed by the wink of her eye. Consequences are sure to follow every action so be careful not to get singed by the flames.

Reference:

Leviticus 18:20, Proverbs 6:29, Matthew 5:28–30

WISDOM TIP 37

Participating in adultery is an act of self-sabotage.

"But the man who commits adultery is an utter fool, for he destroys himself. He will be wounded and disgraced. His shame will never be erased. For the woman's jealous husband will be furious, and he will show no mercy when he takes revenge. He will accept no compensation, nor be satisfied with a payoff of any size."

Proverbs 6:32–35 (NLT)

"Adultery is a brainless act, soul-destroying, self-destructive; expect a bloody nose, a black eye, and a reputation ruined for good. For jealousy detonates rage in a cheated husband; wild for revenge, he won't make allowances. Nothing you say or pay will make it all right; neither bribes nor reason will satisfy him."

Proverbs 6:32–35 (THE MESSAGE)

Recall the woman who had been caught in the act of adultery when Jesus walked the earth. The man fled from the consequences, but the woman was brought to the center of town to be stoned. Jesus' response was, "He who is without sin cast the first stone." I believe Jesus was saying the person who has not slept with this woman or a woman like her cast the first stone. Generations before this scene and for many generations after, men and women have fallen prey to the forbidden fruit of illicit sex. How to accomplish the monumental task of fleeing from all sexual temptation in a culture that is over sexualized and bombarded with sexual images is found in Proverbs 7:4–5, "Talk to Wisdom as to a sister. Treat Insight as your companion. They'll be with you to fend off the Temptress— that smooth-talking, honey-tongued Seductress" (THE MESSAGE).

Further, may the fear of a jealous, raving lunatic of a husband or wife act as an additional insurance policy against messing around with another person's spouse. Crimes of passion are committed daily; many crimes of passion involve members of a secret love affair either revealed to a spouse or unexpectedly caught by a spouse. James Brown put it well when he said, "I don't know karate but I know crazy!" Avoid, getting caught up in the crazy jealous rage of a scorned spouse.

Let me share a story I heard about a young man who lacked wisdom in the area of seduction.

"As I stood at the window of my house looking out through the shutters, watching the mindless crowd stroll by, I spotted a young man without any sense arriving at the corner of the street where she lived, then turning up the path to her house. It was dusk, the evening coming on, the darkness thickening into night. Just then, a woman met him—she'd been lying in wait for him, dressed to seduce him. Brazen and brash she was, restless and roaming, never at home, walking the streets, loitering in the mall, hanging out at every corner in town.

"She threw her arms around him and kissed him, boldly took his arm and said, 'I've got all the makings for a feast—today I made my offerings, my vows are all paid, so now I've come to find you, hoping to catch sight of your face—and here you are! I've spread fresh, clean sheets on my bed—colorful, imported linens. My bed is aromatic with spices and exotic fragrances. Come, let's make love all night, spend the night in ecstatic lovemaking! My husband's not home; he's away on business, and he won't be back for a month.'

"Soon, she has him eating out of her hand, bewitched by her honeyed speech. Before you know it, he's trotting behind her, like a calf led to the butcher shop, like a stag lured into ambush and then shot with an arrow, like a bird flying into a net not knowing that its flying life is over.

"So, friends, listen to me, take these words of mine most seriously. Don't fool around with a woman like that; don't even stroll through her neighborhood. Countless victims come under her spell; she's the death of many a poor man. She runs a halfway house to hell, fits you out with a shroud and a coffin."

If the language of my story sounds a little Shakespearean to you, it is because this scandalous story I've shared with you was taken directly from Proverbs 7:6-27 (THE MESSAGE). Whoever said reading the Bible was boring lied to you.

Reference:

Proverbs 9:16–18

WISDOM TIP 38

When the student is ready, the teacher appears.

"'You—I'm talking to all of you, everyone out here on the streets! Listen, you idiots—learn good sense! You blockheads—shape up! Don't miss a word of this—I'm telling you how to live well, I'm telling you how to live at your best. My mouth chews and savors and relishes truth—I can't stand the taste of evil! You'll only hear true and right words from my mouth; not one syllable will be twisted or skewed. You'll recognize this as true—you with open minds; truth-ready minds will see it at once. Prefer my life-disciplines over chasing after money, and God-knowledge over a lucrative career. For Wisdom is better than all the trappings of wealth; nothing you could wish for holds a candle to her."

Proverbs 8:4–11 (THE MESSAGE)

Those who have sought after a mentor or desired insight from a wise more mature person, I have great news for you! A mentor by the name of Lady Wisdom has been seeking you. Even better, her mentorship is open to all, not just a few select chosen people with the right last name and pedigree. For those of you who have enjoyed the benefits of being molded and directed by strong mentors, I'm sure you will agree that mentorship has given you a "head start" in your life, career, business, or relationships because of the insight and direction you have received from your mentor. However, there are many who have never been mentored closely, not even by a parent. No matter who you are, your background, or what situation you currently find yourself in, Lady Wisdom is the mentor that levels the playing field. Wisdom is calling out to everyone, even everyone in "da streets." All self-proclaimed "idiots and blockheads," Lady Wisdom is inviting you to take a seat at the table. Further, Lady Wisdom is a mentor for all personality types: naïve, easily influenced, gullible, foolish, or those of us who consider ourselves wise in our own eyes. Lady Wisdom announces loudly, "Come to me and receive the instruction that will add value to your life." Lady Wisdom offers numerous tangible, yet intangible, gifts when we open our lives to her mentorship.

Let's take a look at Lady Wisdom's thirty-second "elevator pitch":

> "I am Lady Wisdom, and I live next to Sanity; Knowledge and Discretion live just down the street. The Fear-of-God means hating Evil, whose ways I hate with a passion—pride and arrogance and crooked talk. Good counsel and common sense are my characteristics; I am both Insight and the Virtue to live it out. With my help, leaders rule, and lawmakers legislate fairly; With my help, governors govern, along with all in legitimate authority. I love those who love me; those who look for me find me. Wealth and Glory accompany me—also substantial Honor and a Good Name. My benefits are worth more than a big salary, even a very big salary; the returns on me exceed any imaginable bonus. You can find me on Righteous Road—that's where I walk—at the intersection of Justice Avenue, handing out life to those who love me, filling their arms with life—armloads of life!"
>
> Proverbs 12–21 (THE MESSAGE)

If you desire any of the attributes Lady Wisdom is pitching, then take a moment to welcome Lady Wisdom as your supreme mentor. Because she is a lady, she will not force herself upon you. When the student is ready, the teacher appears. Are you the eagerly awaited student? Open the ears of your heart and the eyes of your understanding, Lady Wisdom awaits you.

WISDOM TIP 39

Before you attempt to "drop" knowledge, know your audience.

> "If you reason with an arrogant cynic, you'll get slapped in the face; confront bad behavior and get a kick in the shins. So don't waste your time on a scoffer; all you'll get for your pains is abuse. But if you correct those who care about life, that's different—they'll love you for it! Save your breath for the wise—they'll be wiser for it; tell good people what you know—they'll profit from it."
>
> PROVERBS 9: 7–9 (THE MESSAGE)

> "Anyone who rebukes a mocker will get an insult in return. Anyone who corrects the wicked will get hurt. So don't bother correcting mockers; they will only hate you. But correct the wise, and they will love you. Instruct the wise, and they will be even wiser. Teach the righteous, and they will learn even more."
>
> PROVERBS 9: 7–9 (NLT)

Any successful public speaker will give you this advice, "know your audience." Wisdom offers the gift of discernment, which allows you to understand exactly who you are addressing, the mocker or the wise. When you hold a conversation with a fellow seeker of wisdom they will welcome your wise counsel and seek to apply the counsel to the area of their life where it fits best. A mocker, on the other hand, is not open to hear wise counsel even if you wrote it on a hundred-dollar bill and taped it to his ear. In fact, a mocker will view you as an enemy to his way of life and treat your words of wisdom as a personal attack. As a result, attempting to correct or teach a mocker will only lead to disagreements, arguments, and strife. Wisdom will allow you to discern between the two. Placing your great grandmother's heirloom pearls on a pig would not stop a pig from playing in the mud. Likewise, wasting your valuable breath, time, and knowledge on a fool who has no plans of receiving your instruction or changing his path will produce frustration and stress that you do not need in your life. Know your audience.

Reference:

Proverbs 10:8, 15:12, 19:25, 23:9; Matthew 7:6; Psalm 141:5

WISDOM TIP 40

Life is choice driven!

"Live wisely and wisdom will permeate your life; mock life and life will mock you."

PROVERBS 9:12 (THE MESSAGE)

"If you are wise, you are wise for yourself [for your own benefit]; If you scoff [thoughtlessly ridicule and disdain], you alone will pay the penalty."

PROVERBS 9:12 (AMPC)

"If you become wise, you will be the one to benefit. If you scorn wisdom, you will be the one to suffer."

PROVERBS 9:12 (NLT)

Your life today is a summation of all the choices you have made up to this point. Life is choice driven, you will live or die by the choices you make. Death will not necessarily occur as a physical death of your body. Death is displayed as the end result of poor choices. Look around and I'm sure you will be able to identify at least one example of death brought on by foolish choices. I also know that you have a deep desire to avoid the dysfunction you may have witnessed. Wisdom is here for the taking to make your life easier and more fulfilled. However, foolishness awaits on the other side. Choose this day the voice you will heed—the voice of wisdom or the voice of foolishness. The choice is yours alone just as the consequences will also be yours alone.

WISDOM TIP 41

Folly is a deathtrap hidden by the appearance of fun.

"The woman Stupidity is loud, gullible, and ignorant. She sits at the doorway of her house. She is enthroned on the high ground of the city and calls to those who pass by, those minding their own business, 'Whoever is gullible turn in here!'

"She says to a person without sense, 'Stolen waters are sweet, and food eaten in secret is tasty.'

"But he does not know that the souls of the dead are there, that her guests are in the depths of hell."

Proverbs 9:13–18 (GW)

"The woman named Folly is brash. She is ignorant and doesn't know it. She sits in her doorway on the heights overlooking the city. She calls out to men going by who are minding their own business. 'Come in with me,' she urges the simple. To those who lack good judgment, she says, 'Stolen water is refreshing; food eaten in secret tastes the best!' But little do they know that the dead are there. Her guests are in the depths of the grave."

Proverbs 9:13–18 (NLT)

The archnemesis of Lady Wisdom is best known as Folly. Folly is as bold as Lady Wisdom, she too stands in the streets summoning the masses to enter her door. The difference with Folly is, once she gets you to the doorway, the horror movie begins as she whisks you into a darkened room called ambiance, sets the mood by offering you food she stole from the market earlier that day, and gets you so drunk that your blurred vision will be unable to see the corpses of her previous victims. It all tastes good going down, exotic even, but wait until the next day when the high wears off and you have the opportunity to see her in the daylight. The problem is, by then, it is too late! You try to move, but you are chained to the bed with unimaginable aches and pains throughout your body. Here comes Lady Folly without her weave, makeup, and lashes. She's removed the Spanx and it's all hanging out, you can finally see her for who she really is. You've come to the realization that you've been hoodwinked and deceived. However, you are now trapped; the most recent victim of her cunning and conniving schemes. Your only relief is to consume the very pleasures that trapped you, this time, as an escape from the reality of your confinement. Her house has one entrance and one exit. Don't get caught up in the fun of Folly's deathtrap.

Reference:

Proverbs 5:6–8

WISDOM TIP 42

What you do to get it, you will have to do to keep it.

"Tainted wealth has no lasting value, but right living can save your life."

Proverbs 10:2 (NLT)

"Wealth you get by dishonesty will do you no good, but honesty can save your life."

PROVERBS 10:2 (GNT)

Whatever you did to get it, you will have to continue to do to keep it. If you stole to get wealth, you will have to continue to steal to preserve the wealth you stole in the first place. If you lied, cheated, and connived to get to your measure of success, then you will continually have to exercise the same means to remain in that place. Not to mention, the enemies you made along the way. The term "more money, more problems" is only true for those who do not have the wisdom required to assign money to pious purposes. This passage is specifically talking to those whose monetary gain is taken rather than earned or earned for the purposes of greater access to shameful exploits. Those "dead presidents" won't be worth the paper they are printed on when you are standing knee-deep in the middle of consequences that will surely come knocking on your door demanding payment in full. The pursuit of a life of luxury without freedom is no life at all, it is just another source of death and destruction. Whatever measure of success you desire to attain, do it the right way so you can enjoy it without looking over your shoulder. Stolen bread is only sweet for a season. When it has been digested, you may find that the hidden worms are eating away at you from the inside out.

Reference:

Proverbs 11:4, 11:18, 21:6

WISDOM TIP 43

Diligence will reward you sooner and later.

"Lazy people are soon poor; hard workers get rich."

PROVERBS 10:4 (NLT)

"Poor is he who works with a negligent *and* idle hand, but the hand of the diligent makes *him* rich."

PROVERBS 10:4 (AMP)

If you are lazy and put absolutely no effort toward anything in life, you will gradually grow poor in both dollars and ability. No grind, no rind. However, if we look a little closer at this proverb, we discover that laziness does not simply constitute the act of doing nothing, but also consists of being negligent in what you do. Basically, if you are doing your job "half-way," then you will one day grow poor. Poor in reliability, poor in trust, poor in opportunity, poor in growth and potential. The list of areas in which you can potentially become poor in based on laziness and negligence are vast. Meanwhile, the opposite holds true for those who are diligent. If you want to prosper in life, be diligent in your efforts. Diligence is simply applying disciplined practices consistently. Over time, consistently diligent efforts produce tremendous results. Diligently working on something for thirty minutes a day turns into 10,950 minutes a year. Diligently saving $50 a month for thirty years turns into $18,000. I purposely used small numbers to show that diligence adds up. The other benefits of diligence are the nonmonetary areas that bring you riches, like a rich reputation, a rich work ethic, a rich skill set, which all have the potential to lead to monetary gain. Diligence will prove to reward you in your present and your future.

Reference:

Proverbs 12:27, 13:4, 18:9, 21:5

WISDOM TIP 44

Sleeping during harvest will land you in an empty barn.

"A wise youth harvests in the summer, but one who sleeps during harvest is a disgrace."

PROVERBS 10:5 (NLT)

"He who gathers during summer *and* takes advantage of his opportunities is a son who acts wisely, *but* he who sleeps during harvest *and* ignores the moment of opportunity is a son who acts shamefully."

PROVERBS 10:5 (AMP)

In order to gather during harvest, you must be vigilant and alert. Taking advantage of opportunities is a form of gathering harvest. Opportunities come to our lives in many shapes and forms; some sit silently by, waiting to be recognized, while others stare us boldly in the face, demanding to be seized and acted upon. Either way, we are wise to act when the opportunity is present. A wise person once said, "An opportunity of a lifetime, must be seized in the lifetime of the opportunity." On the other hand, one who sleeps during harvest, ignoring the lifetime of the opportunity is a person who lacks wisdom on so many levels. Seek out the opportunities that God has placed within your reach. Not all opportunities will be for your benefit, some will be for the benefit of others. However, you will find that even the gathering of the harvest for the sake of others will allow you to gather from the sheaves that fall to the ground. Ask Ruth and Boaz how beneficial gleaning can be. In modern-day language, Ruth was the poor girl getting her food from the local food pantry, not realizing that the handsome director of the pantry was actually the owner of a large grocery store chain who was looking for a good woman to put a "ring on it." She was "gleaning" food in order to feed herself and her mother-in-law based on a vow she was committed to keep. Meanwhile, Boaz was "gleaning" the character of a woman who was wife material. Carpe diem—seize the day! Put your hand to the plow so you can gather your harvest.

Reference:

Proverbs 6:6–8, 30:25

WISDOM TIP 45

Live your life from the standpoint of the memory you want to create.

"We have happy memories of the godly, but the name of a wicked person rots away."

PROVERBS 10:7 (NLT)

"A good and honest life is a blessed memorial; a wicked life leaves a rotten stench."

PROVERBS 10:7 (THE MESSAGE)

The great Roman philosopher Cicero once said, "The life of the dead lies in the memory of the living." Live your life in the way you desire to be remembered. Let's test this proverb. When you hear the names Hitler, Charles Manson, Jeffrey Dahmer, Bin Laden, how do you feel? The very thought of those wicked men makes me want to fumigate the room. Now, think about the names of Mother Theresa, Martin Luther King Jr., Gandhi, and Kyna Williams. Notice the difference in your reaction and your blood pressure. That my friend is the difference between the memory of the righteous and the rotten stench of the wicked. Let's thumb it down to everyday life. We can all remember the unruly neighborhood kids our parents forced us to play with who broke every toy they got their hands on. To this day, some of us can't bear to recall the trauma they caused our favorite toys. Now that just barely touches the surface of the stench the memory of the wicked leaves behind. The wicked are normally people you hate to see coming, you count every second until their departure, and pray they do not return any time soon.

I'm reminded of a lady in the Book of Acts named Tabitha (translated Dorcas in the Greek). She lived her life in such a giving and helpful manner that when she died, the widows of her town gathered in the room where her body lay with all the items she made for them while she was alive. In fact, she was such a generous and helpful person that the local people would not accept that it was her appointed time to die. They immediately sent for Peter and urged him to come at once. When Peter arrived, he found all those whom Dorcas (Tabitha) had encountered during her life lifting up the items she once so graciously blessed them with. I believe one of the compelling reasons why Peter immediately responded with the faith to raise Dorcas from the dead was due to all the good deeds recounted to him by the men and the line of mourners who were no doubt recalling all the good Dorcas once did as Peter made his way to her home. By the time Peter arrived to Dorcas's home, where she lay dead, his faith was ignited to raise her from the dead so her goodness towards God's people would continue. So be it unto us, our lives should reflect helpful and honorable actions that will cause others to thank God for having allowed our paths to cross with every memory.

Reference:

Proverbs 22:1; Psalm 34:16, 112:6

WISDOM TIP 46

Close your mouth and open your ears!

"The wise are glad to be instructed, but babbling fools fall flat on their faces."

Proverbs 10:8 (NLT)

"The wise in heart [are willing to learn so they] will accept *and* obey commands (instruction), but the babbling fool [who is arrogant and thinks himself wise] will come to ruin."

Proverbs 10:8 (AMP)

There is a good reason why we have one mouth and two ears. We are to listen more than we speak. In the area of gaining wisdom and insight, the same holds true. No one enjoys being in the presence of a self-proclaimed know-it-all. In fact, most people avoid such personalities and secretly hope for their demise. Remain teachable no matter how many alphabets you have behind your name (degrees). Likewise, listen to the opinions of others even if you do not agree with them. Listen with the intent of understanding the perspective of someone who thinks completely opposite than you on a subject. Receive instruction with gladness even from someone whom you believe to be your junior. When we get to the point in life where we are no longer willing to learn from others, then we come to ruin not simply due to a lack of counsel, but by way of our limited experiences, relationships, and perspective. Close your mouth, open your ears and heart to receive from others so that your life can continue to expand.

Reference:

Proverbs 1:5, 9:8–9, 10:13–14

WISDOM TIP 47

What's done in the dark will one day be found out, so walk in the light!

"Honesty lives confident and carefree, but Shifty is sure to be exposed."

PROVERBS 10:9 (THE MESSAGE)

"Whoever walks in integrity walks securely, but whoever takes crooked paths will be found out."

PROVERBS 10:9 (NIV)

Wisdom requires us to walk in sincerity, integrity, and uprightness of heart before God and people. Rather than list all the ways of deceit, I will provide a clear picture of what a walk of integrity and moral character looks like. A life of integrity and honesty provides the benefits of security that money cannot buy. Further, honesty eliminates the fear of exposure that prohibits you from living free and authentically. Honesty provides confidence that allows you to be carefree in your mind, giving you a clear conscience about the affairs of your life as well as your dealings with others. Sneaking, creeping, keeping it on the DL (down-low), or however you choose to term "shifty" is sure to be exposed sooner or later, and with it comes the ruin of your reputation and many other things you once held dear. *John Gill's Exposition of the Bible* provides an excellent word picture of the benefits of integrity, "Such a man 'walks surely,' or securely, safely, confidently. Such an one has nothing to fear in his walk; he walks on 'terra firma,' on good ground, in a good way, which leads to life eternal: he has a good guide, the Spirit of God, which goes before him, and will be his guide even unto death, and lead him in the way everlasting, unto the land of uprightness; he has a good guard about him, not only the angels of God that encamp around him, but God himself is a wall of fire to him, and his power surrounds and protects him; he has many precious promises to support him; not only that the Lord will be a buckler to him, but will withhold no good thing from him, Proverbs 2:7; he has the gracious and supporting presence of God, when he passes through the fire and water of afflictions, and even through the valley of the shadow of death, so that he has nothing to fear; and has moreover the testimony of a good conscience; and having a good hope through grace, he walks in hope." **FORWARD, M-A-R-C-H with integrity.**

Reference:

Matthew 10:26, 1 Timothy 5:25, Proverbs 3:23, 26:26, 28:18

WISDOM TIP 48

Watch out for the wink!

"Whoever winks maliciously causes grief, and a chattering fool comes to ruin."

PROVERBS 10:10 (NIV)

"Those who wink their eyes are trouble makers, and the mocking fool will be brought down."

PROVERBS 10:10 (ISV)

In our day, an eye wink generally has a positive connotation; however, during biblical times an eye wink was a "sign of craft, malice, and deceptive plans" (Pulpit Commentary). Furthermore, what is worse than one who practices deceit is one who makes evil plans and talks about them, often termed in the Book of Proverbs as "the one who speaks foolishness." This person will surely come to a downfall. The life lesson here is simple—don't be the malicious eye winker. If you are planning malice, then definitely do not open your big mouth and brag about your plans. Finally, DO NOT hang around or associate with those whom you know or suspect are involved in some type of crazy scheme or plot. The law of association has proven that, more often than not, you become who you associate with. An old wise saying prominent in the African American community is, "If you have four broke friends, you are sure to be the fifth." Beware of the winkers when they cross your path. Most importantly, beware of the schemes cooking in their bag of tricks. When a fool opens his mouth to proudly let you in on his plans, believe that it really is too good to be true and will surely end in ruin.

Reference:

Proverbs 6:13, Job 15:12

WISDOM TIP 49

Refresh others with the words you speak.

"The mouth of a good person is a deep, life-giving well, but the mouth of the wicked is a dark cave of abuse."

Proverbs 10:11 (THE MESSAGE)

"The words of the godly are a life-giving fountain; the words of the wicked conceal violent intentions."

Proverbs 10:11 (NLT)

After spending time in the company of a person whose words are a "fountain of life," you walk away feeling good all over. Words can pick you up or tear you down. Words can bring comfort, peace, encouragement, and wisdom or they can do just the opposite and completely pulverize your spirit. Luke 6:45 says, "out of the abundance of the heart [the] mouth speaks" (author's paraphrase). Did you get that? What's in your heart will either produce a fountain of life or an assassin's bullet. What a person speaks comes directly from what is in their heart. I have often heard people say, "You can't judge me because you don't know what's in my heart." Yes, I do! I know what is in your heart based on your conversation, the words you continually speak. If your words are filled with cursing, filth, deceit, and half-truths, then that's exactly what your heart looks like. You either speak life or death. There is no in between with this one, no shaded gray areas. We must make the decision to choose life with the words we speak and recognize when we do not choose to use our words carefully we are by default making the choice to partner with destruction. The tongue is a powerful rudder that sits in the middle of your mouth. It can either be used for good or bad. Make a decision to be a person who refreshes others with your words. Turn your back on corrupt communication by filling your heart with words of life.

Reference:

Proverbs 10:20–21, 32, 15:7, 20:15; Ephesians 4:29; James 3:5–8; Matthew 12:34–37; Ecclesiastes 10:12

WISDOM TIP 50

Love will eventually conquer all.

"Hatred starts fights, but love pulls a quilt over the bickering."
PROVERBS 10:12 (THE MESSAGE)

"Hatred stirs up quarrels, but love makes up for all offenses."
PROVERBS 10:12 (NLT)

Ever notice when you dislike someone, everything they do is seen from a negative point of view. Your perspective of someone's motives and actions are skewed when you have a healthy disdain for them. While dislike is not as extreme as hatred, the same principle applies. The key to overcoming strife with others is love. Hatred stirs up conflict, while love covers all wrongs. If you want to avoid conflict, strife, and all other sorts of evil transactions brought on by behavior steeped in hatred, you must learn to operate in love. Love does not mean that you will never have to confront someone or call out bad behavior in others. Sometimes confrontation is the exact act of love required. However, confrontation is not synonymous with conflict. Confrontation mingled with hateful words or behavior are creators of conflict. Love can be felt, it can be sensed. Make sure your heart is filled with love and it will be received as such.

Reference:
1 Peter 4:8, Proverbs 17:9, 1 Corinthians 13

WISDOM TIP 51

"Lay up" good things so you can "lay hold" of their benefits in the future.

"The wise accumulate knowledge—a true treasure; know-it-alls talk too much—a sheer waste."

PROVERBS 10:14 (THE MESSAGE)

"The wise store up knowledge, but the mouth of a fool invites ruin."

PROVERBS 10:14 (NIV)

To accumulate or "lay up" means that you are in pursuit of a thing that, once obtained, is stored for the purpose of adding to what already exists. Wisdom should be pursued and stored so it can emerge when needed. Most salaried employees accumulate vacation time for the purpose of taking a break from work to revive themselves through rest and relaxation. Likewise, Proverbs 10:14 confirms that it is essential to put the right things in our heart so we may draw from them upon the proper time. If you continually put garbage in, then garbage is what will come out, proving you to be a fool who invites ruin. What we do on a consistent basis characterizes our lives. If you put the garbage of gossip, backbiting, and slander in your heart, then out of the abundance of the heart your mouth will speak. However, if you consistently seek after wisdom and the things of God that produce the fruits of the spirit, then when needed, love, joy, peace, patience, kindness, goodness, faithfulness, gentleness, and self-control will bubble over from the abundance of your heart through your mouth. What you lay up today will be at your disposal for withdrawal in the future.

Reference:

Proverbs 12:23, Matthew 12:35

WISDOM TIP 52

Enemies are often camouflaged in a layer of the latest gossip.

"Liars secretly hoard hatred; fools openly spread slander."

PROVERBS 10:18 (THE MESSAGE)

"Whoever conceals hatred with lying lips and spreads slander is a fool."

PROVERBS 10:18 (NIV)

Beware of those who pretend to be your friend, but are "secretly" harboring hatred in their heart for you. Young people often refer to this group of individuals as "haters." It's not time to "put your Stevie Wonder on" when it comes to the "haters" who may surround you. This proverb provides a way to recognize "haters" with 20/20 vision. If someone comes to you defaming or bashing someone else, red flag. If you see that same person talking to the person they just spoke evil of in your presence, red flag. If someone is constantly attempting to discredit someone else, red flag. Be leery of this type of person, keep them at arm's length. Not only are they secretly hoarding hatred rooted in envy and jealousy, but they are also showing you their foolish character. As my grandmother would say, "If they talk about them to you, they will talk about you to them."

Reference:

Exodus 23:1; Proverbs 26:24; Jeremiah 9:4; Psalm 5:9, 15:3, 50:20, 101:5

WISDOM TIP 53

Don't be a "mouth almighty, tongue everlasting!"

"The more talk, the less truth; the wise measure their words. The speech of a good person is worth waiting for; the blabber of the wicked is worthless."

PROVERBS 10:19-20 (THE MESSAGE)

"Too much talk leads to sin. Be sensible and keep your mouth shut. The words of the godly are like sterling silver; the heart of a fool is worthless."

PROVERBS 10:19-20 (NLT)

Are you beginning to catch the correlation between wisdom and your mouth? We've looked at the words you speak, now let's work on the frequency and quantity in which you speak them. The wise person knows when to speak and when to be quiet. Whereas, the blabbering fool always wants to be seen and heard. Put a muzzle over your mouth and hold your tongue until you have considered the circumstances, the person you are speaking to, the time, and occasion. Think before you speak. A good starting point for learning to measure your words are:

T - Is it True?
H - Is it Helpful?
I - Is it Inspiring?
N - Is it Necessary?
K - Is it Kind?

Proverbs 10:21 (THE MESSAGE) explains, "The talk of a good person is rich fare for many, but chatterboxes die of an empty heart." The first half of this proverb is where you want to find yourself—a person whose speech feeds, nourishes, and guides others.

Reference:
Proverbs 17:27, Ecclesiastes 5:3, James 1:19

WISDOM TIP 54

God has a sure path to financial security, follow it!

"The blessing of the LORD brings wealth, without painful toil for it."
PROVERBS 10:22 (NIV)

The blessing of the Lord will make you rich. However, God's blessing provides richness that can be seen outside of the financial arena. Richness in your health, mind, spirit, and relationships on top of financial security. These days, pressing the power button on your television or portable electronic device comes with a bombardment of images featuring the latest celebrity flashing all the bling they can afford to wear at one time. However, not many are as vocal about the torment and paranoia financial wealth has added to their lives. On the flip side, there are many people who work their fingers to the bone in pursuit of financial wealth. While hard work is appropriate and definitely a biblical principle to adopt in our lives, our work was never meant to be a sorrowful toil accompanied with dread. Nor were we meant to seek after riches to the point of losing sight of what really matters in life. The new covenant provided through the blood of Jesus made provision for our Spiritual blessing as well as our financial well-being. There are financial principles found in the word of God—namely tithing, giving of offerings, and sharing of resources—that when applied to your life will produce an open window of blessings and heavenly provision. When we pursue financial wealth any other way, it will produce sorrow. When wealth is obtained by honest and righteous means, then the wisdom to maintain and distribute that wealth will come as a result of the blessing of the Lord. Be careful not to confuse the blessing of God with a certain dollar value. If you are reading this, then you are wealthy with education since a portion of the world is still illiterate. If you have clean indoor water and plumbing, then you are wealthier than three-quarters (¾) of the people around the world who live in extreme poverty without clean running water to support basic living needs. You may not see your life this way, but the truth of the matter is that the majority of Americans, including the "working poor," have a percentage of financial wealth and the hope of achieving more in comparison to the majority of the world's inhabitants who live in extreme poverty without the hopes of arising from the dust. Don't allow culture to dictate what the blessing of the

Lord over your life should look like. Appreciate what God has entrusted under your care and be a good steward over that which you consider to be a little because, to someone with nothing, your little is overflowing abundance, a source of the Lord's blessing indeed.

Reference:

Deuteronomy 8:18; Proverbs 8:21, 14:24

WISDOM TIP 55

Wisdom is a seeker of sensibility, while folly is a seeker of mischief.

"An empty-head thinks mischief is fun, but a mindful person relishes wisdom."

PROVERBS 10:23 (THE MESSAGE)

"Doing wrong is fun for a fool, but living wisely brings pleasure to the sensible."

PROVERBS 10:23 (NLT)

Proverbs 10:23 is both a "how to live verse" as well as a "who to avoid" while you are living verse. Wisdom is a seeker of sensibility while folly is a seeker of mischief. What exactly is sensibility? Dictionary.com defines sensibility as "keen consciousness or appreciation." One of my personal favorite definitions is "the capacity for intellectual and aesthetic distinctions, feelings, tastes, etc.; a man of refined sensibilities." In order to be a person of refined sensibilities, you must have wisdom. The way of wisdom brings pleasure to the person of refined sensibilities. Sensibility can be applied to your life by first taking pleasure in wisdom. At this point, I would say that you are a student of wisdom or you would not have read this far. On the other hand, fools delight in mischief. To delight in something means that you take extreme pleasure in the thing in which you delight. Fools not only take pleasure in doing wrong, but they also are not ashamed of it and often wonder what's wrong with you for not wanting a piece of the action. To the fool, sin has become a pastime comparable to their favorite sport. The fool counts down until the Friday night lights will allow him to fully indulge in his pastime of choice. Allow wisdom to form an impression of sensibility that will dictate what folly "looks like" and how to avoid its seepage into your life.

Reference:

Proverbs 15:21, 14:9

WISDOM TIP 56

Only what is built on a solid foundation will stand.

> "When the storm is over, there's nothing left of the wicked; good people, firm on their rock foundation, aren't even fazed."
>
> Proverbs 10:25 (THE MESSAGE)

In recent times, we have witnessed the destruction that can be brought on by storms. In 2017, the United States was hit by several record-breaking, destructive hurricanes within weeks of one another: Hurricane Harvey in Houston, Irma in Florida, and Maria in Puerto Rico. These storms left a magnitude of destruction that has yet to be fully rectified. However, not everyone who lived within those areas suffered the same amount of damage and destruction. Some homes were built on higher levels or had a more intact foundation that withstood the damaging effects of the high winds and flooding waters. If you have spent time in church, I'm sure at some point you have heard these lyrics, "on Christ the Solid Rock I stand all other ground is sinking sand." Standing on Christ the Solid Rock is a biblical principle of truth that can be applied to every area of life. No matter who you are, what you do, or how you choose to do it, a solid foundation is pertinent for success. Although this proverb is reflective of the wicked in reference to sin, we, the righteousness of God in Christ Jesus, also have the ability to operate wickedly (unjustly or unwisely) when we do not follow the principles of God's Word and His guiding. Therefore, we can also experience having nothing left after the storm. Yes, it is true that God's lavish grace and mercy will cover our mistakes, but we are not always completely saved from the consequences of those mistakes. My advice, follow the way of wisdom and build whatever you set out to do on Christ the Solid Rock to ensure a solid foundation that offers guarantees against the demolition brought on by tumultuous storms.

Reference:

Matthew 7:24–27, Proverbs 12:3

WISDOM TIP 57

Be diligent in your work ethic.

"Lazy people irritate their employers, like vinegar to the teeth or smoke in the eyes."

PROVERBS 10:26 (NLT)

"A lazy employee will give you nothing but trouble; it's vinegar in the mouth, smoke in the eyes."

PROVERBS 10:26 (THE MESSAGE)

For most people, a spoonful of plain vinegar is disgustingly distasteful. My personal automatic response would most likely be to spit it out of my mouth immediately. Smoke burns your eyes and hinders your ability to see clearly; it causes you to squint and seek cover far away from the source of the smoke. So does a L-A-Z-Y employee. The best advice on how to lose a job quickly—be lazy! An employer will seek cover far away from a lazy employee by spitting the lazy person back into the unemployment line quick, fast, and in a hurry. The best advice on how to be a valued star employee—be diligent! If longevity is your goal or even if you are only seeking short-term employment and desire a good reference upon the end of your tenure, diligence is key. Whatever your hands find to do, do it diligently and wholeheartedly. You were hired to perform a task, so perform the task during the time slot allotted. The sluggard should look at the ant to learn the habit of diligence. The ant works when it's time to work, carefully, methodically, and diligently. The ant prepares ahead of time during seasons of abundance for seasons of lack. During peak hours, days, or seasons you don't have to wonder where the ant is located or if the ant will show up! Be a model employee, you are representing your name and your God!

Reference:

Proverbs 6:6

WISDOM TIP 58

Grow old gracefully.

"The [reverent] fear of the Lord [worshiping, obeying, serving, and trusting Him with awe-filled respect] prolongs one's life, But the years of the wicked will be shortened."

PROVERBS 10:27 (AMP)

"The Fear-of-GOD expands your life; a wicked life is a puny life."

PROVERBS 10:27 (THE MESSAGE)

I've never met a person who wants to die young. You may be the exception to this rule, but I doubt it. Most young people want to live long even if their youthful, skewed perspective of living long is in their forties. Bottom line, SIN and the effects of SIN kills! You don't have to look much further than your local news station to hear of the number of local deaths from crime, violence, drug usage, and the sorts. All of these acts are the complete opposite of worshiping, obeying, serving, and trusting God. Maybe you don't have outward sins that are immediately apparent. Maybe your sin is secret, remember what goes on in the dark will eventually come to the light! In the Book of Ecclesiastes, Solomon so eloquently offered this advice to youth, "Honor and enjoy your Creator while you're still young, before the years take their toll and your vigor wanes" (Ecclesiastes 12:1 THE MESSAGE). Solomon also warns that "Eventually God will bring everything that we do out into the open and judge it according to its hidden intent, whether it's good or evil" (Ecclesiastes 12:14 THE MESSAGE). There are no secrets where God is concerned, He is the Omnipotent, Omnipresent God. He is all-knowing and in all places at the same time. Why wait another day or another minute? Dedicate your life to pursuing a spiritual journey that leads you along a path of reverently worshiping, serving, obeying, and trusting God. This, my friend, is what embodies growing old gracefully!

Reference:

Proverbs 3:1–2 and 16-18, 9:11–12, 14:27; Ecclesiastes 7:17–18; Psalm 91:16

WISDOM TIP 59

Be careful, little mouth, what you speak!

> "The mouth of the godly person gives wise advice, but the tongue that deceives will be cut off. The lips of the godly speak helpful words, but the mouth of the wicked speaks perverse words."
>
> Proverbs 10: 31–32 (NLT)

> "A good person's mouth is a clear fountain of wisdom; a foul mouth is a stagnant swamp. The speech of a good person clears the air; the words of the wicked pollute it."
>
> Proverbs 10: 31–32 (THE MESSAGE)

One constant we have seen throughout the Book of Proverbs is the link between our words and a wise life. The Message translation compares a wise mouth to "a clear fountain" and clean air. Whereas, a wicked mouth is compared to "a stagnant swamp" and polluted air. In the age of Global Warming, we have witnessed the effects of pollution on our planet and the domino effects pollution has on our weather patterns as well as the health of the human population from consuming the polluted air and water sources. The words of the wise will be like a tree planted in the middle of a polluted swamp. The tree will begin to give out life-giving oxygen and dispose of deadly levels of carbon dioxide. The tree will eventually change the weather patterns of the environment in which it is planted by bringing life-giving rain and providing shade that will block the harmful effects of the polluted air. Are you getting this? Your mouth can be a life-giving tree or the source of "stagnant" pollution that corrupts everything around you. Start taking inventory of how the words you speak change the environment (the mood) of those around you. Are you clearing the pollution levels or adding to the stagnant pollution that's sucking the life out of the atmosphere?

WISDOM TIP 60

Honest business practices balance the scales.

"God hates cheating in the marketplace; he loves it when business is aboveboard."

Proverbs 11:1 (THE MESSAGE)

"A false balance *and* dishonest business practices are extremely offensive to the Lord, but an accurate scale is His delight."

Proverbs 11:1 (AMP)

How you do one thing is how you do everything. This holds true in business. Taking shortcuts for the sake of the bottom line indicates a shortcut business philosophy that will eventually topple. Quality input will produce quality output and the reputation of quality that follows amongst those who consume your product. One shady transaction can put your entire reputation on the line. Seek fairness in all your business transactions and you will garner the reputation of a reputable business person. Otherwise, "one thing" of shadiness stands the chance to tarnish your "everything." Bottom line, "If you do the right thing, honesty will be your guide. But if you are crooked, you will be trapped by your own dishonesty" (Proverbs 11:3 CEV). Let's not limit this principle to business only. Let your "one thing" prove to be consistent across the board. You may not be an entrepreneur, but you are representing "accurate weights" or "honest practices" when you choose not to cheat on a test, when you choose not to allow stereotypical viewpoints and false judgments to determine how you treat one person over another. Make the decision to allow honesty and fairness to balance the scales of your path.

Reference:

Proverbs 20:10, 20:23; Hosea 12:7

WISDOM TIP 61

Humility is the key to elevation.

"The stuck-up fall flat on their faces, but down-to-earth people stand firm."

PROVERBS 11:2 (THE MESSAGE)

"When pride comes [boiling up with an arrogant attitude of self-importance], then come dishonor *and* shame, but with the humble [the teachable who have been chiseled by trial and who have learned to walk humbly with God] there is wisdom *and* soundness of mind."

PROVERBS 11:2 (AMP)

Pride comes before the fall. This sneaky little fox can catch you by surprise, often because you are too proud to admit that you have pride. If you want to identify where you are on the pride meter, record your conversations with others for a day. Your own words will give you away. Did you interject your opinion often? Did you find your comments to be braggadocios or boastful? Did you feel the need to speak of your accomplishments or accolades? Were your comments of others judgmental and critical? If the answer is yes to any of the above, then you may have an issue with pride. Pride is brother to destruction. Jesus spoke of the vast contrast between the proud and the humble by expressing to His disciples the principle of the greatest amongst you being the greatest servant of all. Humble yourself to the point of servitude in your dealings and attitude toward others. Then and only then will you be exalted to a true place of honor. Standing on the firm foundation of humility will cause you to look up to God and out to others.

Reference:

Proverbs 16:18, 18:12, 29:23

WISDOM TIP 62

Developing integrity will increase your focus and faithfulness.

> "If you do the right thing, honesty will be your guide. But if you are crooked, you will be trapped by your own dishonesty."
>
> PROVERBS 11:3 (CEV)

> "The integrity of the honest keeps them on track; the deviousness of crooks brings them to ruin."
>
> PROVERBS 11:3 (THE MESSAGE)

At first glance, this proverb leans toward the development of integrity and honesty. However, once you dig a little deeper, you will discover that honing the character trait of integrity will result in a life characterized by faithfulness, reliability, focus, and determination to name a few. Our scripture tells us that if we seek to do what is right, then honesty (integrity) will guide us. What exactly does honesty guide you to do? What action is integrity guiding you to perform? My answer is reliability, focus, determination, and faithfulness in the work that God has given you. Your "work" may be faithfulness in marriage, reliability in parenting, focus on a long-term project, or volunteer commitment. Whatever that "thing" is, your integrity will cause you to stay focused, committed, faithful, and determined to see it through to the end long after the emotional high has diminished.

Now, let's look at the opposite of the integrity of the honest—the crookedness of the dishonest. Integrity produces the traits of faithfulness and focus, its opposite, crookedness, produces duplicity or what the Bible refers to as double-mindedness. If you are unfaithful to a given vision, you will be swayed by every wind of distraction that provokes you to give up, take shortcuts, or simply find the next best thing that's beckoning for your attention. It simply comes down to this: How do you want to be remembered? As a starter who was faithful to her calling, guided by integrity through all the rough patches, and eventually crossed the finished line. Or as a starter who, somewhere along the way, became a dishonest double-minded person by not staying true to the path God had destined for her, losing authenticity along the way. Allow integrity to keep you on track by giving you a fixed focus and the faithfulness to remain on the course.

Reference:

Proverbs 11:5, 13:6

WISDOM TIP 63

Money can't buy everything.

"A thick bankroll is no help when life falls apart, but a principled life can stand up to the worst."

PROVERBS 11:4 (THE MESSAGE)

Ever heard the saying, "Character will keep you at the top"? Same holds true when the storms of life bring boisterous winds across your path. You may be loaded with a "thick bankroll," but only principled character will sustain you when the going gets tough. Money does not equate to character. We can turn on the evening news to see the daily occurrences of wealthy individuals who lack character and just act a plum fool in view of the entire world. When the going gets tough in your life, it's your character that will sustain you. Money will not sustain a vibrant marriage, only a principled life that honors your spouse can lead to a vibrant marriage. Money will not sustain a healthy lifestyle. Money affords one the vast opportunities to healthy food choices, health and fitness experts and facilities, but without a principled life that enforces the discipline necessary to take advantage of the access to those healthy venues, the hopes for a healthy physical body will be far out of reach. I think you get the message. Money can't buy everything. In all you are striving to obtain, do not forget to grasp the godly principles that will sustain your life and your money.

Reference:

Matthew 16:26, Proverbs 10:2

WISDOM TIP 64

It's a "hard knocks" life for those who follow a treacherous path.

"Moral character makes for smooth traveling; an evil life is a hard life."

PROVERBS 11:5 (THE MESSAGE)

> "The righteousness of the blameless will smooth their way *and* keep it straight, but the wicked will fall by his own wickedness."
>
> Proverbs 11:5 (AMPC)

> "If you are truly good, you will do right; if you are wicked, you will be destroyed by your own sin."
>
> Proverbs 11:5 (CEV)

The musical, *Annie*, is one of my childhood favorites. The song "It's a Hard Knocks Life" has been sung, remixed into hip hop records, and quoted by children and adults alike over the past thirty-years. This proverb tells you exactly what produces a hard knocks life—wickedness. Unfortunately, for the orphans featured in *Annie*, as well as for many true orphans around the globe, their hard knocks life was at no fault of their own, but perhaps brought on by the wickedness of a parent, family member, government, or a stranger. However, no matter the source, wickedness is behind the hard knocks we experience or observe through the experiences of others. The life of a person who chooses to go the opposite direction of God's guidance is treacherous. Take inventory of your family members. Think about those whom you know have had a hard life and some of the choices they made along the way. Now think about those whom you would consider to have a good life and some of the choices they made along the way. If you are a young adult, I challenge you to have a conversation with both sets of family members and ask them what contributed to experiences that they would characterize as smooth and straight and likewise what contributed to experiences that were treacherous and hard. I'm sure sin will be the root of everything treacherous and hard. Likewise, doing the right thing (moral character) is one of the key ingredients to a smooth and clear path. Having said all of that, the lavish grace of God cannot be quantified. The grace of God will keep you from making the wrong choices just as it will redeem you from the wrong choices you may have made, purely because of the goodness of the Lord our Shepherd who guides us along paths of righteousness for His name's sake (Psalm 23:3).

Reference:

Proverbs 3:6, 5:22, 21:29, 11:3

WISDOM TIP 65

Lustful enticements will eventually trap you.

"Good character is the best insurance; crooks get trapped in their sinful lust."

PROVERBS 11:6 (THE MESSAGE)

"The righteousness of the upright delivers them, but the treacherous are taken captive by their lust."

PROVERBS 11:6 (ESV)

James 1:4 (NASB) tells us that each person is tempted when "he is carried away and enticed by his own lust." Wisdom causes you to turn away from the hidden lusts of the heart to pursue God's way of doing things (righteousness). As in Proverbs 11:4, this passage reminds us that good character will deliver you from death (sin, lust, evil). If you are tempted by something or someone today, seek the route of wisdom and ask for the righteous response that will result in building good character instead of the captivity that comes from following lustful desires. Often, the word lust is related only to sexual temptation; however, you can lust after food, promotion, attention, status, power, or a position. Whatever the "lust" area is in your life, seek God's wisdom to avoid the pathway of crookedness. When we make the choice to follow our own way, we become "treacherous" in our pursuit of that particular action. The pursuit of a thing is what qualifies it as a lust of your heart. Anything I pursue more than God becomes lust in my life and eventually an idol that leads to destruction. Most people do not intentionally plan on being so captivated with something that they become "trapped" by it. The drug addict, sex addict, workaholic, kleptomaniac, compulsive gambler, and habitual liar never planned to become the "crook" who just can't get enough of the lust that drives their entire life. Take your clue from this proverb and let "good character" become your life insurance from anything that could lead to the development of lust in your life. Good character is simply turning away from the temptation the first time it is presented before you; it is saying no even if no one will find out about it this time. Your character is a reflection of who you really are, while your reputation is a glimpse into who others think you are.

Reference:

Psalm 7:16; Proverbs 5:22; Genesis 30:33, "and my honesty shall answer for me in the future" (author's paraphrase).

WISDOM TIP 66

Don't allow your words to spread infection to yourself or others.

"The loose tongue of the godless spreads destruction; the common sense of the godly preserves them."

PROVERBS 11:9 (THE MESSAGE)

"Dishonest people use gossip to destroy their neighbors; good people are protected by their own good sense."

PROVERBS 11:9 (CEV)

Have you ever heard a nasty rumor about someone before you actually had the opportunity to meet them, only to find that your interaction with that person was completely opposite of what you heard? The "common sense" that preserves the godly allows them to use their own knowledge to form their individual opinion of a person without falling prey to the destructive gossip of those who seek to annihilate the character of others. A gossiper uses lies, insinuations, and slander to destroy the reputations of their victims. You who are seeking to be preserved or saved from the destruction produced by a gossiper can do so by first, not listening to their death talk, and secondly, by following the principles of speech that promote peace and life. Life and death are in the power of the tongue and those who love it (life or death) will EAT the fruits thereof (reap the consequences) (Proverbs 18:21). Those who are constantly speaking death will eventually find death at their doorsteps. Not necessarily a physical death, but death nonetheless. Likewise, those who have heeded wisdom and made the choice not to participate in gossip and slanderous attacks are making the choice to pursue life. This is how the righteous are preserved. Further, Proverbs 18:8 (NIV) tells us that, "The words of a gossip are like choice morsels; they go down to the innermost parts of the body." Whose body? The body of the one who spreads the gossip by being a willing participant in either speaking or hearing it. Just imagine all the compounded gunk of gossip piling up over the years, eventually making the gossiper a ball of filth with a stench that is recognized by anyone who comes into their presence. Remember, you are what you eat! This principle works with your words as well. What you eat gets chewed up into pieces (thought about), taken into your digestive system (meditated upon), and finally dispersed into your bloodstream as either life preserving nutrients or life destroying waste. You will either have the energy to sustain a healthy life or be sapped of all your strength as your organs attempt to survive on the grime of deadly words.

Reference:

Proverbs 11:12

WISDOM TIP 67

A trustworthy person will not disclose what he is trusted with, unless the real good of society or others require it.

"A gossip goes around telling secrets, but those who are trustworthy can keep a confidence."

Proverbs 11:13 (NLT)

"A gadabout gossip can't be trusted with a secret, but someone of integrity won't violate a confidence."

Proverbs 11:13 (THE MESSAGE)

Proverbs 20:19 (NIV) warns, "A gossip betrays a confidence; so avoid anyone who talks too much." Likewise, make it your business not to be the gossiper! In fact, be cautious of any acquaintances you have who has a tendency to talk about others. You may not want to reveal any private matters to this person. If they talk about someone else to you, you can be sure they are talking about you to someone else. A trustworthy person will not betray your confidence even at the threat of their own reputation. However, this is not a "snitches get stitches" doctrine. Remaining trustworthy does not mean keeping a secret that will destroy the life of a friend or the lives of others. There are times when confidence must be breached in order to save that person or others from fatal harm. The following series of questions may assist you with identifying circumstances that may compel you to speak up for the greater good of all: (1) Can this information place someone in prison if I do not come forward? (2) Will this information result in the death of someone if I do not come forward? (3) Will this information result in the bodily harm or emotional breakdown of someone if I do not come forward?

If still in doubt, seek wise counsel from a trustworthy person and allow that trusted adviser to assist you in determining the consequences of remaining quiet.

Reference:

Proverbs 20:19, 25:9–10; 1 Timothy 5:13; Leviticus 19:16

WISDOM TIP 68

Always plan to get counsel.

"Without good direction, people lose their way; the more wise counsel you follow, the better your chances."

PROVERBS 11:14 (THE MESSAGE)

"Where there is no guidance the people fall, but in abundance of counselors there is victory."

PROVERBS 11:14 (NASB)

In 2 Corinthians 13:1 (NIV), it is explained that "Every matter must be established by the testimony of two or three witnesses." Likewise, when making plans, we plan to fail when we do not seek counsel from at least two sources. When we follow the pattern of decision making in the Bible, we will find that key decision makers had many advisors who provided counsel before action was taken. In present day, the President of the United States has a cabinet of advisors who provide counsel in their areas of expertise relating to domestic and global affairs before vital decisions are made. Likewise, we as leaders of our lives should seek counsel from subject matter experts prior to making significant decisions. Your first source of counsel should come from Him who is named Wonderful Counselor (Isaiah 9:6). Prayer and the Word of God will direct your path. In Psalm 119:24–25, David proclaims, "Your statutes are my delight; they are my counselors" (NIV). "Your laws please me; they give me wise advice" (NLT). Further, the Wonderful Counselor will see to it that He sends someone or something across your path to confirm the direction you believe you have received from Him through prayer and the study of His Word. Why is it important to have counsel? One reason is because wisdom says so. *John Gill's Exposition* sums it up perfectly, "but in the multitude of counsellors there is safety; because what one may miss another may hit upon; and, if they agree in their advice, it may be the more depended upon; and, if not, yet their different sentiments being compared together, and the reasons of them, a person may the better judge which is best to follow, and what is fit to be done." As you walk through this journey of life, you will find it advantageous to periodically seek counsel from others in one form or another.

Reference:

Proverbs 15:22, 20:18, 24:6

WISDOM TIP 69

Cosigning for the debts of others is not a wise move.

"There's danger in putting up security for a stranger's debt; it's safer not to guarantee another person's debt."

PROVERBS 11:15 (NLT)

The Color Purple, a book written by Alice Walker, was adapted to screen by director Steven Spielberg. This movie is amongst one of my all-time favorites. Toward the end of the movie, the character Shug Avery walked into her father's church and began singing, "Can't sleep at night and you wonder why, maybe God is trying to tell you something, RIGHT NOW!" That "something" is do not fall into the trap of cosigning or taking on debt for others. I'm not saying that you are not to help others because we are definitely called to help, serve, share with, and bless the lives of others. However, you can only give based on the means you have been provided. If you are asked to give, help, or share to the point of going into debt or by increasing debt because you are required to add your "good name" as a cosigner or put up collateral for another, then I refer you back to Wisdom Tip 68; plan to get counsel, godly counsel. Maybe this wisdom tip has been written specifically for you as a source of wise counsel. Heed the voice of wisdom before "guaranteeing another person's debt." *John Gill's Exposition* explains this concept in Old English, just in case you need to hear it in two languages, "he engaging or becoming a bondsman for one whose circumstances he knew not; and these being bad bring a load upon him, such a heavy debt as crushes him to pieces." You've heard it from Solomon, Gill, and Kyna. Maybe God is trying to tell you something "right now!" Can I get an AMEN?

Reference:

Proverbs 6:1–5, 17:18, 20:16, 22:26–27, and 27:13

WISDOM TIP 70

Honey attracts more bees than vinegar.
Kindness will reward you.

"When you're kind to others, you help yourself; when you're cruel to others, you hurt yourself."

PROVERBS 11:17 (THE MESSAGE)

"Your kindness will reward you, but your cruelty will destroy you."

PROVERBS 11:17 (NLT)

"You reap what you sow." "What you give is what you get." "What you did to me has already been done to you." How about this oldie, but goodie, "You can catch more bees with honey than with vinegar." The origin of such wisdom is straight from the Bible. Whatever you attempt to do in life, do it with kindness. The kindness you give out will come back into your life in more ways than you can imagine. As it is with cruelty, meanness, and rudeness. These will eventually catch up with you and when they show up, they will pierce like self-inflicted wounds. People will look and say, "He brought all this upon himself." How about, "I would help him, but he has never done anything good for anyone, so let him finally see how it feels." I could go on and on with things that I've heard said of others when their lifestyle of cruelty finally caught up to them. Just as insects are attracted to the sweetness of honey and natural sugars, you will find that human nature is also attracted to kindness, mercy, and gentleness. Take a look at your attitude today and identify where you are on the "honey scale." You will accomplish more in life when you are kind, for your kindness will reward you.

Reference:

Proverbs 11:16, Matthew 5:7

WISDOM TIP 71

Not all money is good money.

"Bad work gets paid with a bad check; good work gets solid pay."

Proverbs 11:18 (THE MESSAGE)

"Evil people get rich for the moment, but the reward of the godly will last."

Proverbs 11:18 (NLT)

Not all money is good money! You heard me! My inner New Orleans coming out. Bad work gets paid with a bad check! In other words, it will cost you something. Some opportunities presented to you in life will be in the form of "bad works" that stand against every moral fiber in your body. Unfortunately, the "bad works" often come wrapped in layers of the almighty dollar! You may be rich for a moment as you cash that bad check, but it will produce insufficient funds in another area of your life. Never allow money to be your driving force nor your deciding factor when making a decision. When opportunities are presented that require you to compromise your beliefs or higher life priorities, then it's time to step back and ask yourself if its "good money." Opportunities that represent "good work" will produce solid payments. Pay that extends beyond the form of monetary gain and etches into eternal glory. Don't get it twisted, what you do in the marketplace, classroom, boardroom, in your living room at home all have the potential to impact your life and the lives of others for eternity. Find your good work and be intentional about converting it into solid pay that will last.

Reference:

Galatians 6:8–9, Proverbs 10:16

WISDOM TIP 72

Those who insist on doing wrong will be overtaken with wrong doing.

"Anyone who is determined to do right will live, but anyone who insists on doing wrong will die."

PROVERBS 11:19 (GNT)

"Always do the right thing, and you will live; keep on doing wrong, and you will die."

PROVERBS 11:19 (CEV)

I've witnessed a few people in my life who have insisted on doing wrong. Allow me to identify what "insisting on doing wrong" is and what it is not. "Insisting on doing wrong" is not making a mistake nor is it giving into temptation here or there. "Insisting on doing wrong" is the eager pursuit of wrongdoing. It is making detailed plans to do wrong and carrying it out to no avail. Very similar to premeditated murder. Being determined to do right does not mean that you will always make the right decision or that you will always do everything perfectly in line with God's Word and His wisdom. We must remember that God is not a hard task master. His way of doing things are not hard. They are life-giving principles designed to make life easier and less burdensome. I love the way Proverbs 21:16 (NIV) puts it, "Whoever strays from the path of prudence comes to rest in the company of the dead." When you stray from the path of prudence (wisdom), you will find yourself resting in the company of the dead instead of the company of Jesus who invites us to lay down every heavy burden and every sin that so easily entangles and find rest in HIM (Matthew 11:28–30 and Hebrews 12:1). Proverbs 13:15 (KJV) tells us that "the way of transgressors is hard," it's a hard life and it is hard work to keep it going. Heed the words you have just read and seek after life. Your heart knows the difference. For every situation you will face today or in the future to come, wisdom will guide you along the path of life if you aggressively and intentionally pursue the way of wisdom. Seek to do the right thing with an internal power that consumes your pursuit. That internal power is the very Spirit of God who is wisdom personified.

Reference:

Romans 6:23; James 1:15; Proverbs 12:28, 19:23, 21:16

WISDOM TIP 73

Beauty is as beauty does!

"As a ring of gold in a swine's snout, so is a beautiful woman who is without discretion [her lack of character mocks her beauty]."

PROVERBS 11:22 (AMP)

"Like a gold ring in a pig's snout is a beautiful face on an empty head."

PROVERBS 11:22 (THE MESSAGE)

Calling all the "ladies" out on this one. Yes, it's finally in black and white. Beauty without discretion, modesty, and wisdom is as foul as swine shuffling around in a muddy puddle. To all my singles, when searching for your spouse, what good is a gorgeous face with an empty head or heart for that matter? Take a close look at the person's ways and consider if your choice of good looks over discretion will eventually muddy up your life. That's not to say that you can't have both. You can have good looks, discretion, wisdom, and modesty all together in one package, but if it is not present, don't become so entrapped with looks that you make it fit. Get my drift!

The God's Word translation reads, "Like a gold ring in a pig's snout, so is a beautiful woman who lacks good taste." "Good taste" here is not referring to material preferences that boast of affluent elegances found amongst the rich and famous. You can watch any episode of "The Real House-Fools" to see an example of beauty with poor taste. Also, think about how despised pigs were in biblical times and still are in many parts of the Eastern world. A beautiful woman who lacks good taste is likened to a creature that is looked upon with disgust. What we see played out in today's culture is often beauty that has lost all sense of "modesty, virtue, and honor" that it actually looks disgusting to the eye, sounds degrading to the ear, and produces drought of thought to anyone with good sense. "Good taste" is in line with behavior that is tasteful, full of flavor and life. The flavor we give off should be in line with the biblical requirement to be the salt of the earth (Matthew 5:13–16). A woman's taste should bring salt to her life and those around her by enhancing and giving them true meaning. If your beauty does not leave a good taste in the hearts and minds of those around you, then you are muddying up and polluting the atmosphere with ugliness. Beauty is as beauty does!

Reference:

Proverbs 31:30, 1 Peter 3:3–4

WISDOM TIP 74

Generosity never leaves your life.

"Give freely and become more wealthy; be stingy and lose everything."

PROVERBS 11:24 (NLT)

"It is possible to give away and become richer! It is also possible to hold on too tightly and lose everything. Yes, the liberal man shall be rich! By watering others, he waters himself."

PROVERBS 11:24 (NLT)

A family member of mine is employed by a billionaire couple whose ultimate goal is to give away over 90% of their wealth during their lifetime. During a brief catch up conversation, my family member casually mentioned that during a business meeting, the couple shared the fact that although they are tenaciously giving away money, they are faced with one problem—they keep making more money. Most of us will not become billionaires who face the challenge of allocating the majority of our earnings during our lifetime; however, according to this proverb, the way to become richer is by giving generously. Those who generously scatter their monetary wealth from a heart that seeks to refresh others will continue to increase in riches. It doesn't matter if you have $2 or $2 million to give, the heart behind your giving should be that of generosity. Selfishness will lead to poverty in more ways than one; financial poverty, relational poverty, and heart poverty because you will fail to know the joy of giving. Remember this, what leaves your hand never leaves your life, it travels ahead of you and returns with friends.

Reference:

Proverbs 11:25, 2; Corinthians 9:6–8; Deuteronomy 15:10; Luke 6:38

WISDOM TIP 75

Generosity brings refreshment to your life.

"The generous will prosper; those who refresh others will themselves be refreshed."

PROVERBS 11:25 (NLT)

Think about refreshing others so you can be refreshed in return in terms of watering a garden. You water your garden for the purpose of refreshing it with the vital substance needed to maintain its life and growth. Physical Science 101 tells us that plants need three essential things to live: water, sunlight, and the right soil composition. In the case of a vegetable garden, your refreshment will come in the form of food that will refresh your physical body. Both gardens return the refreshment it received from your actions back into refreshment for your life. Likewise, your generosity and kindness toward others will be reciprocated back to you directly from the bulb that your generous act has watered.

Reference:

Matthew 5:7, 2 Corinthians 9:6–7, Job 29:12–13, Isaiah 58:7–11

WISDOM TIP 76

What you pursue will one day pursue you.

"If you search for good, you will find favor; but if you search for evil, it will find you!"

PROVERBS 11:27 (NLT)

An Indian proverb says, "When men are ripe for slaughter, even straws turn into thunderbolts." Whatever you are itching for will eventually rise up and scratch you, good or bad. I know this is very similar to some of the other wisdom tips we have already explored, but its fabric is threaded throughout the entire Book of Proverbs as a hint that this concept is worthy of repetition. What you seek after, you will find. What you pursue will pursue you. What's in your thoughts will show up in your life. Make sure you are itching for the right things in life, the right way, and the right kind of people to surround you. Don't set traps for others or you will find yourself attempting to dig out of the same hole. This idea sums up a very important theme of the Bible: Do unto others as you would have them do unto you; love your neighbor as yourself. Sow only what you want to reap. Itch only where you are sure you want to be scratched because what you pursue will one day pursue you.

Reference:

Esther 7:10, Psalm 7:15–16, Psalm 57:6

WISDOM TIP 77

Place your trust in God alone.

"A life devoted to things is a dead life, a stump; a God-shaped life is a flourishing tree."

PROVERBS 11:28 (THE MESSAGE)

"Trust in your money and down you go! But the godly flourish like leaves in spring."

PROVERBS 11:28 (NLT)

Money is not the root of all evil, it is the love of money that forms the root of all evil. Devoting your life to the pursuit of money represents a deep rooted trust in monetary assets. If you have any American money in your possession, pull it out for a moment. Notice this motto, "In God We Trust." Even your money has enough sense to understand that it has to trust in God. American money is declaring, "I'm nothing without God." Trusting in money or things that money can buy leads to a life of uncertainty. The value of money fluctuates from day to day. The stock market rises and falls daily, sometimes several times within one day. God is the same yesterday, today, and forever! He changes NOT! Take note of what you are truly pursuing in your life. Did you pick your college major because of the amount of money you can make? Do you drive a certain automobile because it gives you the appearance of a certain status? Are you working two jobs just to provide your children with a "lifestyle" when what they really need is your time and affection? Check your motives and intentions. If they all point back to the almighty dollar instead of the Almighty God, then your trust is misaligned. Be as wise as the money you pursue and make a declaration with me, "In God We Trust"!

Reference:

1 Timothy 6:17, Jeremiah 17:7, Job 31:24–25, Psalm 49:6–9

WISDOM TIP 78

Don't bring shame on the family name.

"Whoever brings ruin on their family will inherit only wind, and the fool will be servant to the wise."

PROVERBS 11:29 (NIV)

First, let's review the definition of a fool. A fool is a self-willed, hard-headed individual who will not listen to the advice of others and drives himself to a dead-end street called ruin as a result. I have known countless men who strongly demand of their sons to do good by the family name. In some cases, the sentiment shared was, "All I have is a good name so don't do anything to destroy the only solid thing I truly own in this world." Although this is mostly expressed to a son from a father, the same holds true for all children. Don't cause trouble for your family by doing something that dishonors the family name. On the flip side, what about causing trouble within the family? Psalm 133:1 (ESV) declares, "How good and pleasant it is when brothers dwell in unity!" Therefore, the opposite must also be true—how dreadful it is when brothers are divided by conflict. The person at the root of the conflict will not only lose monetary or material inheritance, but also the intangible inheritance of healthy and loving family relationships. If you are at odds with a family member, seek wisdom and pursue peace. If you are the source of conflict and disunity in your family, take heed while you still have time lest you find yourself "grasping for wind," unable to hold on to your family ties. If you happen to come from a family filled with fools and all they know is disunity and strife, remember that you have been adopted into a new family of royalty, so live in a manner worthy of your calling as an heir of God and joint heir with Jesus Christ. Whatever the case, rep your family name and model a new legacy for the generation that will follow in your footsteps.

Reference:

Proverbs 11:17, 12:24, 15:27

WISDOM TIP 79

Learn to love discipline.

"If you love learning, you love the discipline that goes with it—how shortsighted to refuse correction!"

PROVERBS 12:1 (THE MESSAGE)

"To learn, you must love discipline; it is stupid to hate correction."

PROVERBS 12:1 (NLT)

The purpose of discipline is growth. Discipline, when administered correctly, is designed to make you better by promoting personal growth. Almost every endeavor in life comes with something called a learning curve. Even if you have a God-given talent, you have a learning curve in identifying how to properly use that gift or talent or how to develop in that area. You have to develop the discipline to learn. Just as you have to develop the discipline to receive correction. The word "discipline" often gets a bad rap, but discipline is what you see on the football field during the Super Bowl. Discipline is what you see walking across the stage at a graduation. Discipline is what you see in the life of a man who is committed to loving one woman well for a lifetime. Discipline is the learning and correction that takes place along the journey that brings you to your final destination. The destination that so many people admire, but many are not disciplined enough to walk out on a daily basis in order to arrive at a similar destination. Stupidity is doing the same thing over and over again after being corrected, but expecting the same results as the one who applied the discipline of learning. You are smarter than that, now put discipline to use in your life.

Reference:

Psalm 50:17, Proverbs 5:12

WISDOM TIP 80

Men, find a wife of noble character. Women, be a wife of noble character.

"A wife of noble character is her husband's crown, but a disgraceful wife is like decay in his bones."

PROVERBS 12:4 (NIV)

While this wisdom tip is geared toward wives, it can also be adhered to by single women who one day desire to be a wife. Nobility versus disgrace is the theme of this passage. While the responsibilities of a wife may extend beyond the home for the modern-day wife, noble character is a universal and timely truth. What does noble character look life for a wife? Let's look at Proverbs 31 for the answer in its entirety. Verse 12 (NASB) reads, "She does him good and not evil all the days of her life." Noble character as a wife looks like doing good toward and for your husband, and turning away from anything or anyone that remotely gives the appearance of an evil connection. If you still aren't sure what that looks like in every situation, then ask yourself, "Would I still do or say this if my husband were standing next to me?" Even better, "Would I still do or say this if my pastor, mother, father, or person I admire or want to impress were standing here?" If the answer is no, then act nobly and reframe from the act or conversation. If the answer is yes, then proceed as a representative of your husband and his last name in which you now represent as his wife. Such display of noble character will personify Proverbs 31:11 (NIV) in your life, "Her husband has full confidence in her and lacks nothing of value."

Reference:

Proverbs 18:22, Proverbs 31:10–11

WISDOM TIP 81

Never allow your mouth to murder others.

"The words of the wicked are like a murderous ambush, but the words of the godly save lives."

PROVERBS 12:6 (NLT)

"The words of the wicked kill; the speech of the upright saves."
PROVERBS 12:6 (THE MESSAGE)

Words coming from the mouth of a wicked person is compared to a murderous ambush. Just as "if looks could kill," words in the mouth of the wrong person can have murderous intent and can in fact kill, steal, and destroy the life of another. On the contrary, the words of the godly have the power to save lives. In fact, *Matthew Henry's Concise Commentary* says, "A man may sometimes do a good work with one good word." Imagine that for a moment, one good word can equate to a good work, potentially a good work that can save the life of another. Do you have the gift of gab? Be sure to use your gift to save lives by building others up around you with the words you speak. Gifts are strange phenomena because they often take on a completely different life than the intended purpose of the gift giver. Once gifted, the receiver of the gift has complete control over how the gift is utilized. Will you use your words to prepare a murderous ambush against someone's reputation, their career, their marriage, their children, or will you use your gift to speak an on time word to build others up, to fight injustices, and ultimately save lives? Let not your mouth be found guilty of murder.

Reference:

Proverbs 14:3

WISDOM TIP 82

Fake prosperity is a trap of poverty.

"Better to be ordinary and work for a living than act important and starve in the process."

Proverbs 12:9 (THE MESSAGE)

"Better to be an ordinary person with a servant than to be self-important but have no food."

Proverbs 12:9 (NLT)

John Gill's Exposition describes the person who fakes prosperity as one who "boasts of his pedigree, and brags of his wealth; dresses out in fine clothes, keeps a fine equipage, makes a great figure abroad, and has scarce bread to eat at home, and would have none if his debts were paid." Respectful mediocrity is better than boastful poverty. Beware of the person who is always boasting about money, their status, or their family pedigree. A word to the wise, wealthy people by large do not make constant mention of their wealth and most who can boast of their ancestral pedigree have last names that speak for themselves. Step out of the keeping up with the Jones's mentality, faking prosperity for the sake of appearances. Better to be an ordinary worker, living modestly with money in the bank than a "fake it till you make it" with no plans of ever making it beyond appearances. Another nugget—never let your net worth be invested in your closet and the latest gadgets, cars, and equipment. Wisdom will direct you to live below your means (respectful mediocrity) and set aside a portion of what you earn for the future, so the money you earn today becomes your servant tomorrow.

Reference:

Proverbs 13:7

WISDOM TIP 83

Pet owners, be kind to your animals.

> "Good people are good to their animals; the 'good-hearted' bad people kick and abuse them."
>
> PROVERBS 12:10 (THE MESSAGE)

> "The righteous care for the needs of their animals, but the kindest acts of the wicked are cruel."
>
> PROVERBS 12:10 (NIV)

Hear ye! Hear ye! If you are going to take on the life of an animal, then you must care for the needs of that animal. I'm personally not a pet owner. I have three kids and a husband, so the idea of caring for the needs of one more living thing makes me cringe. While I am in no way an animal activist, I do believe that God has given us dominion over animals, not to abuse and misuse them, but for our enjoyment. If you own a pet, the B-I-B-L-E, not Kyna, says that you are to care for its needs. If you cannot adequately care for the needs of the pet, then wisdom directs you to give that pet to someone who can, so your good intentions are not converted to cruelty. Why is this principle important? Because it speaks to the nature of your character. Wisdom is a whole life concept, not a method or algorithm that can be applied here or there and left untouched in other areas. Valuing the earth and all the creatures in which inhabit the earth flows in line with a lifestyle of wisdom. Just think of the effects pollution, mass hunting, and inhumane treatment of animals have had on our society. A person of wisdom will recognize the need to properly regard the life of animals and their long-term preservation for the benefit of society at large.

Reference:

Exodus 23:9, Proverbs 27:23, Deuteronomy 22:6–10

WISDOM TIP 84

Hard work brings prosperity.

"A hard worker has plenty of food, but a person who chases fantasies has no sense."
PROVERBS 12:11 (NLT)

"The one who stays on the job has food on the table; the witless chase whims and fancies."
PROVERBS 12:11 (THE MESSAGE)

How you spend your time will either bring prosperity or poverty. This passage offers a bit of an incentive as well as a warning. The incentive lures you to "stay on your job" with diligent hard work that produces food and satisfaction. The warning tells us that those who decide not to heed the incentive and seek after fantasies or chase whims will waste valuable time and one day find themselves in a state of ruin. We each have a calling in life, that calling may be pursued in a variety of different platforms. Whatever it is that we are called to do, we are to diligently pursue that work with the vigor and tenacity known as "hard work." Staying on the job is a way of saying, "do not quit when the going gets tough, stay the course." Don't faint in your pursuits because, in the end, it will pay dividends in the form of a life of satisfaction and plenty. Do not get wrapped up in the package in which plenty presents itself. Plenty comes in various forms based on the desires of the individual and their personal capacity to "fill up." I cannot define plenty for you, nor can I look to you for my definition of plenty. What I can offer is the fact that plenty is not narrowed down to a certain amount of financial gain or provision. Yes, you need food, shelter, clothing, and proper means to maintain, but the degree to which you desire such provision differs from person to person. True prosperity is living a life of contentment, doing something you love, surrounded by people you love. Whatever you find to do, work at it with all your might as unto the Lord, for it is He who has given you both the power and ability to prosper in the activities in which you diligently work towards.

References:

Proverbs 28:19

WISDOM TIP 85

You are what you speak.

"From the fruit of their lips people are filled with good things, and the work of their hands brings them reward."

PROVERBS 12:14 (NIV)

"Well-spoken words bring satisfaction; well-done work has its own reward."

PROVERBS 12:14 (THE MESSAGE)

I recently viewed a commercial that compared how we treat our bodies to how we treat our cars. The commercial shows the interior of a car splattered with fast food items, carbonated beverages and common fast food condiments. The commercial ends with the statement, "What if you treated your car the way you treat your body?" Ouch! I must admit that every time I enter a fast food drive thru, that commercial plays in my mind and makes me think twice about my order. This proverb makes a correlation between the words we speak and the capacity in which our lives are filled with good things. Very similar to the foods you eat that cause your internal system to be filled with good or not so good things. What are you feeding your life by the words you continuously speak? If your words are seeds, what kind of crop would they produce? Bitterness, anger, envy, jealousy, defeat, loneliness, excuses? If you don't want to see a particular fruit in your life, then don't speak it. Of course, you need to vent from time to time, it's healthy for you. However, you should not have the same venting sessions day after day, week after week, month after month, and year after year. "I'm so fat, my husband is so lazy, my children have lost their minds. I'm broke busted and disgusted." Guess what, you will continue to see all of that and more if that's what you continue to speak. Fill your mouth with good things so the fruit of those good things will manifest internally, in your mindset, and in your actions. The work that you put into watching the words you speak will be its own reward.

Let's have a brief "speak" exercise. Repeat after me:

1. I'm on the earth for a purpose.
2. I'm filled with the strength to overcome all obstacles.
3. I make wise decisions.
4. I reflect love to others and I receive love from others.
5. I manage my finances responsibly and I'm getting better with financial management.
6. I have a beautiful smile.

7. I brighten the day of others with my smile.
8. I love life.
9. I love myself.
10. I love my life.

I know you feel better already. Take a few minutes to come up with your own list of fruitful words and purpose to add to your list every month. As you see your words reflected in your life, check off that item and add something new. Words precede attitude and attitude determines the altitude and quality of your life. Remember, you are what you speak, so go ahead and speak good things so you can enjoy the fruits. UMM! That sounds delicious!

Reference:

Proverbs 13:2, 18:20

WISDOM TIP 86

Always take heed before you proceed.

"Fools are headstrong and do what they like; wise people take advice."

Proverbs 12:15 (THE MESSAGE)

"A stubborn fool considers his own way the right one, but a person who listens to advice is wise."

Proverbs 12:15 (GW)

I am a strong advocate for being your own person and thinking for yourself. However, I am also a strong advocate for not falling into the trap of being stubborn and high-minded. Meaning, can't nobody tell you nothing! Yes, that is my best English for the foolish. The quickest way to go down the road to ruin is to be stubborn and head strong. As my Southern peers and I would say, "Too grown for your own good!" Your parents may not have as much education as you, they may not have been exposed to as many of the finer things in life as you have, but what they do have is life experience that has given them wisdom and judgment beyond what books can teach. Your auntie can see straight through that boy or girl. Your uncle can point out the deception in that offer without knowing the full terms of the contract. Word to the wise, you better humble yourself and listen to the advice of those around you who love and care about you. They want to see you succeed more than you want to succeed, but they want to see you do it the right way, under the right circumstances. Do yourself a favor by heeding the advice of the wise. Others of age, experience, wisdom, and most importantly those who seek to walk in the way of the Lord can provide you with a wealth of knowledge that your limited judgment and reasoning could never conjure up. Take heed before you proceed.

Reference:

Proverbs 14:12, 16:2, 16:25, 19:20, 21:2

WISDOM TIP 87

The power of self-control should never be underestimated.

"A fool is quick-tempered, but a wise person stays calm when insulted."

PROVERBS 12:16 (NLT)

"Fools have short fuses and explode all too quickly; the prudent quietly shrug off insults."

PROVERBS 12:16 (THE MESSAGE)

A few years back, Gospel artist Canton Jones had a hit song entitled "Stay Saved." The hook reminds the listener that wisdom is a verb, meaning it requires action. A fool's quick temper will constantly land him right in the middle of trouble. If you can master your temper then the rest is smooth sailing. When you can stay calm in the face of the person who is purposely insulting you and walk away for the benefit of that person and yourself, that's wisdom in action. Too many of us have a pride issue. I can hear you now, "Ain't nobody gone talk to me like that!" What you are really saying is, "To save my reputation, I'm willing to get suspended from school, get arrested, catch a case, and possibly face probation or jail time because my pride wouldn't let me walk away." You better go talk to some people sitting in jail right now who have been there for months just awaiting a trial, not sentencing, a trial just to explain what happened. Is it really worth it to lose weeks, months, and in some cases years of your life over a few minutes? A wise person knows the power of walking away and leaving a fool to argue by himself. In fact, a wise person will gain more credit for being the bigger person when the act of walking away saves their future and possibly their life. It takes two to tango, so eliminate yourself from the competition of rage. Your grand prize is freedom and the true power that comes from self-control.

Reference:

Job 5:2, Proverbs 29:11

WISDOM TIP 88

Truth is the same yesterday, today, and forever.

"Truthful words stand the test of time, but lies are soon exposed."
PROVERBS 12:19 (NLT)

"Truth lasts; lies are here today, gone tomorrow."
PROVERBS 12:19 (THE MESSAGE)

Truth is truth. No matter who likes it or dislikes it. Truth will not cease being truth due to the opinions, schemes, or changing tides of men. Likewise, lies will be lies today, tomorrow, and forever. Just as it is with truth, it may take some time to uncover a lie, but rest assured it will be exposed when truth breaks forth like the light of day. Truth is constant, unshakable, and permanent. Tell the truth and the end result will stand the test of time. Tell lies and exposure is sure to come. Lying never stands, it is sure to be found out one way or another.

Reference:
Proverbs 19:9, Proverbs 12:22, Proverbs 17:7

WISDOM TIP 89

Joy can be found in peaceful plans.

"Deceit fills hearts that are plotting evil; joy fills hearts that are planning peace!"
PROVERBS 12:20 (NLT)

"Evil scheming distorts the schemer; peace-planning brings joy to the planner."
PROVERBS 12:20 (THE MESSAGE)

People who plot and scheme only end up hurting themselves. They always find themselves in the middle of some mess! If they are not headed into strife with someone currently, they are looking over their shoulder because of some mess they pulled in the past. Evil schemers live a life of fear and worry. Their hearts are so full of suspicion of others, based on the wickedness in their own hearts, that they miss the joy of living in peace. Remember the concept of "what you do to me has already been done to you." You reap what you sow! Peacemakers are simply people who try to carry out the golden rule, do unto others as you would want them to do to you. When you make this concept your life's mantra, not only will you bring joy to the lives of others, but to yourself and your conscience.

Reference:

Proverbs 26:24

WISDOM TIP 90

Pass along wisdom when the right opportunity presents itself.

"Prudent people don't flaunt their knowledge; talkative fools broadcast their silliness."

Proverbs 12:23 (THE MESSAGE)

"The wise don't make a show of their knowledge, but fools broadcast their foolishness."

Proverbs 12:23 (NLT)

There's nothing worse than being with a know-it-all who feels the need to provide their opinion on every subject matter during every conversation. A wise person is aware of something called timing and saves their knowledge until the right opportunity presents itself. People don't care how much you know until they know how much you care. A fool will blabber every fact he has consumed with such an aura of boasting that his words fall on deaf ears. Let your ambition lead you to become a caring listener so when you open your mouth to communicate knowledge to others, their ears perk with excitement because your reputation is of one who shares from a heart that cares.

Reference:

Proverbs 10:14, 15:2, 18:2

WISDOM TIP 91

Diligence paves the way to success.

"Diligent hands will rule, but laziness ends in forced labor."
PROVERBS 12:24 (NIV)

"The diligent find freedom in their work; the lazy are oppressed by work."
PROVERBS 12:24 (THE MESSAGE)

Diligence, steadfastness, persistence, tenacity, and resolve are just a few English words synonymous with good old-fashioned hard work and consistency. People who possess these qualities end up winning in life. They win over obstacles, they win over excuses, and they win over haters. However, winning is not always about conquering those outside forces. Applied diligence also rules over internal fears and self-doubt. You have the opportunity to silence internal fears every time you resolve to remain diligent, to persist until you succeed, and to move forward steadfastly. Diligence wins! Laziness will put you in the category of all the would have, could have, should haves who are still talking about what they accomplished twenty years ago in high school. Idleness and laziness are often companions. Work is oppressive to the lazy person because they have never gained the joy of accomplishment that diligence produces. If it's easy, they are fair game. As soon as the obstacles show up, lazy people go back to idleness until circumstances force them to get up and show a little effort. If you are diligent with your current opportunities, then greater opportunities will come your way. You will rule because diligence will pave the way.

Reference:

Proverbs 10:4, 13:4, 17:2, 22:29

WISDOM TIP 92

Worry is the fear of what could be, not what actually is.

"Anxiety weighs down the heart, but a kind word cheers it up."
PROVERBS 12:25 (NIV)

"Worry weighs us down; a cheerful word picks us up."
PROVERBS 12:25 (THE MESSAGE)

Worry produces anxiety that is displayed in different ways for different people. Worry and anxiety deprives you of the ability to enjoy the moment. They zap you of the joy you would otherwise receive from living your life with great expectations of good things happening. If the well-being of your life stems from your heart, then worry and anxiety will be the negative emotions that disband the vigor required to fulfill the pertinent tasks of life. When I say life, I'm not merely speaking of working a job, running a business, or maintaining a career. Your true life goes beyond what you do and delves into who you were created to be, who you are at your core. When you know who you are at your core, you are better equipped to navigate the cares of life, jump over the hurdles brought along your journey, and do it all with a joy and hope that tomorrow will be better. The good news is that an encouraging word has the power to lift you out of the stupor of worry and anxiety. An encouraging word spoken at the correct time can go into the depths of your heart and seize fear as cold water on a hot summer day seizes thirst. Just as water refreshes your body, a timely word will refresh your soul.

Reference:

Proverbs 15:13; 17:22, 18:14

WISDOM TIP 93

Don't just talk about it, rise up and be about it!

"Lazy people don't even cook the game they catch, but the diligent make use of everything they find."

PROVERBS 12:27 (NLT)

"A lazy life is an empty life, but 'early to rise' gets the job done."

PROVERBS 12:27 (THE MESSAGE)

This proverb reminds me of stories my husband tells about his grandparents who raised hogs, planted vegetable gardens, and fruit trees to sustain their lives. As the story goes, during hog slaughter, they used every part of the hog. The meat was cured and smoked, the fat was melted and used to make soap and oil for hair and skin. The snout, tail, and feet of the hog were all used. The head was used to make hog's head cheese. Every part of the hog was used for a worthy purpose. The same with the vegetables and fruits. They were canned, preserved, baked, sliced and diced into dishes and cakes. This is an example of diligent living. On the other hand, a lazy person will sit on the sofa all day and not even get up to cook the packaged meat purchased from the grocery store. The Message translation provides a different perspective, "A lazy life is an empty life." It's empty because lazy people tend to not accomplish much. A person's sense of accomplishment in life is what produces a sense of value to oneself and those around them. The early bird gets the worm because the early riser is the seeker, the pursuer, the one who doesn't just talk about it, but gets about the business of making it happen. Don't just talk about it, be about it!

Reference:

Proverbs 10:4, 13:4

WISDOM TIP 94

Intelligent children listen to their parents; foolish children do their own thing.

"A wise child accepts a parent's discipline; a mocker refuses to listen to correction."

PROVERBS 13:1 (NLT)

"Intelligent children listen to their parents; foolish children do their own thing."

PROVERBS 13:1 (THE MESSAGE)

This wisdom principle hits home for me because I was the mocker who refused to listen to the instruction of my parents and others as a teen. Somewhere around the age of fifteen, I completely lost my right mind. As the old people would say, "I started smelling myself." It was nothing but the sheer grace of God that covered my life during the next three years, shielding me from my own foolishness. I look back over those years and shake my head at the opportunities I passed up and the good things that had the potential to give me a leg up in life that I turned away from. Wisdom will cause you to recognize how good you have it when you have parents who love you enough to help guide you along the right path. Our country has seen its fair share of delinquent parents who provide neither godly advice nor the proper guidance required to live a good life. Wisdom will also cause you to listen, heed, and obey instructions even when it comes in the form of correction. The way to receive less correction is to obey the instruction you have already received. I urge you to embrace the wisdom of those who have been placed in your life. Doing your own thing places you on the path of the foolish. Remember, experience is not the best teacher, wisdom is. Thus, learning from the experience and wisdom gained from others will help you avoid traps and obstacles along your journey of growing all the wiser.

References:

Proverbs 9:8, 10:1, 15:12, 15:20

WISDOM TIP 95

Fill your mouth with good fruit so your life can produce goodness.

"The good acquire a taste for helpful conversation; bullies push and shove their way through life."

Proverbs 13:2 (THE MESSAGE)

"From the fruit of their lips people enjoy good things, but the unfaithful have an appetite for violence."

Proverbs 13:2 (NIV)

Your life today is a sum total of all the things you have vocalized in the past. Your words, the fruit of your lips, have played a role in producing the good you see in your life. Just as the rotten fruit of your lips have played a role in producing the not so good you currently see in your life. Test it out today. Let's deem today the "Positive Fruit of the Lips Challenge Day." Practice speaking good and only good about yourself, those around you, and your current circumstances. If you can't find anything good to say, then say nothing at all. Better yet, make today a day of gratitude and allow the fruit of your lips to express thanksgiving to God for all the good things He has given you to enjoy. If you are having a difficult time thinking of something to be grateful for, allow me to recommend a few: air to breathe, the sun to provide warmth, eyes that see, ears that hear, and teeth to chew your food. Speaking of teeth, we don't recognize what a blessing they are until we meet someone without teeth who has to gum their food, then we suddenly become thankful for our own chompers. If you still don't know where to start then try this, "I receive good things coming into my life today. God give me the ability to recognize them when they come today so I can be grateful to you." When you discover the power of filling your lips with "good fruit," you are on your way to filling your tomorrows with goodness.

Reference:

Proverbs 12:14, 18:21

WISDOM TIP 96

Learn to be "slow to speak" in order to carefully craft your speech.

"Those who guard their lips preserve their lives, but those who speak rashly will come to ruin."

PROVERBS 13:3 (NIV)

"Careful words make for a careful life; careless talk may ruin everything."

PROVERBS 13:3 (THE MESSAGE)

I am a recovering Lip Warrior. For all my Lip Warriors out there, you probably chuckled when you read that. Notice I said recovering to insinuate a continual process. While I am much better than I was a year ago, I'm still not where I should be when it comes to guarding my lips and speaking rashly. If you rub me the wrong way at the wrong time, on the wrong day, then you may meet Kyna the Lip Warrior instead of Kyna the Bible Study Teacher and that's real talk as the young people would say. My lip wars do not involve profanity or verbally abusive phrases, but they represent words that are not in keeping with guarding my life from strife, impatience, or defending my own cause. My lip wars have the complete goal of ensuring the subject in question understands without any uncertainty that he or she has just come across an educated woman who knows her rights and understands how to articulate them precisely in a passive aggressive way. Not guarding my tongue has put me in situations where I have spoken rashly, without thinking or without considering the consequences. The person who flows in wisdom understands that to look over an offense promotes peace. Therefore, the wise person will guard his lips and consequently guard his very life. Especially these days with all the "cray crays" rolling around with concealed weapons! Can I get an amen? Today's wisdom tip is to simply think before you speak. It's better to save a relationship from the ruin of harsh words that cannot be withdrawn than to "rightly" defend your cause by speaking rashly. Be slow to speak and slow to anger, you just might literally save your life from ruin.

Reference:

James 3:2; Psalm 34:13, 141:3; Proverbs 10:14, 18:21, 21:23

WISDOM TIP 97

A dream without action is simply a day dream.

"Indolence wants it all and gets nothing; the energetic have something to show for their lives."

PROVERBS 13:4 (THE MESSAGE)

"A sluggard's appetite is never filled, but the desires of the diligent are fully satisfied."

PROVERBS 13:4 (NIV)

Whew! This one is a mouthful. If you are a sluggard, you can't even imagine chewing and swallowing the words that cause your mouth to be fully satisfied. However, the diligent are all over this one. The sluggard, aka lazy, aka don't want to work for nothing, aka gives up at the first sign of trouble, aka entitlement minded, aka everyone is to blame but me GETS NATHAN! Excuse me, that means "nothing" for all of my proper English speaking readers. All your dreams will eventually fall to the wayside because a dream without action is simply a day dream. We all remember what happened to the day dreamers in class, they always came up short when the teacher caught them slipping. They couldn't answer the question, never knew where to begin the next reading segment, and were completely cut off from the reality of what was really going on around them. Don't get me wrong, sometimes your dreams will cause others to believe that you are living in a fantasy world, but your actions will one day prove them wrong. Not so the sluggard, his inactions find him in the same predicament year after year while the desires of the diligent are fully satisfied because of the effort and work they have contributed to make their dream a reality. One thing I know for sure is once you sit down to do the work, God's supernatural empowerment becomes ever more visible. He's always there because He is the one who gives us the dream, idea, concept, or endeavor to begin with. However, it is not until we put action behind the dream that the products we desire are realized, resulting in a satisfaction that only comes as a result of completion.

Reference:

Proverbs 6:6, 10:4, 12:27, 20:4, 21:25

WISDOM TIP 98

Extravagant living does not equal an extravagant bank account.

"One person pretends to be rich, yet has nothing; another pretends to be poor, yet has great wealth."

PROVERBS 13:7 (NIV)

Many financial advisors will attest to the fact that their wealthiest clients are not always the most visually extravagant people. I've heard that many of their wealthiest clients drive fifteen-year-old automobiles and wear generic brand clothing. The one who pretends to be rich versus the one who pretends to be poor yet has great wealth. Don't get me wrong, I like nice things just as much as the next person, but nice things in their right place, in the right season of life, when all other things are in order. Take a look at your finances. Are you pretending to be fabulous while suffering silently with lack? Put first things first and get your financial life in order. It's not how much you make that makes you rich, it's how much of the income you generate that you are able to keep and apply toward money making endeavors that causes wealth to accumulate. Handling finances in accordance with biblical terms means returning back to God the tithe (10% of your income) and being a good steward over the 90% that is left to freely distribute at your discretion. If you haven't started, try the 20% rule to start—10% back to your local church and 10% back to yourself in terms of savings, investments, and future wealth building endeavors. Once you get accustomed to this lifestyle, increase it a few percentages every year, or every other year. Stop being more consumed with having a net worth that consists of the latest and greatest designer fashions and technological devices. If your finances are literally drowning you right now, seek professional help and a personal accountability partner to help you though this time. Tough times don't last, but the desires of the diligent will be satisfied in time.

Reference:

Proverbs 11:24, 13:8, 12:9

WISDOM TIP 99

Setting aside a little here and a little there will produce exponential results.

"Wealth from get-rich-quick schemes quickly disappears; wealth from hard work grows over time."

PROVERBS 13:11 (NLT)

"Easy come, easy go, but steady diligence pays off."
PROVERBS 13:11 (THE MESSAGE)

In the end, get-rich-quick schemes dwindle away; it's like chasing after the wind only to feel it breeze through your fingers. You know why, dishonest money is normally in the hands of an unwise person. Money without wisdom is a dwindling situation, because life handled foolishly eventually dwindles. Those who work hard and gather what some would call chump change, but has the wisdom to put aside a little bit here and a little bit there can wisely build a nest egg. I recall hearing of a woman who worked as a domestic helper all her life and lived in a modest home. However, this woman died a millionaire and left an estate that invested in the collegiate endeavors of a number of underprivileged children. This woman was born during a time when many educational options were not offered to her because of her race, but the wisdom expressed in this verse prompted her to put away a little bit at a time in order to be a blessing to herself and others in her later years. Rumor is she started saving pennies when she first began putting away money for the future. Those pennies turned into millions that produced lasting fruit in the lives of many children who may not have otherwise had the opportunity to pursue their educational pursuits.

Reference:

Proverbs 20:21, 28:8

WISDOM TIP 100

Choose your friends wisely.

"Walk with the wise and become wise; associate with fools and get in trouble."

PROVERBS 13:20 (NLT)

"Become wise by walking with the wise; hang out with fools and watch your life fall to pieces."

PROVERBS 13:20 (THE MESSAGE)

Birds of a feather flock together. I don't understand the rationale behind the birds of a feather instead of just saying the same species of birds. However, it has proven true nonetheless. If you walk with the wise you will gain wisdom, but if you walk with fools you will suffer harm because of the foolishness of your peer group. First, let's put "walk with" in its correct context, which really means to hang out with or closely associate with. There is a group of young men who made a pact as children for each of them to graduate from medical school. They encouraged each other when times were hard and rejoiced with one another when victories were won. Most importantly, because they made the choice to walk with like-minded young men, they all walked across the stage to receive their medical degrees and are all doctors. Similarly, I've heard of otherwise good kids hanging around with the wrong crowd and going to prison for their first offense because they were accessories to a crime in the wrong place at the wrong time with the wrong people, often without being fully aware that what they were actually walking into would result in a serious criminal offense. Your friendships have the potential to influence you for the better or corrupt and destroy you. Word to the wise, choose your friends carefully.

Reference:

Proverbs 2:20, 9:6, 15:31; 1 Corinthians 6:15:33–34

WISDOM TIP 101

A legacy of honorable living will outlast a monetary inheritance.

"Good people leave an inheritance to their grandchildren, but the sinner's wealth passes to the godly."

Proverbs 13:22 (NLT)

"A good life gets passed on to the grandchildren; ill-gotten wealth ends up with good people."

Proverbs 13:22 (THE MESSAGE)

Good people intentionally set out to leave a generational inheritance. While some will characterize an inheritance solely on the grounds of monetary assets, I urge you to look beyond the financial realm for a moment and look to a legacy of faith, a legacy of commitment, and a legacy of service to name a few. I'm not refuting the financial aspect of an inheritance because we've already learned that wisdom will guide you in your financial affairs to put away little by little, allowing the growth to expand into exponential increase. However, let's not seek to leave wealth for our offspring without the wisdom required to manage it properly and the character to enjoy it. In keeping with most sayings of the wise, there is a warning attached. A crooked person's monetary wealth and assets that were amassed by dishonest means will eventually find its way into better hands. Partly because the inheritance was void of the wisdom and life skills required to assign it a purpose beyond the life of the beneficiary. There's no way to get around it, make an effort to intentionally live a life of integrity and honor and your life will be an inheritance that can produce far greater dividends than wealth alone.

Reference:

Proverbs 28:8, Ecclesiastes 2:26

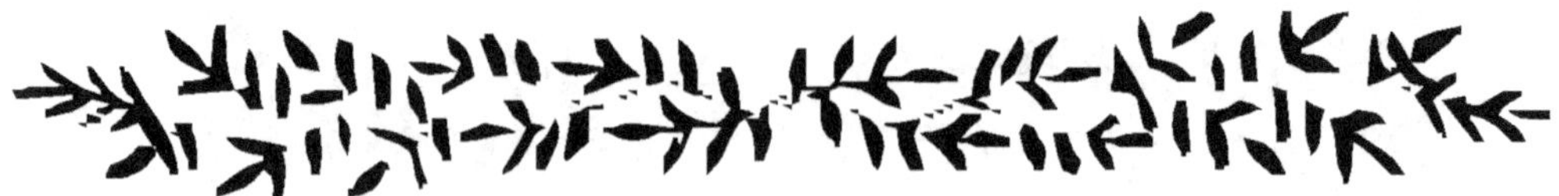

WISDOM TIP 102

Love your children enough to discipline them.

"Those who spare the rod of discipline hate their children. Those who love their children care enough to discipline them."

PROVERBS 13:24 (NLT)

"A refusal to correct is a refusal to love; love your children by disciplining them."

PROVERBS 13:24 (THE MESSAGE)

"Spare the rod, spoil the child" is a phrase that has been repeated by the best and most well-intentioned parental advisors. However, many have a limited perspective on the term "rod," narrowing their idea of discipline to corporal punishment alone. As a mother of three very different and distinct personalities, I've wisely observed that discipline comes in many forms and must properly reflect the lesson to be learned. Additionally, discipline changes as children grow in their understanding. Wherever you may fall along the spectrum of the "rod," wisdom makes it clear that we are to discipline our children and discipline them promptly as an act of love. Some modern parents unwisely believe that friendship should precede discipline. The truth is, friendship with our adult children will arise out of respect as a result of properly disciplining them when they were younger. There is a season for everything. Parent while your children need a parent and become a friend later in life after they have learned that your parenting methods have proven to literally and figuratively save their lives from destruction. Do yourself and society a huge favor by teaching your children the right way to live, so they can one day grow to be productive citizens of society instead of future terrors that both you and others are terrified to deal with. The right form of discipline now will save your precious little angels from the wrong form of wrath in the future.

Reference:

Proverbs 3:12, 19:18, 22:15, 23:13–14, 29:15, and 29:17

WISDOM TIP 103

Women, you have the power to build a lovely home or to demolish it with your own hands, brick by brick.

"A wise woman builds her home, but a foolish woman tears it down with her own hands."

PROVERBS 14:1 (NLT)

"Lady Wisdom builds a lovely home; Sir Fool comes along and tears it down brick by brick."

PROVERBS 14:1 (THE MESSAGE)

Ladies, if you were not aware of how much power you have over the condition of your home and the people who live within its walls, my hope is that this truth will speak to your heart. This verse could have been inspired to read "a wise man builds his home," but God, in His infinite wisdom, is trying to relay a deep message to women directly reflective of our value in His eyes and our worth to society at large. During my years as a stay-at-home wife and mother, I often had pity parties and felt sorry for myself because in my mind, "Life was passing me by." Nevertheless, being the Type A personality that I am, I made myself busy at home by training and teaching my children, maintaining a spotlessly clean and comfortable home for my family, managing the finances to ensure we thrived on a budget that supported good stewardship, serving in my church, volunteering in the local community, and mentoring the military families that fell under my husband's responsibility. Hum! Sounds like life was really passing me by! Ladies, please grasp the importance of what you do and the power that lies within your possession to either wisely build your home and your community or to foolishly tear it down with your own doing. Let wisdom guide your affairs with discretion as you build your home brick by brick, for better or for worse.

Reference:

Proverbs 31:10, 19:13, 9:13–15, 21:9 and 19

WISDOM TIP 104

The muscle that brings a beating is not your fist, it's your mouth.

"A fool's proud talk becomes a rod that beats him, but the words of the wise keep them safe."

PROVERBS 14:3 (NLT)

"Frivolous talk provokes a derisive smile; wise speech evokes nothing but respect."

PROVERBS 14:3 (THE MESSAGE)

If we can learn to control the flappy piece of muscle that we call a tongue, then we have found one of the keys to conquering life. Our words will either cause us to dwell in safety or cause us to walk right into harm's way. If I were to take a poll amongst each of you reading this today, I'm sure most of you will say you personally know or have heard of someone who talked himself right into trouble. Some would say, his mouth wrote a check that his behind could not cash! If we are truly wise, we will learn to use our words with care, and care sometimes means to just "shut up" and use no words at all. Other times, our carefully chosen words will promote peace and goodwill.

Reference:

Proverbs 12:6, 18:6

WISDOM TIP 105

Take frequent inventory of your life to remain fully aware of the value of your chosen path.

"The prudent understand where they are going, but fools deceive themselves."

PROVERBS 14:8 (NLT)

"The wisdom of the wise keeps life on track; the foolishness of fools lands them in the ditch."

PROVERBS 14:8 (THE MESSAGE)

Learn to examine well your own way before you decide to act. When you truly examine your way, you will consider the consequences of your action, the motive behind your action, and the result your action will have on your life and the lives of others. The direct opposite of a prudent person is ... drum roll please ... you guessed it, the F-O-O-L! The fool only cares about me, myself, and I. The fool's sole purpose of existence is to con his way into what he wants out of life, in other words, to attempt to deceive others while not having possessed enough good sense to understand that the joke is actually on him. Deception has a hefty price tag attached to it and the deceiver does not have the liberty of choosing the payment plan. Listen carefully, you only fool yourself if you think you will profit from deception. Oh, what a tangled web we weave when at first we practice to deceive! Wisdom, on the other hand, gives careful thought to the consequences of an act. Notice the proverb is already giving credence to the fact that it is the wisdom that you have already accepted and applied that urges a person to seek out more wisdom, so that it may also be applied in order to stay on the right track. You heard it right, this wisdom thing is a lifelong journey. The more you get the more you want, and the more you want it the more you realize how much you need it. If you don't care for the picture you currently see painted on the canvas of your life, then you and you alone control the stroke of the paintbrush. At any given moment, you can change the scenery by allowing wisdom to pave the way.

Reference:

Proverbs 14:15, 15:21; 1 Corinthians 3:19; 2 Timothy 3:13; Ephesians 5:15

WISDOM TIP 106

Do not allow your heart to lead you, allow your authentic spirit to lead your heart.

"There is a path before each person that seems right, but it ends in death."

PROVERBS 14:12 (NLT)

"There's a way of life that looks harmless enough; look again—it leads straight to hell. Sure, those people appear to be having a good time, but all that laughter will end in heartbreak."

PROVERBS 14:12–13 (THE MESSAGE)

The phrase "follow your heart" is loosely thrown around on T-shirts, advertisements, and advice columns just about everywhere these days. We've heard it so much that "follow your heart" has become a common mantra to the young and old alike when making major decisions. I submit to you the notion that your heart can be tainted by hidden motives, unchecked biases, and self-will. Your heart can only be trusted to be your guide to the degree that your heart has been submitted to the wisdom and reverence of God Almighty who knows and measures the motives of every person's heart. Wisdom is based on lasting and proven universal truth steeped in the Word of God, but your heart is wavering given the circumstances. Sometimes in life, you may believe with everything in you that this is the best thing to do or the best way to handle a situation, but it will end with unexpected detrimental results because you didn't heed that little check in your spirit. When in doubt and when you are almost certainly sure, check your heart against God's highest way and check your thoughts against God's highest thoughts. Always check the leading of your heart against "the way" to see how they align prior to making a final decision.

Reference:

Proverbs 12:15, 16:25, Matthew 7:13–14, Romans 6:21

WISDOM TIP 107

Believe half of what you see and none of what you hear!

"Only simpletons believe everything they're told! The prudent carefully consider their steps."

PROVERBS 14:15 (NLT)

"The gullible believe anything they're told; the prudent sift and weigh every word."

PROVERBS 14:15 (THE MESSAGE)

Believe half of what you see because your eyes can deceive you and none of what you hear because second-hand information can be twisted. When someone brings something to you, good or bad, you must have the ability to consider what you are being told and the source of the information prior to taking it to the bank. A gullible person is a person who is easily persuaded or easily swayed to one side or the other. Gullible people believe every sob story and every voice of eloquence promising a pie in the sky. A gullible person is easily persuaded because they have yet to establish their lives on firm principles, such as the biblical wisdom principles found in this book. Therefore, you can tell a gullible person that the sky is now red and persuade them that it was never blue but purple, and eventually, they will come to accept your position and believe it as a firm truth. Don't be an Eve in the Garden and give up your royal position for a piece of fruit when you own the entire orchard based on the word of a sly talking, smooth walking, slithering snake. Wisdom responds with the careful consideration of information, sifting it for the truth and all the elements that lie in between. As my husband would say, "Trust but verify."

Reference:

Proverbs 17:4, 4:26, 1 John 4:1

WISDOM TIP 108

Self-control is a by-product of wisdom.

"Short-tempered people do foolish things, and schemers are hated."

PROVERBS 14:17 (NLT)

"The hotheaded do things they'll later regret; the coldhearted get the cold shoulder."

PROVERBS 14:17 (THE MESSAGE)

Fill in the blank. "That fool gon' mess around and get himself __________________!" If I had a dime for every time I've heard that phrase uttered about someone who is so hotheaded and short-tempered that they react without thinking. Self-control is a by-product of surrendering to the wisdom of God. Tired of doing foolish things only to regret them later? Try wisdom. Tired of blowing up and losing control at the slightest offense? Try wisdom. Tired of all the broken relationships and trouble caused by your explosive temper? Try wisdom. If you struggle in this area, go back and find all the proverbs dealing with controlling your mouth and emotions. Study them and focus on putting them into practice until you begin to notice a change in your temperament. After that, continue to study and practice them and the reference scriptures until someone close to you comments on how much you've changed. If Peter can go from cutting off ears and ready to rumble at the drop of a hat to the calm shadow healing apostle, then there is hope for you and I, my friend.

Reference:

Ecclesiastes 7:9; Proverbs 14:16, 16:32, 22:24

WISDOM TIP 109

How you treat the "least of them" is the true judge of your character.

"It is a sin to belittle one's neighbor; blessed are those who help the poor."

PROVERBS 14:21 (NLT)

"It's criminal to ignore a neighbor in need, but compassion for the poor—what a blessing!"

PROVERBS 14:21 (THE MESSAGE)

How you treat someone who has nothing to offer you is closely related to who you really are when all the masks are pulled back. Let's not trivialize the word neighbor by defaulting its meaning to the exclusivity of those who live next door to us in our community. The parable of the Good Samaritan correctly defines a neighbor as anyone who has a heart of compassion toward another, regardless of their differences. I challenge you to identify the biases you may have in your heart against your neighbor and to remember the Great Commandment that requires us to love our neighbor as ourselves and the Golden Rule that teaches us to "do unto others as you would have them do unto you." Likewise, the poor cannot be limited to those poor in resources. You may be called upon to help those poor in attitude, poor in emotions, or poor in their outlook of those who are physically different from them. There is a difference between compassionate charity and philanthropy. You can display philanthropic acts and still have a poor attitude toward those your money is servicing. Compassionate charity finds its motives in the purity that comes from faith in God who is Creator and Father of all mankind. To witness your neighbor suffering is to witness your brother suffering; therefore, the act of compassionate charity is extending love and grace to your brother in honor of your Father.

Reference:

Psalms 41:1; Proverbs 14:31, 19:17, 1 John 3:17

WISDOM TIP 110

Lip labor produces nothing but empty words.

"Work brings profit, but mere talk leads to poverty!"
PROVERBS 14:23 (NLT)

"Hard work always pays off; mere talk puts no bread on the table."
PROVERBS 14:23 (THE MESSAGE)

Too much talking and not enough doing will profit you none. Ecclesiastes tells us there is a time for everything under the sun. When it's time for working, all talk must be put aside and all distractions hidden. In this world of constant connection to social media, I often wonder how much work is actually going on in the workplace when so much time is directed at updating your status with superficial pictures of what you ate for lunch. Allow your diligent work ethic to update your real status in life. Talk is cheap! Lip labor produces nothing but empty words. I agree with Missouri, show me what you are working with!

Reference:
Proverbs 12:24, 28:19; Ecclesiastes 5:3

WISDOM TIP 111

Understand what makes you tick and be wise enough to avoid it.

"People with understanding control their anger; a hot temper shows great foolishness."
PROVERBS 14:29 (NLT)

"Slowness to anger makes for deep understanding; a quick-tempered person stockpiles stupidity."
PROVERBS 14:29 (THE MESSAGE)

This temperament issue must be important! Here it is again in the same chapter. Just in case you missed the concept the first time, it was reworded to catch your attention the second go-round. Self-control is linked to wisdom. Those who control their anger are described as people of understanding, but a quick-tempered person is described as a person who builds upon his or her stupidity. Basically, every time you fly off the handle, another shovelful of stupidity is dumped into your barn. Now you have the task of digging your way out of all that stupid so you can begin to see the light of day. An explosive temper is not who you are, but if not careful, it will define the entire trajectory of your life. A person of understanding will identify his or her own trigger points and learn how to control his or her reactions before the heat of the moment. Understand what makes you tick and be wise enough to avoid it.

Reference:

James 1:19; Proverbs 15:18, 16:32, 17:27, 19:11; Ecclesiastes 7:9

WISDOM TIP 112

Living your best life begins with a peaceful heart.

"A peaceful heart leads to a healthy body; jealousy is like cancer in the bones."

PROVERBS 14:30 (NLT)

"A sound mind makes for a robust body, but runaway emotions corrode the bones."

PROVERBS 14:30 (THE MESSAGE)

A peaceful heart and a sound mind are free of the rotten emotions that erode both your body and your soul. The kings of negative emotions are jealousy and envy; nothing can destroy your well-being like rotting away with obsession over the life of someone else. The self-debilitating diseases of jealousy and envy release all of your best energy toward the benefit of someone whose best energy is aimed at accomplishing the thing in which you envy. Transfer your attention and energy to living your best life and you'll reap the priceless benefit of a peaceful heart and sound mind along with contentment with yourself and all that God has blessed you with.

Reference:

Proverbs 15:13, Job 5:2, Psalm 112:10

WISDOM TIP 113

The whispers of a bona fide lady can be seen more loudly than the acts of a bona fide fool.

"Wisdom is enshrined in an understanding heart; wisdom is not found among fools."
PROVERBS 14:33 (NLT)

"Lady Wisdom is at home in an understanding heart—fools never even get to say hello."
PROVERBS 14:33 (THE MESSAGE)

Wisdom is a lady who acts accordingly. Gentlemen, this does not exclude you. The partner to a lady is a bona fide gentleman who graciously yields to the lady on his side. A lady does not expose all her goodies in full view for the public eye. A lady knows how to enter a room with such grace that the announcement of her entry alone will begin to shift the atmosphere of the room. Likewise, when Lady Wisdom rests in a heart that understands her force and her grace, then the actions of that heart will follow accordingly. Not so with the loud mouth woman known as "Folly." She must be heard and seen at the same time. You've seen her in Walmart, in the mall, and walking down an otherwise quiet street. You can hear her from a mile away, ranting and raving about everything under the sun with amusement, to the disgust of all those within hearing range. Folly never gets to say hello to Lady Wisdom because she will not keep her mouth shut long enough to hear the announcement of Lady Wisdom's entrance. So like the lady she is, Lady Wisdom passes by without interrupting. Moral of the story, "turn down" long enough to hear a gentle voice that you may not recognize at first. Become familiar with her voice so even in a crowded room with many competing voices, your ear will catch the tune of her gentle whisper.

Reference:

Proverbs 2:10, 13:16

WISDOM TIP 114

Represent the brand of your employer well.

"A king rejoices in wise servants but is angry with those who disgrace him."

PROVERBS 14:35 (NLT)

"Diligent work gets a warm commendation; shiftless work earns an angry rebuke."

PROVERBS 14:35 (THE MESSAGE)

Hold the brakes … we no longer have kings who we employ lifelong servitude too, but we do have companies or organizations that employ us for the services or talents we provide. Just as in biblical days, the servant of the king represented the king and all that his kingdom stood for, so do you Mr. or Ms. Employee. You represent the brand, the name, and the CEO of the organization that hired you to perform a certain task. If you want to make your boss happy, then produce superior work in a timely manner. If you want to make them angry, then do just the opposite. It's not rocket science, but it is wisdom. Start with coming to work on time with breakfast already in your stomach so you are prepared to work when you get there. Next, do the work you were hired to do and that you get paid handsomely to do without the bad attitude that believes you are doing the employer and their customers a favor. Work when it's time to work; work does not mean talk unless you were hired to talk; work does not mean be the office's social bee and moral booster, unless you were given this duty; and work definitely does not mean checking your social media, text messages, and Snapchat every fifteen minutes unless it's included in your job description. Work can be defined as diligent attention and activity to the task in which you have been hired to accomplish. Lastly, if you fail to apply yourself, you will get an "angry rebuke" (i.e. write-up, demerit, warning). This is the time to sit down and be humble. Accept that you messed up and make the decision to straighten up before the brand removes its seal and you become just another generic name standing in the unemployment line.

Reference:

Matthew 24:45–47, 25:21–23; Proverbs 5:12, 17:2

WISDOM TIP 115

A gentle answer stops wrath in its tracks.

"A gentle answer deflects anger, but harsh words make tempers flare."

PROVERBS 15:1 (NLT)

"A gentle response defuses anger, but a sharp tongue kindles a temper-fire."

PROVERBS 15:1 (THE MESSAGE)

Mild and respectful words have the hidden potential to defuse a hostile environment. In some instances, the right words softly spoken with the right attitude may even save your life. In this modern age of freedom of speech and individual rights, a respectful mild response may be viewed as weak, but respect never goes out of style. You have two options: match the anger of the other person involved and see the situation escalate from fists to cuffs, or in some cases even death. The second option is only chosen by the wise: humble yourself and speak reasonably with the person whose anger has already gone from 0 to 100 and begin walking away. I've seen both options play out in my home with my spouse and my children. I can match their anger and add fuel to the fire, or I can decide to speak a calm word that allows flaring tempers to simmer. Remember the words of Jesus, "Blessed are the peacemakers." As much as it depends on you, be a peacemaker with your words and stop a storm before it begins to brew.

Reference:

Proverbs 15:18, 25:15

WISDOM TIP 116

Hone the skill of tact; know what to speak, when to speak it, and to whom.

"The tongue of the wise makes knowledge appealing, but the mouth of a fool belches out foolishness."

PROVERBS 15:2 (NLT)

"Knowledge flows like spring water from the wise; fools are leaky faucets, dripping nonsense."

PROVERBS 15:2 (THE MESSAGE)

There's nothing more annoying than a dripping faucet. Not only is it annoying to hear the constant "plip-plop" of the water, but it can be costly over the long term. Compare the dripping of a leaking faucet to the dripping of nonsense that seeps from the mouth of a fool; it is constant, annoying, and costly. A fool has what I have characterized as an unrestrained mouth. You can't take a fool nowhere and I do mean nowhere—not anywhere. The unrestrained mouth of a fool gossips, lies, tells all of your business, his business, and her business. Fools scheme and connive with their words in order to conjure up as much discourse as the listener will allow. A fool doesn't know when to be quiet or when to stand down. A wise person has learned to hone a very valuable skill known as tact. Tact directs the tongue of the wise to speak with appropriate language, at the proper occasion, during the opportune time. The tongue of the wise makes knowledge appealing by knowing what to speak, when to speak it, and to whom. Thus, the edifying and knowledgeable words that flow from the mouth of the wise refreshes the listener in a timely manner, provoking the hunger for knowledge within.

Reference:

Proverbs 12:23, 13:16, 15:7, 15:28; Ecclesiastes 10:14

WISDOM TIP 117

Aim to speak words that bring healing rather than pain.

"Gentle words are a tree of life; a deceitful tongue crushes the spirit."

Proverbs 15:4 (NLT)

"Kind words heal and help; cutting words wound and maim."

Proverbs 15:4 (THE MESSAGE)

Kind and gentle words spoken at the right time bring soothing comfort as refreshing as water to a dying plant. Words can lift you out of a pit of depression just as words can send you down a spiraling road of destruction. One of the worse things you can do to a person who is already down is speak words that will drag them down lower by "wounding and maiming" their spirit to the point of crushing. Life and death are powerful derivatives of your words, they either ignite a spark of life or they drain the life out. There is not a gray area when it comes to the power of words. Take a tally of your words this week to discover where you are. If you need to make a change, start with filling your mind with scriptures, such as this one that highlight the power of your words until your mind and your mouth begin to agree with habitually producing life-giving words that overflow from your heart to others.

Reference:

Proverbs 12:18, 16:24

WISDOM TIP 118

Welcoming correction is a mark of good sense.

"Only a fool despises a parent's discipline; whoever learns from correction is wise."

Proverbs 15:5 (NLT)

"Moral dropouts won't listen to their elders; welcoming correction is a mark of good sense."

PROVERBS 15:5 (THE MESSAGE)

Somewhere over the rainbow or around the corner, someone has tried to offer you correction. Possibly a teacher, a coach, a grandparent, aunt, uncle, a friend's parent, or the lady at the grocery store. When I was growing up, a fool who would not listen to correction was termed "hard-headed." I guess we can assume the opposite of those who would listen and call them "softheaded." Think about this for a moment. If your head is soft, it has the potential to soak up correction like a sponge. Soft things are generally pliable and easy to work with, versus hard, stone-like items that require strenuous labor in order to penetrate the surface. Anyone with good sense will choose the soft, pliable route over the hard, laborious route. That's the difference, my friends, between those who listen to correction and those who despise being corrected. Hardheads eventually find themselves saying something very similar to this, "How I hated instruction and despised reproof!" (Proverbs 5:12). Stop learning everything the hard way; wisdom is soft and pliable which makes it easy to apply.

Reference:

Proverbs 13:18, 15:32

WISDOM TIP 119

Despising correction is like digging the ditch to your own grave.

"Whoever abandons the right path will be severely disciplined; whoever hates correction will die."

PROVERBS 15:10 (NLT)

"It's a school of hard knocks for those who leave God's path, a dead-end street for those who hate God's rules."

PROVERBS 15:10 (THE MESSAGE)

If you continue to make the choice to defy correction and sound judgment, then you are digging the ditch to your own grave. Correction is meant to steer you back on the right path, especially when it comes from a loving source. To continue to reject discipline will land you in a place that will make you lift your eyes to heaven, one way or another. If you lay your bed hard, you will one day have to lie down in that hard bed. My prayer is that you do not perish before you get the opportunity to wake up with a stiff back from the bed of lessons learned.

Reference:

Proverbs 22:6, 10:17, 2:13; 2 Peter 2:15

WISDOM TIP 120

Knowledge fuels the hunger of the wise.

"A wise person is hungry for knowledge, while the fool feeds on trash."

Proverbs 15:14 (NLT)

"An intelligent person is always eager to take in more truth; fools feed on fast-food fads and fancies."

Proverbs 15:14 (THE MESSAGE)

I once heard a commentator say, "The wise man knows that he knows nothing, so he always seeks to learn more." I've also heard it put this way, "When you stop learning you stop living." Statements such as these are what fuel the hunger of the wise. Trash denotes stale and expired food no longer fit for consumption. Feeding on trash will result in a malnutritioned body that will eventually break down your immune system, making you susceptible to all kinds of sickness and disease. The same can be applied to fast-food. It may taste good, but it's not good for you to feed on over a consistent time period. The types of trash that a fool feeds on are too numerous to list, but you can recognize it by the stench. Just as money produces more money, wisdom breeds more wisdom and foolishness produces more of the same stinky trash that pollutes and malnourishes your life. Join the wise and allow the nutrients of knowledge to fuel your hunger.

Reference:

Proverbs 18:15, 9:9, 1:5

WISDOM TIP 121

When life gives you lemons, add some sugar and make lemonade.

"For the despondent, every day brings trouble; for the happy heart, life is a continual feast."

PROVERBS 15:15 (NLT)

"A miserable heart means a miserable life; a cheerful heart fills the day with song."

PROVERBS 15:15 (THE MESSAGE)

Misery check: If you are happy and you know it, clap your hands. If you are happy and you know it, clap your hands. If you are happy and you know it and your face will truly show it, if you are happy and you know it, clap your hands. All my happy people sang the lines to the tune of the song in their heads and all my really, really happy people are singing out loud and clapping their hands. In fact, the exuberantly happy people went back to a fond childhood memory and are now floating on cloud nine. The despondent "can't get happy about 'nothing,'" and "can't stand to see you happy" people are annoyed right now. We all have known a doom and gloomer. If it's sunny outside, they complain about the light and warmth of the sun. If it rains, they complain about the clouds and the wet grass. These are the people who always find the worst in every situation and are sure to let everyone around them know about it. How can two people with very similar circumstances respond differently? It's a matter of the heart. What have you allowed to fill your heart? Bitterness, anger, anxiety, and pity will produce misery. When you learn to focus on the good in life, your heart will fill up with joy that overflows with the happy song. It's all about the condition of your heart. A guarded cheerful heart says, "Thank you for providing all of these sour lemons, I'm going to add the sweetness of joy to make some tasty lemonade we can enjoy until the storm passes over."

Reference:

Proverbs 17:22, Ecclesiastes 12:2

WISDOM TIP 122

Great treasure with inner turmoil is poverty at its best.

"Better to have little, with fear for the Lord, than to have great treasure and inner turmoil."
Proverbs 15:16 (NLT)

"A simple life in the Fear-of-God is better than a rich life with a ton of headaches."
Proverbs 15:16 (THE MESSAGE)

Many times in life, we find ourselves striving to achieve the next big thing. In all your striving, where is your desire to strive for the things of God? What does it profit you to gain the "rich life" and have inner and outer turmoil? Without reverence for the Lord who has given you the ability to get wealth, it is all meaningless. The headache and turmoil that comes with the "rich life" without God has to do with the anxiety and care it requires to guard your treasures. You gotta watch out for thieves, your boy from high school who wants the hook up, your distant cousins who just need to hold $20. All that pressure that comes from trying to keep what you got and not knowing who to trust is fertile soil for inner turmoil. As Biggie once said, "More money, more problems!" I'm not advocating poverty because I believe the Bible is clear about the righteous being made whole in every area of our lives, that includes your financial status. If you make God your partner you can have a rich life that far exceeds monetary wealth; it includes contentment and riches that thieves cannot steal.

Reference:

1 Timothy 6:6, Psalm 37:16, Proverbs 16:8, Proverbs 28:6

WISDOM TIP 123

Simplicity with love is better than abundance with strife.

"A bowl of vegetables with someone you love is better than steak with someone you hate."
Proverbs 15:17 (NLT)

"Better a bread crust shared in love than a slab of prime rib served in hate."

PROVERBS 15:17 (THE MESSAGE)

Love creates an environment of contentment and cheer. I'm reminded of the apartment my husband and I shared as newlyweds. It was no larger than 700 square feet. I selected that particular apartment over others because it came fully furnished and we owned nothing but ourselves, our clothes, and our love for one another. The size of the apartment did not bother me because I shared it with the love of my life. The fact that we didn't own any furniture didn't bother me either. Oh, I almost forgot to say that we were surviving on bare necessities because we were working toward eliminating debt, but that didn't bother me either, ugly nails and all. When faced with the choice between simplicity with love or abundance with strife, choose love every time. The contentment and cheer that love produces will set the tone for the commodity of abundance.

Reference:

Proverbs 17:1, 21:19

WISDOM TIP 124

Comfort is the enemy of greatness, it breeds inaction and laziness.

"A lazy person's way is blocked with briers, but the path of the upright is an open highway."

PROVERBS 15:19 (NLT)

"The path of lazy people is overgrown with briers; the diligent walk down a smooth road."

PROVERBS 15:19 (THE MESSAGE)

Lazy people look for any and every excuse in the book to justify their impending progress (inaction). Every time an obstacle presents itself, the fight or flight instincts of a lazybone signals to retreat and take cover. Not so with the diligent, they bust down the brick walls and clear the debris so they can move steadily toward their goals and ambitions. Lazy people will sit around and talk about every situation imaginable that could go wrong, whether it is highly unlikely or not, any excuse to justify getting back on the couch to binge on TV and social media. It comes down to how bad you want to make it happen. Comfort often is the enemy of greatness. Make up your mind to walk it out come hell or high water, whatever obstacles may come. A made up mind is often the first defense against the retreat of should've, could've, would've, but what had happened was … lazybones.

Reference:

Proverbs 22:5, 13; Proverbs 26:13

WISDOM TIP 125

Accumulate a village of wise counselors on the road to success.

"Plans go wrong for lack of advice; many advisers bring success."

PROVERBS 15:22 (NLT)

"Refuse good advice and watch your plans fail; take good counsel and watch them succeed."

PROVERBS 15:22 (THE MESSAGE)

You can look though the annals of history to find the importance of counsel and advisers in just about every culture. African tribes had and still have village counsel. Native American tribal leaders meet to gather and discuss important matters. The President of the United States has a cabinet of advisors, Great Britain has Parliament, and even mobsters are said to have the "bosses" who determine the fate of organized crime. I hope I have successfully built the case for the historical need for counsel and advisors across cultural and generational entities. Mature deliberation often requires advice from others in order to come to a proper and well-rounded resolution. Not only should your advisers be a source of wise counsel, but they should also be your accountability to ensure that you stick to the plan when the going gets rough. During the rough patches, you will have the confidence of knowing that you have the backing of others and their encouragement along the way.

Reference:

Proverbs 11:14, 20:18

WISDOM TIP 126

The seasoned grace of wisdom will flow through your words when you allow wisdom to take up residence in your heart.

"Everyone enjoys a fitting reply; it is wonderful to say the right thing at the right time!"
PROVERBS 15: 23 (NLT)

"Congenial conversation—what a pleasure! The right word at the right time—beautiful!"
PROVERBS 15: 23 (THE MESSAGE)

The right words spoken at the right time bless the giver and the receiver. Timely advice cannot be conjured up, it has to already be stirred up in your heart by previous consistent exposure to wisdom. Once you begin to live in the realm of wisdom, it will begin to shape your life, your thoughts, and your words. Therefore, when needed, wisdom is there because it has taken up residence in your heart, in your way of life. When you rely on wisdom, you can defeat the fear of putting your foot in your mouth by speaking the wrong words at the wrong time. A deep sense of fulfillment is found in being in the position to assist someone in need with the seasoned grace of wisdom that will direct, encourage, and comfort their lives when they need it most.

Reference:
Proverbs 24:26, 25:11–12; Isaiah 50:4; Ephesians 4:29

WISDOM TIP 127

Riches ill won bring ruin in tow.

"Greed brings grief to the whole family, but those who hate bribes will live."
PROVERBS 15:27 (NLT)

"A greedy and grasping person destroys community; those who refuse to exploit live and let live."

PROVERBS 15:27 (THE MESSAGE)

Riches ill won are acquired by unlawful means. Unlawful according to God's law, not necessarily man's law. Generational wealth has been acquired and passed down based on the unjust laws and business practices such as slavery, gambling, and pornography just to name a few. But what are the costs associated with obtaining wealth through such means? The law of wisdom calls for a strict moral code that cannot be compromised by the sway of popular opinion, or the blinding eye of bribes meant to buy your soul as you turn a deaf ear to corrupt and shameful business methods for the sake of making a dollar. Our modern society is full of politicians who promote and support legislation based on kickbacks or election funding from lobbyist who support industries that are knowingly poisoning our food supply, offering astronomically priced prescription medications, and condoning military style weapons in the hands of private citizens despite the countless mass murders we have seen across this nation over the past ten years or more. Let's not forget about the banks who knowingly provided mortgages to financially unqualified individuals just to recoup the properties when the inevitable loan default occurred. Judges accepting bribes to overrule or sustain the presentation of evidence on behalf of wealthy but overwhelmingly guilty defendants will eventually pay the piper of justice. These are just a few examples of riches ill won based on the principles found in the Word of God. The source behind all of this ill-gotten gain is greed. When you feed on greed, it will ruin you and those you love most. Nothing good ever comes from actions motivated by greed nor the money earned as a result of greed.

Reference:

1 Timothy 6:9–10, Exodus 23:8, Deuteronomy 16:19, Proverbs 23:4

WISDOM TIP 128

Think before you speak!

"The heart of the godly thinks carefully before speaking; the mouth of the wicked overflows with evil words."

PROVERBS 15:28 (NLT)

"Prayerful answers come from God-loyal people; the wicked are sewers of abuse."

PROVERBS 15:28 (THE MESSAGE)

Take time to consider what you are about to say and the repercussions of your words. It's a sin of the mouth to speak and only later think about what you said after the words have found a resting place in the atmosphere. That's like releasing your money to a used car salesman before you get the car inspected. Caution is the fruit of wisdom. Caution in your words and your actions. Lives have been destroyed, families torn apart, and governments overthrown based on foolish words spoken in haste. Never be fearful to utter these words, "Let me think about it before I answer," or "Let me pray about it and get back to you." How about, "I don't have an answer for you just yet, I'll get back to you as soon as I do"? Sounds very elementary, doesn't it? However, it takes maturity to implement in the face of pressure to respond immediately.

Reference:

1 Peter 3:15; Psalm 59:7; Proverbs 10:32, 15:2, 16:23, Ecclesiastes 5:2, 6

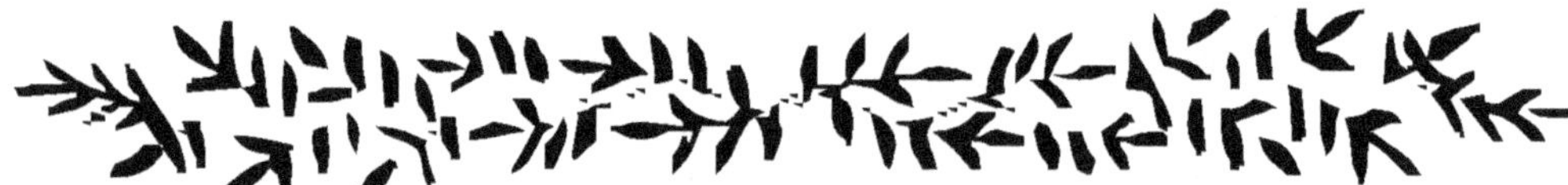

WISDOM TIP 129

Those who construct upon wise advice will find a home amongst the wise.

"If you listen to constructive criticism, you will be at home among the wise."

PROVERBS 15:31 (NLT)

"Listen to good advice if you want to live well, an honored guest among wise men and women."

PROVERBS 15:31 (THE MESSAGE)

Constructive criticism is synonymous with good advice. Criticism that is constructive will be offered in a warm and earnest manner wrapped with words that are both insightfully wise and helpfully applicable. The term constructive means you are able to gain insight that will enable you to construct or build upon the information that has been offered. Once you have proven to have a teachable spirit, the wise are more apt to offer additional advice as the situation is fitting. Applying the wise advice you receive by constructing or building upon the information sets you at home among the wise.

Reference:

Proverbs 13:20, 15:32, 18:15, 25:12, 19:20; Ecclesiastes 7:5

WISDOM TIP 130

Wisdom is the prescription that will save your life from the disease of foolishness.

"If you reject discipline, you only harm yourself; but if you listen to correction, you grow in understanding."

PROVERBS 15:32 (NLT)

"An undisciplined, self-willed life is puny; an obedient, God-willed life is spacious."

PROVERBS 15:32 (THE MESSAGE)

Refusing to receive correction is a form of self-hate. Correction may come in the form of a whispered warning until it reaches the full course of agonizing regret staring you dead in the face. However, even at this point, some people still refuse to accept the correction that has been dealt. If you are warned of self-destruction and you continue on the same path, then you are headed to a puny existence. Let your imagination bring to mind all the ways in which your life could become puny (stunted, frail, feeble, tiny, and weak). The one who loves his life and wants to see his life flourish into a spacious place receives the correction necessary to align his life with God's purposeful will. Receive the medicine that wisdom provides to save you from the disease of foolishness that causes your life to waste away one puny moment at a time.

References:

Proverbs 1:7, 8:33, 8:36, 13:18; Isaiah 3:9

WISDOM TIP 131

Never judge a book by its cover.

"People may be pure in their own eyes, but the LORD examines their motives."

PROVERBS 16:2 (NLT)

"Humans are satisfied with whatever looks good; God probes for what is good."

PROVERBS 16:2 (THE MESSAGE)

What you see is not always what you get. We have a tendency to be attracted to people who aesthetically appease one of our five senses. The Message translation paints the word picture of God probing for what is good. My mind's eye envisions God probing with a medical instrument during a medical examination. We may be able to deceive ourselves and others, but God probes until He finds the perfect location to make the incision that exposes the true intentions and motives of the heart. A wise person will freely offer themselves to the probes of God's spirit as a form of preventative health care. Regular self checkups will prevent the cancer of self-righteousness and the pride that accompanies it. By allowing God to examine our hearts regularly, we remain in constant reminder that the renewing grace of God alone prepares the heart for every good work. When we allow God's probing scalpel to expose self-flattery, we are able to fully rely and depend on His robe of grace that fits perfectly for every occasion.

Reference:

1 Samuel 2:3, 16:7; Proverbs 12:15, 21:2, 30:12; Daniel 5:27

WISDOM TIP 132

Your first plan of action should always be to secure God's blessing.

"Commit your actions to the LORD, and your plans will succeed."

PROVERBS 16:3 (NLT)

"Put GOD in charge of your work, then what you've planned will take place."

PROVERBS 16:3 (THE MESSAGE)

Tell God what you want to accomplish. Once you tell Him, trust Him with the heartfelt desires and intentions you have committed to His hearing. God is the best listener and accountability partner you could ever ask for. Not only is He an active listener, but He will provide you with the support and sustenance required to make your plan a reality. This initial action step does not disqualify you from also seeking wise counsel from others. Often, God Himself will direct you to the person or group of people He has chosen to act as your village of counsel with the plan He has blessed. When your plans are undertaken according to the will of God, they will be directed to completion by His guidance (comp. Proverbs 19:21; Psalm 90:17; 1 Corinthians 3:9).

Reference:

Psalm 37:5, 55:22; Proverbs 3:6, 19:21; 1 Corinthians 3:9

WISDOM TIP 133

Love is greater than hate, right will win over wrong, and peace will endure long past war.

"When people's lives please the LORD, even their enemies are at peace with them."

PROVERBS 16:7 (NLT)

"When GOD approves of your life, even your enemies will end up shaking your hand."

PROVERBS 16:7 (THE MESSAGE)

Experience proves that nothing succeeds like success. When a man is prosperous and things go well with him, even his naysayers, aka "haters," will disassemble when they realize he can't be stopped. Following the way of wisdom will disarm opposition, arouse reverence and love, give no occasion for disputes, and spread around an atmosphere of peace. I'm reminded of a documentary on the Civil Rights Movement I recently viewed. Congressman John Lewis told a story about a former Klansman who had been involved with brutally beating Congressman Lewis during one of his freedom marches in 1963. The former Klansman came to the office of Congressman Lewis in 2009 and apologized for his role in the beating. Congressman Lewis remarked, "I have seen that man four times since that day, he calls me brother and I call him brother." Love is greater than hate, right will win over wrong, and peace will endure long past war. Congressman Lewis's way of life pleased the Lord all the way from the streets of Selma, AL to Washington, D.C. where a former enemy now calls him brother in his legislative chambers. God is able! Won't He do it!

Reference:

Proverbs 3:17, Romans 8:31; 1 Peter 3:13

WISDOM TIP 134

Doing what is right will yield a level of peace and comfort that money cannot buy.

"Better to have little, with godliness, than to be rich and dishonest."
PROVERBS 16:8 (NLT)

"Far better to be right and poor than to be wrong and rich."
PROVERBS 16:8 (THE MESSAGE)

"Wish thou with scanty means pious to live, rather than rich with large, ill-gotten wealth." Actually, if I were a wishing woman, my wish would be wealth with godliness and right with riches. If you have been paying attention, then you know that you do not have to wish for such because it is perfectly attainable with wisdom by your side. Wisdom and godliness should be valued above riches, but all can exist simultaneously. If the choice must be made between the two, then choose the honest way instead of the dishonest way because, in the long run, honesty will benefit your life. Doing what is right will yield a peace and comfort that money cannot buy. Store up for yourself the richness of knowing that you've done the right thing versus the abundance of guilt that bombards a conscience overwhelmed with dishonest actions.

Reference:
Psalm 37:16, Proverbs 15:16, Ecclesiastes 4:6

WISDOM TIP 135

Aspire to be a leader who motivates with truth and integrity of action.

"The king speaks with divine wisdom; he must never judge unfairly."
PROVERBS 16:10 (NLT)

"A good leader motivates, doesn't mislead, doesn't exploit."
PROVERBS 16:10 (THE MESSAGE)

The highest aspiration of any leader who seeks after the way of wisdom should be to lead people with justice. This desire is what distinguishes a leader of integrity from a pawning opportunist. Wisdom will allow you to decipher a true leader from a pawn by the words that he speaks, but will also cause you to lead justly when you aspire to lead in accordance with integrity and wisdom. In biblical days, the word of the king was likened to a word spoken directly from God. This concept was lost to some leaders and they were severely punished as a result. Today, we see our elected leaders falling left and right when exposed for their unjust dealings. Aim to be a leader who motivates with truth and integrity of actions, one whose lips drip with divine wisdom afforded to those who aspire to lead righteously.

Reference:

Proverbs 16:12–13, 1 Kings 3:28

WISDOM TIP 136

Both the keeping and maintaining of truth and justice in commercial affairs are under God's watchful eye.

"The LORD wants weights and measures to be honest and every sale to be fair."
PROVERBS 16:11 (GNT)

"God cares about honesty in the workplace; your business is his business."
PROVERBS 16:11 (THE MESSAGE)

Your business transactions should be fair and equitable. So much for those who thought your Christian life on Sunday is the exception to what you practice during the weekdays. God requires fair trade and ethical business practices at a higher standard than the regulatory requirements of our capitalistic society. This great principle of truth and justice should cover every transaction of buying and selling. Both the keeping and maintaining of truth and justice in commercial affairs are under God's watchful eye. Those operating in wisdom will look upon this principle as a command and a responsibility to operate in a manner that God approves of in order to receive the blessing of the Lord that will cause a business to flourish in the midst of famine.

Reference:

Proverbs 11:1, 20:10, 23; Leviticus 19:35, 36; Deuteronomy 25:13–15; Ezekiel 45:10; Micah 6:11

WISDOM TIP 137

It is the moral foundation of a leader and not his leadership style or operational talent that will stand the test of time.

"Justice makes rulers powerful. They should hate evil."
PROVERBS 16:12 (CEV)

"Good leaders abhor [hate] wrongdoing of all kinds; sound leadership has a moral foundation."

PROVERBS 16:12 (THE MESSAGE)

Lawmakers should not be lawbreakers. This truth of leadership covers any and every domain of leadership. A leader should set the example, and not just any example, but the right example. A leader should have a moral foundation that is anchored in wisdom. The leader empowered by wisdom will above anything else operate in truth and justice and require the same from those around him. It is the moral foundation of a leader and not his leadership style or operational talent that will stand the test of time. Modern society has witnessed the collapse of moral leaders and we have also witnessed the results as leader after leader spanning from government to entertainment industries have fallen and been exposed for their indecent behavior. Please note that none of these fallen leaders were exposed because of incompetence, they were all exposed because of moral failures or allowing a culture of moral indecency to permeate their organizations. A leader who receives his direction from the way of wisdom will uphold a standard of truth and justice by setting an example of what it looks like to the people within his authority, and he will be swift to remove those who dishonor his authority with immoral behavior. And by doing so, he will gain a reputation as an honorable and fair leader.

Reference:

Proverbs 16:13, 25:5, 29:14; Psalm 99:4

WISDOM TIP 138

The commitment to provide truthful advice is the greatest expression of unyielding loyalty.

"A king wants to hear the truth and will favor those who speak it."
PROVERBS 16:13 (GNT)

"Good leaders cultivate honest speech; they love advisors who tell them the truth."
PROVERBS 16:13 (THE MESSAGE)

Itching ears want to hear whatever tickles their feathers at the moment. The only problem is that tickles fade. In other words, they want to hear what makes them feel justified in their actions. Advisors who speak lies, flatter, and gratify the pride, ambition, and love of power in a leader do so to their detriment and the detriment of society at large. A real leader—I say real because of the many who are perpetrating a fraud—will desire to hear truth at all costs. Further, he will surround himself with people whom he knows will tell him the truth when he wants to hear it and especially when he does not want to hear it. A wise leader will not surround himself with "Yes" men. A wise leader will surround himself with advisors who are loyal to the advisement of truth, for the commitment to advise with truth is in fact the greatest expression of unyielding loyalty to a leader. If you are a leader, seek to surround yourself with people of integrity who are not enamored with titles and positions. If you are an advisor or support staff of a leader, make a commitment to speak the truth in season and out of season.

Reference:
Proverbs 22:11

WISDOM TIP 139

Avoid the head-on collisions of life by taking the bypasses offered by wisdom.

"The path of the virtuous leads away from evil; whoever follows that path is safe."

PROVERBS 16:17 (NLT)

"The road of right living bypasses evil; watch your step and save your life."

PROVERBS 16:17 (THE MESSAGE)

"Keep out!" should be the sign posted in your brain as a warning to steer clear of any and everything that has the appearance of evil. Bypass means to avoid by going another route. Wisdom is the flashing signal light that warns you against life-altering detours. Wisdom cautions you to look straight ahead, being careful not to turn to the right nor to the left. Wisdom is the life energy drink that keeps you focused on the right road as you move forward on a certain path. It keeps you alert to snares, temptations, troubles, dangers, and downright evils too unspeakable to mention so that your very life is shielded and preserved. Avoid the head-on collisions of life … take the bypass offered by wisdom.

Reference:

Proverbs 19:16, Isaiah 35:8

WISDOM TIP 140

Grace has no room for pride, for it is a place that rests in humility.

"Pride goes before destruction, and haughtiness before a fall."

PROVERBS 16:18 (NLT)

"First pride, then the crash—the bigger the ego, the harder the fall."

PROVERBS 16:18 (THE MESSAGE)

Anything that gets puffed up too far will pop! Yes, egos are included in this category. If your head is too far up in the clouds, then you cannot see the rocks that will cause you to stumble and fall. The higher you are, the harder the fall. Let's not confuse confidence with pride. Self-confidence is a fallacy because it implies a total dependence on self to achieve. No man is an island. Any measure of success achieved in this life is the result of help along the way. No one— and I do mean, no one—has made it in life without the assistance of someone in one way or another. Allow your confidence to be established in the virtues of wisdom and the God who undergirds those virtues. This is true wisdom because you look around and realize beyond a shadow of a doubt that you are who you are and have what you have by the sheer grace of God.

References:

Proverbs 8:13, 11:2, 18:12; Psalm 29:23; Jeremiah 49:16

WISDOM TIP 141

Pleasant words persuade people.

"The wise are known for their understanding, and pleasant words are persuasive."

PROVERBS 16:21

"A wise person gets known for insight; gracious words add to one's reputation."

PROVERBS 16:21 (THE MESSAGE)

Pleasant does not mean flattery for flattery is steeped in fallacy. Pleasant has more to do with the care behind the words and the tone in which they are spoken. It's not what you say, it's the way you say it that matters most. The ability to express yourself appropriately is a gift of wisdom. There is no profit in wisdom that is hidden, nor in treasure that is hoarded up. The treasures of wisdom become profitable to ourselves and others when we speak them in the appropriate manner that will be pleasantly received by the person who hears them. Wisdom and harshness do not go hand in hand. Don't get me wrong, there are times when you will need to be firm, but firm and harsh are two different attributes. Be a person of persuasive wisdom, your delivery matters.

Reference:

Proverbs 16:23, 15:7, 27:9; Psalm 45:2; Ecclesiastes 12:10; Isaiah 50:4

WISDOM TIP 142

Sweet speech is the physician of a troubled soul.

"Kind words are like honey—sweet to the soul and healthy for the body."

PROVERBS 16:24 (NLT)

"Gracious speech is like clover honey—good taste to the soul, quick energy for the body."

PROVERBS 16:24 (THE MESSAGE)

Gentle and kind words give the body health by soothing the mind. The medicinal remedies of honey have recently made a comeback. For ages, across cultural barriers, honey has been known for its sweetness as well as its healing properties. Likewise, sweet words have saved lives, stopped destructive tyrants in their paths, and calmed storms before they were given the opportunity to surge. The sweetness of your speech may be the very words that will save someone's life today, encourage them in the midst of troubled circumstances, and literally bring a source of life to a troubled soul.

Reference:

Proverbs 12:18, 15:23, 15:26, 23:16, 25:11–12, 27:9; Deuteronomy 32:2; Jeremiah 15:16; Psalm 119:103

WISDOM TIP 143

Diligence is a duty due to self, for wants require labor.

"It is good for workers to have an appetite; an empty stomach drives them on."

PROVERBS 16:26 (NLT)

"Appetite is an incentive to work; hunger makes you work all the harder."

PROVERBS 16:26 (THE MESSAGE)

"A worker's appetite works for him because his hunger urges him on."

PROVERBS 16:26 (HCSB)

One day, while working out on my elliptical machine, jamming to Christian Hip-Hop, a song came on with this chorus, "being poor made me rich." Wow! That's a mouthful. The rapper's lyrics went on to describe the hard times he lived through as a child that produced a "hunger" to succeed in life. A Latin gnome says, "The belly is the teacher of all arts." This proverb directly reflects that pattern of thought. The desire to succeed develops a hunger in a person that cannot be quenched until success is obtained and the goal is met. The desire to succeed will give you strength when you physically feel as if you can no longer endure. That same desire will also make you mentally tough. Obstacles will not cause you to whimper and turn, but will build an ingenuity in your mind to figure out a way to "make it happen." What's churning in the pit of your belly, stirring your appetite? Develop an insatiable appetite to fulfill your divine calling in life. Allow the desire to please God to incentivize your drive to work harder and smarter. After all, the Bible does say, "If you do not work, neither shall you eat" (2 Thessalonians 3:10). You have to put in the work in order to receive the fruit of your labor.

Reference:

Proverbs 6:30, 14:23; 2 Thessalonians 3:8

WISDOM TIP 144

Troublemakers follow their namesake, they make trouble; do not expect anything less of them.

"A troublemaker plants seeds of strife; gossip separates the best of friends."

PROVERBS 16:28 (NLT)

"Troublemakers start fights; gossips break up friendships."

PROVERBS 16:28 (THE MESSAGE)

Troublemaker and gossiper are characterized here together because the gossiper is a troublemaker and a troublemaker is a gossiper. This pair of thieves uses lies and deception to start strife that builds wedges in relationships. The troublemaking gossiper goes from place to place and from house to house, carrying tales and whispering slanderous lies that destroy the character of others. Why are we surprised when we open the door of our lives to a troublemaking gossiper and soon discover the trouble that their names suggest? When you go to the circus you expect to see acrobats perform acrobatics and stuntmen perform stunts; likewise, troublemakers make trouble. You don't have to look far to find an example, the discord brought on by a troublemaker at your family gatherings, in your school, your church, and your workplace are easy to spot. Avoid the company of such a person as well as the temptation to use your tongue as a fiery weapon that incites the flames of trouble.

Reference:

Proverbs 6:14, 16:27, 26:20

WISDOM TIP 145

When a violent person speaks of their tendencies, believe them the first time. Don't stick around to witness their calloused actions.

"Violent people mislead their companions, leading them down a harmful path."

PROVERBS 16:29 (NLT)

"Calloused climbers betray their very own friends; they'd stab their own grandmothers in the back."

PROVERBS 16:29 (THE MESSAGE)

The violent person is one who wrongs others by injurious, fraudulent, and oppressive conduct. They will lead you directly to the slaughter and walk away with a smile. This person has got to be rotten if they are capable of stabbing their own grandmother in the back, as The Message translation indicates. Proverbs chapter one describes in detail some of the attitudes of their heart. They can't wait to do wrong. They conjure up evil deeds in their daydreams and seek to carry them out. What the violent person is capable of goes beyond what many of us can imagine. A full description is not possible. However, you will know when you are in the presence of such a person. Your gut will tell you that this person is up to no good, and their own words will be the final confirmation you need to turn and run away from their presence. Listen to the voice of wisdom and flee before it is too late.

Reference:

Proverbs 1:10, 12:26

WISDOM TIP 146

Respect and honor your elders.

"Gray hair is a crown of glory; it is gained by living a godly life."
PROVERBS 16:31 (NLT)

"Gray hair is a mark of distinction, the award for a GOD-loyal life."
PROVERBS 16:31 (THE MESSAGE)

Respect for our elders has almost become a lost virtue. In many cultures, the elderly are amongst the highest revered and respected individuals in society. Rightfully so because elders have earned every streak of gray that graces their heads. Even a foolish person who lives long enough will gain some wisdom over the course of his life, even if it's simply what not to do. They have been there and done that many times over and can tell you what's waiting on the other side. A person of wisdom will respect and honor the elderly. Listen and heed their words even when you do not see the benefit of applying their words to your life. The older I get, the more respect I have for those who have graced this world for sixty or more years. They've seen countless changes over their lifetime and endured heartache more than we can imagine, yet they obviously mastered the art of getting back up and pressing forward in spite of it all. If nothing else, we can learn resilience from our elders. They can teach us how to take a licking and keep on ticking. If you have the honor of knowing someone sixty years or older, clear your schedule from time to time and give them a call or pay them a visit. Ask questions about their life and sit back with your notepad as all the wisdom gained over the years flows gracefully without thought from the experiences they share. Even the old neighborhood wino can kick some truth if you have ears to hear. He's not walking around quoting Bible verses for nothing!

WISDOM TIP 147

Self-control is a serious feat. The ability to overcome self requires more might than obtaining a forceful victory over an enemy.

"Better to be patient than powerful; better to have self-control than to conquer a city."

PROVERBS 16:32 (NLT)

"Moderation is better than muscle, self-control better than political power."

PROVERBS 16:32 (THE MESSAGE)

The person esteemed by society as powerful may have the ability to overcome external foes with force, but will not master the full measure of a peaceful existence without the ability to overcome the inner turmoils. A man that is slow to anger is esteemed by the Lord, respected by men, and is happy within himself. This type of man is preferable amongst my list of "men of valor". The self-controlled have command of temper, govern their behavior and actions with character, and keeps their "stinky thinking" in check with wisdom. The religious philosopher Cicero said, "Fewer men are found who conquer their own lusts than that overcome the armies of enemies." Be amongst the few, the truly courageous, the self-controlled.

Reference:

James 1:19; 1 Corinthians 9:27; Proverbs 14:29, 19:11, 25:28; Ecclesiastes 7:8

WISDOM TIP 148

Peace and tranquility are more nourishing to your body than the grandest cuisine set at the table of strife.

"Better a dry crust eaten in peace than a house filled with feasting—and conflict."

PROVERBS 17:1 (NLT)

"A meal of bread and water in contented peace is better than a banquet spiced with quarrels."

PROVERBS 17:1 (THE MESSAGE)

It's better to have a stale, moldy slice of bread for dinner in a peaceful atmosphere than the best grade Kobe steak and lobster meal with quareling and hatred. Propose this stipulation to any self-proclaimed food connoisseur such as myself—good food or tranquility? I really have to stop and think twice; trust me, with three kids, I have learned to ignore just about anything for the five to ten minutes it will take me to gobble down a good meal. Upon deeper reflection you will find that this wisdom concept is laying down a foundational principle concerning identifying and assigning value to the intangible substances of life. What you value most in life will be identified in your surroundings and what and who you allow to enter into the most intimate settings of your life. Why should peace be chosen over all else? I'm glad you asked. The Bible warns that, where there is confusion and strife, every evil work is at play. While you may believe you can handle it, the evil that exists behind the force of strife will come up and strike you in unexpected ways at the least opportune time. Peace is a necessity in life that often gets overlooked until all the pieces start to crumble. Pursue peace at all costs and when you have it, cherish it. Don't allow any person, place, or thing to come along and rob you of this great intangible treasure.

References:

Proverbs 15:17

WISDOM TIP 149

Eloquent words look just as crazy on a fool as lies on a leader.

"Eloquent words are not fitting for a fool; even less are lies fitting for a ruler."

PROVERBS 17:7 (NLT)

"We don't expect eloquence from fools, nor do we expect lies from our leaders."

PROVERBS 17:7 (THE MESSAGE)

We expect a fool to speak lies and foolishness as much as we expect leaders to speak eloquent truths. When the opposite occurs, we have mass chaos. What's the lesson to be had from all of this, especially in times when fools are leaders and those who should be leading are cowering like fools? This wisdom lesson is about character and standards of conduct that enforce character. We are all called to be leaders in our own right. Even if the only person you are currently leading is yourself, you must decide to behave in a manner that honors the character traits of a person who leads with wisdom and integrity. Character is not suddenly created when you are placed in a position to lead others. Character is developed as you master self-leadership in the unknown corners of your life. Character is walked out day by day and built upon with every act of integrity along the way. Evading character development on your journey will cause foolishness to show up at your destination.

Reference:

Proverbs 16:12–13, 24:7, 26:1; Psalm 50:16

WISDOM TIP 150

While love forgives, it also seeks not to offend.

"Love prospers when a fault is forgiven, but dwelling on it separates close friends."

PROVERBS 17:9 (NLT)

"Overlook an offense and bond a friendship; fasten on to a slight and—good-bye, friend!"

PROVERBS 17:9 (THE MESSAGE)

To overlook an offense means to conceal and lovingly excuse any act commited against you. This can be done by forgiving and choosing to move forward in the relationship without constant reminder of the wrong committed. You can take it a step further by choosing to overlook the matter altogether by simply never making it known that an offense ever occurred. I must admit that the latter option is for the very mature. In recent years, I've adopted the following when I'm presented with the challenge of either confronting or remaining silent. When presented with this challenge I ask myself if I believe the offense is worth the relationship. Meaning, are you prepared for a possible rift in this relationship if you bring this matter to the attention of the person whom you believe has offended you with their words or actions? If the answer is no, then make the choice to overlook the offense by forgiving and moving forward without mentioning the matter. However, if the opposite is true and you feel you must confront the person, do it in a loving and noncombative manner and allow the offender the opportunity to make it right. However, prepare for the possibility that you may end up one acquaintance shorter. If you are dealing with a wise person, it will be easy to forgive and move on because they will value your concern enough to change and not reinjure the relationship in the future with the same mistake. Now let's note the second half of the verse, the one who repeats the matter separates a friendship. You are not a doormat and you do not have to take the same offensive behavior over and over and over again. You do have to forgive, but you do not have to remain in a relationship with the person. Their actions or words will be the ultimate cause for the demise of the relationship.

References:

1 Peter 4:8; Proverbs 10:12, 16:28 1 Corinthians 14:1

WISDOM TIP 151

Correction lacks the opportunity to travel the distance from the head to the heart of a fool.

> "An intelligent person learns more from one rebuke than a fool learns from being beaten a hundred times."
>
> PROVERBS 17:10 (GNT)

> "A quiet rebuke to a person of good sense does more than a whack on the head of a fool."
>
> PROVERBS 17:10 (THE MESSAGE)

A wise person receives correction in two places—their head and heart. They learn from correction and become better. Not so with the foolish. Correcting a fool is just as much a waste of time as punishing a fool will be a waste of effort. You would think that after 100 beatings, 100 chances, 100 days in jail, or 100 hours of community service that a fool would have learned his lesson. Wrong! A fool will return to his folly after correction has been heaped upon him because a fool's hardhead will not allow correction to seep into his heart.

Reference:

Proverbs 9:8–9; Proverbs 13:1, 15:5, 19:25, 27:22, 29:19; Psalm 141:5; Revelation 3:19

WISDOM TIP 152

A fool in pursuit of his foolish desires will devour you faster than an enraged wild animal.

"It is safer to meet a bear robbed of her cubs than to confront a fool caught in foolishness."
PROVERBS 17:12 (NLT)

"Better to meet a grizzly robbed of her cubs than a fool hellbent on folly."
PROVERBS 17:12 (THE MESSAGE)

Among wild animals, there is none fiercer than a mother bear when she seeks to protect her cubs. And yet, as dangerous as it is to meet up with an enraged mother bear, it is by far safer than meeting a fool in the height of his folly. A fool in the pursuit of his foolish desires will bring injury to any and all without rhyme or reason; at least the anger of the bear is brought on by the thought of a harm suffered by her little ones. Not so a fool. A fool will hurt anyone who stands in the way of his evil plots and schemes. Think about the shootings that have occurred in playground areas, at schools, and random family venues. That's a fool with a vengeance that will only be quenched by carrying out the wicked plots of his heart without regard to anyone or anything that may suffer as a result. A fool will attack for the sheer pleasure of suffering harm upon another person because they are less rational than an angry wild beast. Avoid the company of foolishly furious people.

WISDOM TIP 153

Paying back evil for good is the vilest form of ingratitude.

"If you repay good with evil, evil will never leave your house."
PROVERBS 17:13 (NLT)

"Those who return evil for good will meet their own evil returning."
PROVERBS 17:13 (THE MESSAGE)

Ingratitude is a form of paying back good for evil when someone has been good to you. I was always taught that people are not obligated to do anything for you, so be sure to show your gratefulness when someone does something nice for you. Having an entitlement attitude is one of the surest ways to diminish the goodness of others. A person with an entitlement attitude believes they are owed something by just about everyone in society so they reject goodness with their display of ungratefulness. Some of you have opened your home or your life to someone only to have them betray you in an unspeakable way. No need to try to take vengeance into your own hands because they have just thrown a boomerang of evil that is sure to return when they are least expecting it. Develop a heart of gratitude so you will appreciate the goodness others have shown you. One of the greatest ways you can express gratitude is by taking the goodness you have received and paying it forward to others. This is the optimum gift you can return to the one who bestowed goodness upon you.

Reference:

Psalm 35:12, 109:5; Jeremiah 18:20; Romans 12:17; 1 Peter 3:9; 1 Thessalonians 5:15

WISDOM TIP 154

Resist the earliest display of strife in order to avoid a full-fledged battle.

"Starting a quarrel is like opening a floodgate, so stop before a dispute breaks out."

PROVERBS 17:14 (NLT)

"The start of a quarrel is like a leak in a dam, so stop it before it bursts."

PROVERBS 17:14 (THE MESSAGE)

The beginning of strife is likened to allowing water to seep out of a reservoir. The small crack in a reservoir of water, if not immediately secured, will grow beyond control, resulting in widespread destruction. Likewise, from what first appeared to be an insignificant disagreement, which might at first have been easily checked, arises disputes and tiffs which extend in a wide circle, resulting in widespread ruin and destruction. Anger is a very real emotion that can be felt welling up in the pit of your belly before you actually lash out. Strife can also be sensed before it begins. All it takes is for one person to be the "bigger man" and say it's not worth it, keep his anger under wraps and lips closed. It's best to not get implicated in strife at all by closing the faucet, aka your mouth, before the reservoir of anger is allowed to rush out beyond the point of no return.

Reference:

Proverbs 20:3, 25:8

WISDOM TIP 155

You are not obligated to be indebted to the debt of others.

"It's poor judgment to guarantee another person's debt or put up security for a friend."

PROVERBS 17:18 (NLT)

"Only someone with no sense would promise to be responsible for someone else's debts."

PROVERBS 17:18 (GNT)

Only someone with no sense would promise to be responsible for someone else's debt, these words are hard to take in. Think about it in these terms—the person in need of a cosigner is likely in need of one due to poor money choices, so why would you believe that they are now going to start making wise money choices when your good name and credit history is now placed on the table? Pause. Consider. Allow the light bulb to go off. The flip side is why on earth would someone who really cares about me ask me to cosign for them or to put something in my name on their behalf in the first place? Most people who do this have a serious issue with selfishness; they will never admit it, but the root of not being willing to wait for something to the point of putting another person at risk is selfishness. I want what I want, when I want it. Some will even clean it up by calling it a bona fide need. There are a few exceptions to this generalization, so you have to depend on the spirit of wisdom to know when a person is truly in need of help and when you are being preyed upon to fulfill someone's selfish desires. I know you love your family and your best friend, but you are not obligated to put yourself or your family at risk to the point of taking on the debt of others.

Reference:

Proverbs 6:1, 11:15, 22:26

WISDOM TIP 156

"Man's words his character reveal, but often they his mind conceal?"

"The crooked heart will not prosper; the lying tongue tumbles into trouble."

PROVERBS 17:20 (NLT)

"A bad motive can't achieve a good end; double-talk brings you double trouble."

PROVERBS 17:20 (THE MESSAGE)

Hidden agenda, ulterior motives, two-faced objectives, and talking out the side of your mouth are all phrases that address this proverb. You will not win in life when these are your mode of operation. When you start something with a crooked motive, then the results will be crooked because of the foundation. Double talk and a lying tongue go hand in hand with a crooked heart and a bad motive. You have to lie, cheat, scheme, and scam in order to keep your agenda hidden, your motive concealed, and your real objective on the other side of your face. This proverb is both an example of what not to do as well as what to be on the lookout for. The keen application of wisdom is the only offensive and defensive plan against this hidden mode of operation.

Reference:

James 3:8; Proverbs 6:12–14, 10:31, 24:20

WISDOM TIP 157

Workers of death are sorrow and disease.

"A cheerful heart is good medicine, but a broken spirit saps a person's strength."

PROVERBS 17:22 (NLT)

"A cheerful disposition is good for your health; gloom and doom leave you bone-tired."

PROVERBS 17:22 (THE MESSAGE)

It has been proven that a cheerful attitude can play a profound role in the healing of the body. Happy people are generally more healthy people. Likewise, it has been proven that a gloomy attitude can cause a health condition to deteriorate more rapidly than one with a cheerful attitude with the exact diagnosis. The workers of death are disease and sorrow. The sorrow of the mind is responsible for the hopelessness that plagues those who self-medicate themselves to death, make the decision to end their journey early, and deteriorate inwardly and outwardly as a result of the gloom brought on by a sickness. The joy or sorrow of the mind can be a huge determining factor in any form of mental or physical illness of a person. Those passions of the soul, joy and sorow, have a very great influence upon the body, either for its good or harm. Here's my best advice on how to age gracefully—choose joy and cheer over sorrow no matter what diagnosis or prognosis arrives at your door.

Reference:

Proverbs 15:3, 16:24, 18:14; Ecclesiastes 9:7

WISDOM TIP 158

The ability to keep an even temper will win over many enemies and keep many friends.

"A truly wise person uses few words; a person with understanding is even-tempered."

Proverbs 17:27 (NLT)

"The one who knows much says little; an understanding person remains calm."

Proverbs 17:27 (THE MESSAGE)

"Those who are sure of themselves do not talk all the time. People who stay calm have real insight."

Proverbs 17:27 (GNT)

Once again, the avoidance of rash speech and a hasty temper is the word to the wise. A person has the ability to display wisdom by keeping his temperament in check and by the management of his tongue. A person of wisdom is careful to ensure that when he speaks, his speech is laced with purpose. Thus, "he that hath knowledge spares his words and he that spares his words has knowledge." Be a thinker, a person of reflection, so when it is time to open your mouth, you will actually have some knowledge and wisdom to share with others. Also, when you are a person of reflection, you will ponder the position of others before quickly becoming angered by the words or arguments of others. Having the ability to keep an even temper will win over many enemies and keep many friends.

Reference:

James 1:19; Proverbs 10:19, 14:29, 15:28

WISDOM TIP 159

It is not good for man to be alone, living as an isle to himself.

> "People who do not get along with others are interested only in themselves; they will disagree with what everyone else knows is right."
>
> PROVERBS 18:1 (GNT)

> "A man who isolates himself seeks his own desire; He rages against all wise judgment."
>
> PROVERBS 18:1 (NKJV)

We have seen many examples of religious compounds that can serve as prime examples of isolation gone wrong. If you subscribe to the belief that we all have been given innate gifts and responsibilities that are to be used for the betterment of all mankind starting with those within our local community, then you can clearly see the harm in a lifestyle of isolation. Not only can you learn from others, but others can learn from you. When isolation is dismantled, the concept of TEAM, Together Everyone Achieves More, thrives. On the other hand, isolation tends to foster an environment of distrust and paranoia on both sides of the fence that can prove to be detrimental.

Reference:

Proverbs 17:14, Hebrews 10:25

WISDOM TIP 160

Communication is a two-way street, listen with the intention of understanding instead of providing a comeback response.

"Fools have no interest in understanding; they only want to air their own opinions."
PROVERBS 18:2 (NLT)

"Fools care nothing for thoughtful discourse; all they do is run off at the mouth."
PROVERBS 18:2 (THE MESSAGE)

A self-opinionated fool is obsessed with his own thoughts to the point of airing his opinions obsessively and frequently without regard to anyone else. To attempt to communicate with such a person is to cast your pearls before swine. It would be a waste of your treasured store of breath and wisdom in the same sense as throwing money down the toilet is known to be a wasted endeavor. If you have regular interactions with such a person, the best recourse is to pray for them and for the wisdom to keep your mouth shut so you don't get swallowed up into a lecture you had no intention of hearing. Seriously, if you believe in the power of prayer, then pray that their heart will be opened to receive truth and the blinders of self-conceit will be removed from their mind. It's a possibility that you may be the person described in this passage. Hint, if you read this and thought, this doesn't apply to me. Maybe, just maybe. The truth is we can all benefit from a refresher course on effective communication, in particular, the need to converse with others with the intention of understanding instead of responding. It is not necessary to agree with someone to learn something insightful from them. Stay teachable and look at all experiences as an opportunity to learn.

Reference:

Proverbs 12:23, 12:28, 13:16, 15:2, 18:3; Ecclesiastes 10:3

WISDOM TIP 161

Justice leads the way for peaceful outcomes.

"It is not right to acquit the guilty or deny justice to the innocent."

PROVERBS 18:5 (NLT)

"It is not right to favor the guilty and keep the innocent from receiving justice."

PROVERBS 18:5 (GNT)

Justice should be blind, but it has been proven to favor the wealthy well connected groups of society. God's view of justice is equitable and distributed without any respect of persons, meaning no matter who you are, how much money you have, what your last name may be, or the ethnic group that you comprise, you will get a fair and equitable opportunity. Our streets have erupted in violence and chaos across the United States as the result of a historical volcano that has been bubbling up the hot lava of civil and judicial injustice for generations. When we acquit the guilty and deny justice for the innocent or play any part in allowing it to go forth with our silent approval, then we are violating the way of wisdom. Find a way to make your voice heard when you see injustice displayed. Not all will march in the streets with picket signs, some will write letters, some will pray, and others will teach. Whatever action you decide upon, let it be constructive, but do not let it be silence! To know justice is to know a peaceful society.

Reference:

Exodus 23:2, 23:6; Leviticus 19:15; Deuteronomy 1:17, 16:19; Proverbs 17:15, 17:26, 24:23

WISDOM TIP 162

A fool's mouth will be the direct cause of his destruction.

"Fools' words get them into constant quarrels; they are asking for a beating. The mouths of fools are their ruin; they trap themselves with their lips."

PROVERBS 18:6-7 (NLT)

A fool's lips enter into contention, And his mouth calls for blows. A fool's mouth is his destruction, And his lips are the snare of his soul."

Proverbs 18:6-7 (NKJV)

A fool's contentious words start quarrels, invite lawsuits, and sometimes open up a can of lickings on the backside. You can't take a fool nowhere; the double negative here is to promote the double negative effects of hanging with a fool. He will consistently say things he should not say, entangle himself in word squabbles that end in broken relationships and in some extreme cases, violence. In fact, his mouth is the weapon of choice. He has a loud bark and not much to back it up with except more bark. Do yourself a favor and steer clear of mouth fools; better yet, make sure you aren't the mouth fool that others must steer clear of. In the words of my Louisiana relatives, "You heard me!"

Reference:

Psalm 64:8, 140:9; Proverbs 10:14, 12:13, 13:3, 18:8; Ecclesiastes 10:12; Matthew 12:35; James 3:6

WISDOM TIP 163

Listening to gossip creates word tumors that will block the flow of your blessings.

"Rumors are dainty morsels that sink deep into one's heart."
Proverbs 18:8 (NLT)

"Listening to gossip is like eating cheap candy; do you really want junk like that in your belly?"

Proverbs 18:8 (THE MESSAGE)

Itching ears want to hear the rumors of the day. Not only do they hear them, they also store the rumors up as their own future ammunition. A person whose ears perk up when a rumor goes forth most likely has an agenda that includes spreading it and adding to the original tale as it is passed on to the next set of itching ears. The question is, "Do you really want that junk inside of you?" It feels good to hear that the girl you thought was perfect has a hidden flaw, or that your rival nemesis is about to go down for fraud, but in the interim, what is the bad news floating around in the rumor mill really doing to you? If we have acknowledged wisdom, we must also acknowledge the power of life and death that lies within each word we hear and each word we speak. Be careful of swallowing down the reputation of others because your reputation may just go down with it.

Reference:

Leviticus 19:16, Proverbs 26:22

WISDOM TIP 164

Lazy and Sloppy are two brothers that destroy your future abilities and opportunities.

"A lazy person is as bad as someone who destroys things."
Proverbs 18:9 (NLT)

"Slack habits and sloppy work are as bad as vandalism."
Proverbs 18:9 (THE MESSAGE)

Neglect of duty causes as much harm as active wrongdoing. The saying goes, "An idle mind is the devil's workshop." The "devil's workshop" is run by two brothers known as Laziness and Sloppiness. The only process improvements they implement are stagnancy and destruction. Laziness will eventually destroy you and destruction comes as an end result of sloppiness. To be slack in your responsibilities, no matter the area, is to destroy the experience and the learning process that the responsibility was meant to bring about. Thus, hindering your ability to move forward; thereby, destroying your future abilities and opportunities.

Reference:

Proverbs 10:4, 23:30–34; Hebrews 6:12; Proverbs 12:11 and 24, 23:21

WISDOM TIP 165

Stay humble or pride will create circumstances that cause you to crash and burn.

"Haughtiness goes before destruction; humility precedes honor."
PROVERBS 18:12 (NLT)

"Pride first, then the crash, but humility is precursor to honor."
PROVERBS 18:12 (THE MESSAGE)

The superior attitude produced by pride comes before the crash. Haughtiness is the arrogance that fills a person's heart to the point of completely "believing your own hype." For those unaware of the slang term of hype, it goes a little like this: "My money, my position, my last name, my title, my this, and my that gives me the right to judge anyone and any situation that is not up to my standards." News flash, your possessions, stature, or current standing in life does not make you any better than the next man, and they definitely do not exclude you from feeling the plights of life. It is my opinion that pride brings on destruction because we all have the potential to experience the trials of life no matter how much money and power we have at our disposal. Your child has the ability to make a mistake just like my child. Poor health in the slums has the same effect on your body as poor health in a mansion. Marital strife in the ghetto creates the same family insecurity as marital strife in the suburbs. Life is life and we are all experiencing the ups and downs of the issues of life. The attitude in which we go through life determines our altitude. Honor comes to those who are humble. Humility is not a lowly "bow your head to the next man" type of attitude. Humility is what causes you to extend your hand to another, knowing that but by the grace of God, there go I. Humility is the atmosphere you create that makes others feel welcomed and unjudged in your presence. Humility causes you to be honored where it really counts—in the hearts of people and of God.

Reference:

Proverbs 11:2, 15:33, 16:18, 29:23.

WISDOM TIP 166

Take your time to know the "why" behind your answer before you open your mouth to provide one.

"Spouting off before listening to the facts is both shameful and foolish."

PROVERBS 18:13 (NLT)

"Answering before listening is both stupid and rude."

PROVERBS 18:13 (THE MESSAGE)

Running off at the jib is what we, mature people, prefer to call spouting off before listening. Translation, running your mouth without all the facts. Yacking without knowledge. This person gives you an answer before hearing you out and interrupts you mid-speech to add their two cents without hearing the entire story. It is foolish to give a reply without thoroughly understanding what is being said or required of you. Not only is it foolish, but it is downright rude. No one likes to be interrupted when speaking and it shows that you are not listening with the intention of understanding, but listening only with the intention of spouting off as soon as you hear a brief pause. Listen with the intent to understand and hold off on your response until you have the ability to gather facts. Remember, it's alright to say, "I do not have an answer for you right now, I'll have to get back to you on that." This is appropriate for business and personal matters. Take your time to know the "why" behind your answer before you open your mouth to provide one.

Reference:

John 7:51, Proverbs 20:25, Deuteronomy 13:14

WISDOM TIP 167

Remain teachable!

"Intelligent people are always ready to learn. Their ears are open for knowledge."

PROVERBS 18:15 (NLT)

"Wise men and women are always learning, always listening for fresh insights."

PROVERBS 18:15 (THE MESSAGE)

When it comes to gaining wisdom, it's okay to be a little greedy. The wise person is always seeking to expand their knowledge, to learn something new, and increase their store of wisdom. Mainly because the wise are teachable. When I say teachable, they learn lessons from five-year-olds as they watch their interactions on the playground. It is their willingness to receive knowledge, insight, and wisdom that causes them to know it when they see it. What you seek out will start to find you. What you seek changes your perspective and vantage point as you interact with others. The key here is to have an ear open to instruction and a heart ready to receive.

Reference:

Proverbs 15:14, 15:31, 23:23

WISDOM TIP 168

Do not be hasty in judgement. Instead, let everything be established by the mouth of two or three witnesses.

"The one who states his case first seems right, until the other comes and examines him."

PROVERBS 18:17 (ESV)

"The first speech in a court case is always convincing—until the cross-examination starts!"

PROVERBS 18:17 (THE MESSAGE)

Parents, teachers, legal professionals, and all people in between, hear these words, "There are two sides to every story and the truth normally rests somewhere in between." That's why one-sided statements are not reliable sources unless they come with two or three trustworthy witnesses. These days, camera phones are everywhere and technology has served as a credible witness for neighborhood disputes to criminal cases. However, technology will provide evidence that in many cases lacks the human aspects that a technological device cannot offer. It is wise to seek out both sides when judging a matter as well as nonbiased witnesses who can validate the positions of the parties involved. The Bible says, "Do not be hasty in judgement. Let everything be established by the mouth of two or three witnesses." If this wisdom tip were followed, our criminal justice and educational disciplinary measures would be reduced dramatically.

WISDOM TIP 169

Guard your relationships from offenses brought on by petty arguments.

"An offended friend is harder to win back than a fortified city. Arguments separate friends like a gate locked with bars."

PROVERBS 18:19 (NLT)

"Making up with a friend you have offended is harder than breaking through a city wall."

PROVERBS 18:19 (CEV)

How do you go from being BFFs who share everything from clothes to opinions to potent enemies? Offense will do it every time. Good friendships go from strong to wrong so fast because of the investment that was poured into the relationship. You cannot be hurt by the actions or words of a stranger to the same degree as someone whom you have loved and trusted. That's why it is so hard to mend contentions with a close friend once the breach has been established. People begin to put up defenses to guard against a broken heart. What should you do? Take care to see that you do not fall out with a good friend. Remember the wisdom tip that urged you to overlook an offense. Wisdom and grace make it easy to forgive, but also make sure you are not the source of the contentions by remaining loyal and loving to your friends.

WISDOM TIP 170

You will have to live with the consequences of every word you speak.

"From the fruit of his mouth a man's stomach is satisfied; he is filled with the product of his lips."

PROVERBS 18:20 (HCSB)

"Words satisfy the mind as much as fruit does the stomach; good talk is as gratifying as a good harvest."

PROVERBS 18:20 (THE MESSAGE)

You must be prepared to accept the consequences of your words, good or bad. Imagine if the words you spoke directly reflected the nourishment of your body. Would your physical body look more like Black Panther, representing a strong physical stature, or the stick figure people drawn by most preschool students, representing severe malnutrition? The satisfaction of your stomach is the source of the satisfaction of your life. Your words can represent the savory speech of creole seafood gumbo or they can represent a junk food diet. Whatever the case, remember your output is determined by your input. What comes out of you is a direct reflection of what you have first put inside. Further, what comes out will produce results that you will be forced to live with.

Reference:

Proverbs 12:14, 13:2

WISDOM TIP 171

Observe your words in order to observe your future.

"What you say can preserve life or destroy it; so you must accept the consequences of your words."

PROVERBS 18:21 (GNT)

"Words kill, words give life; they're either poison or fruit—you choose."

PROVERBS 18:21 (THE MESSAGE)

It is said that speech is the picture of the mind. If this is true, then your self-talk as well as the words you speak to others and receive in conversations are forming mental images that form your thoughts, which form your words, which form your behavior, which form your habits that translate into what you do consistently, which dictates the trajectory of your life. Funny how that little, seemingly insignificant part of your body holds so much power. The power to steer your life toward good or bad. The good thing is that you are in complete control of the steering. Do a word check today. Write down every negative word or phrase you find yourself saying today. At the end of the day, review the list and ask yourself this important question, "Do I want to see these things in my future or the future of the person I spoke them about?" As the captain, you can choose to course correct at any time. Today looks like just as good of a day as any other.

References:

Matthew 12:37; Proverbs 13:2–3; Proverbs 21:23; Proverbs 12:1, 18; 26:28

WISDOM TIP 172

Happy wife, happy life!

"A man's greatest treasure is his wife—she is a gift from the LORD."
PROVERBS 18:22 (CEV)

"Find a good spouse, you find a good life—and even more: the favor of GOD!"
PROVERBS 18:22 (THE MESSAGE)

The ad reads, "Chickenheads need not apply!" In my day, a chickenhead was a ratchet female who was loud, messy, and lacking in every form of moral character you can imagine. I'm not sure what the current term may be for this millennial generation. Betty Wright had a song entitled "No Pain, No Gain," her exclusive lyrics described what constituted a good woman. I know some of you are turning the book facedown right now, but this advice is consistent with the Bible's version of a good spouse. She can be a cook, translation—industrious. She can be a lady in the streets, translation—virtuous. She can't show her teeth to every man she meets, translation - modest and loyal. She can be sweet, translation—kind and good-natured. A woman who is also a mother to her kids, translation—wise in handling your family and household. And in the sheets…translation—your breast will satisfy him (your husband) all the days of your life. All of this packaged into one woman equals a gift from the Lord. Men, make sure you model the same character because like attracts like. When you find her, marry her, and receive more than a treasure, but evidence that God has greatly favored your life.

Reference:

Genesis 2:18; Proverbs 12:4, 19:14, 31:10; Ecclesiastes 9:9; 1 Corinthians 7:2

WISDOM TIP 173

Reliable friends are priceless, hold on to them.

"One who has unreliable friends soon comes to ruin, but there is a friend who sticks closer than a brother."

PROVERBS 18:24 (NIV)

"Friends come and friends go, but a true friend sticks by you like family."

PROVERBS 18:24 (THE MESSAGE)

Show me a person who hangs with a group and I'll ask you to point out the select few reliable friends. Always remember that it is not the number of so-called friends, social media followers, or arm-length acquaintances you have floating around, but the quantity of true reliable friends that add value to your life. It's often hard to identify who your true friends are until some type of catastrophe hits your life. It may be a public or private struggle, but the instant you go through something that requires someone to be in your corner, you will know promptly who your real friends are and who was just going along for the ride. When you identify the reliable ones, keep them near, don't allow petty disagreements to separate your bond. For in them, you have found family.

Reference:

Proverbs 17:17, 20; 27:10

WISDOM TIP 174

Honesty is a "best practice" that will never cease.

"It is better to be poor but honest than to be a lying fool."

PROVERBS 19:1 (GNT)

"Better to be poor and honest than a rich person no one can trust."

PROVERBS 19:1 (THE MESSAGE)

Honesty is more valuable than all the possessions this world has to offer. My advice is to be both honest and rich, but the truth behind this wisdom tip is the correct distribution of value. Value the good intangible qualities of life in yourself and others over superficial and foolish things that will not profit your life without wisdom. Integrity, uprightness of heart, sincerity, kindness, and loyalty are but a few traits that money cannot buy, earn, or give. Seek the true riches and the other riches will enhance your life.

Reference:

Proverbs 28:6, 4:24

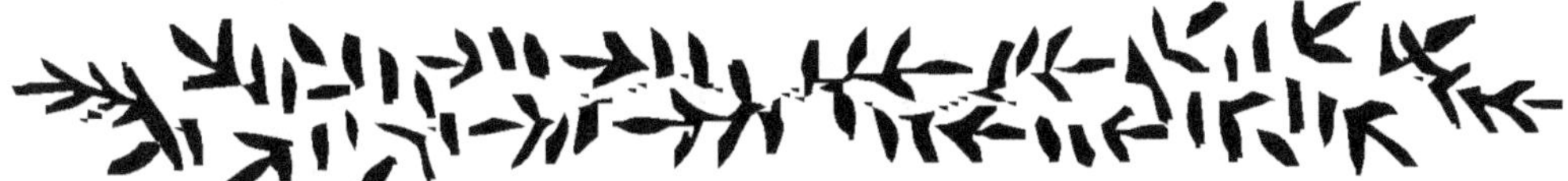

WISDOM TIP 175

Enthusiastically pursue the knowledge you need to make fully viable decisions.

"Enthusiasm without knowledge is no good; haste makes mistakes."

PROVERBS 19:2 (NLT)

"Desire without knowledge is not good—how much more will hasty feet miss the way!"

PROVERBS 19:2 (NIV)

Just as foolishness leads down the wrong path, so does ignorance. You need to be both intellectually and morally sound in order to establish a clear objective for your path. When acting in haste, you have not taken the time to ponder the results of your actions, and most times, you make a decision without the full knowledge available. Just being one degree off on a map can land you in a location not intended, and so it is in life. Ignorance, the opposite of wisdom, leads to mistakes. Equally, wisdom, synonymous with knowledge, leads to awareness, familiarity, and comprehension. Let's put it all together now—wisdom or knowledge will guide you down a path of awareness that, although new, will be an experience that is familiar to your comprehension of wise choices. Rashness, the result of ignorance, brings trouble. Be enthusiastic about getting the knowledge you need to make a fully aware decision. *Comprende!*

Reference:

Proverbs 21:5, 28:20, 29:20

WISDOM TIP 176

Your "ride or die" friends will be there for richer or poorer, for better or for worse.

"Wealth makes many "friends"; poverty drives them all away."
PROVERBS 19:4 (NLT)

"Wealth attracts friends as honey draws flies, but poor people are avoided like a plague."
PROVERBS 19:4 (THE MESSAGE)

Flies will swarm to a piece of candy dropped on the sidewalk in a blink of an eye. That's the mental picture I want you to keep in mind when it comes to the wealthy and friends. When a person is "all the way up," everybody wants a piece of the action. They will get to know somebody who may know somebody who knows you just for the possibility of being in the same room for a potential introduction. Get near the flies and shoe them away. Afterwards, you will find that rare one of two flies that are not easily scattered by the threat of being smashed by a shoe, still buzzing. These are your ride or die friends. Rich or poor, for better or for worse friends. When the swarm is long gone, they will be there like, "What? We not scared of a little shoe action; we can find us another spot until it's time to come up again!" Spoken with my best "ride or die" lingo.

Reference:

Proverbs 14:20, 19:6

WISDOM TIP 177

The conscience of a liar is never clear, their minds are always racing with the fear of being found out.

"A false witness will not go unpunished, nor will a liar escape."
PROVERBS 19:5 (NLT)

"Perjury won't go unpunished. Would you let a liar go free?"
PROVERBS 19:5 (THE MESSAGE)

Before you tear me down with your shouts of, "But what about such and such who lied and got away with it?" or "Such and such who was lied on and caught a case". We must first come to an understanding that the judgment this side of heaven is not the end nor the beginning of true judgment. God's law is greater and His way of doing things higher than any of our puny minds can imagine. Just because there is an external appearance that a person has gotten off scot-free does not identify the internal prison they are held captive in as a result of the lies they have told. The conscience of a liar is never clear, their minds can be found racing with the fear of being found out. Living in fear is not freedom. Life without mental freedom equates to a death row sentence.

Reference:
Exodus 23:1; Deuteronomy 19:16, 19:9, 21:28

WISDOM TIP 178

Acquiring wisdom is the ultimate form of self-love.

"To acquire wisdom is to love yourself; people who cherish understanding will prosper."
PROVERBS 19:8 (NLT)

"Grow a wise heart—you'll do yourself a favor; keep a clear head—you'll find a good life."

PROVERBS 19:8 (THE MESSAGE)

By now, you should understand that wisdom is not a matter of the intellect only, but also includes your mind, will, emotions, imagination, and values as well. These are all things that comprise your soul, what makes you the unique individual you are. To acquire the wisdom needed to correctly manage your mind, will, emotions, imagination, and values is the ultimate form of self-love. To turn away from wisdom is the ultimate form of self-hate. What you are saying to yourself is "I do not value you enough to follow the right path. I do not value you enough to believe that you even deserve the good things that are promised to those who make wisdom their friend and understanding their relative." The one who cherishes understanding prospers in life because he walks a course that is sure and proven. Even if ending well means you are able to sleep like a baby on a cot in a tent with a clear conscience and a sure love of God, self, and others. With wisdom by your side, your story has the ability to transform from that cot into a plush Tempur-Pedic mattress.

Reference:

Proverbs 16:20, 17:16

WISDOM TIP 179

"When they go low, you go high!"

"Sensible people control their temper; they earn respect by overlooking wrongs."

PROVERBS 19:11 (NLT)

"Smart people know how to hold their tongue; their grandeur is to forgive and forget."

PROVERBS 19:11 (THE MESSAGE)

"Hold your peace" is an old phrase that means "keep your mouth closed right now and all your opinions to yourself." Hold your peace is compatible with keeping the peace in a situation where there is great potential for strife. That little pink rudder that is pierced between your lips has the ability to flap open at the wrong moment and cause an explosion of tempers. I must admit that this is a wisdom point that I am still attempting to master and will probably revisit daily for the rest of my time on earth. I am a talker and a very opinionated talker. However, I will say that the more of God's ways and wisdom that I allow into my life, my opinions are steeped in God's truths and I have a greater degree of self-control that comes through the empowerment of the

Holy Spirit. I've learned that it is an honor and a greater use of power to pardon a person who offends without their knowledge of the wrong. Instead of being of the mindset that you have to defend your honor with the flap of your lip, you learn that honor is defended when you actually give no credence to the wrong behavior of others. When they go low you rise in sensibility!

Reference:

Proverbs 14:29, 16:32, 29:11

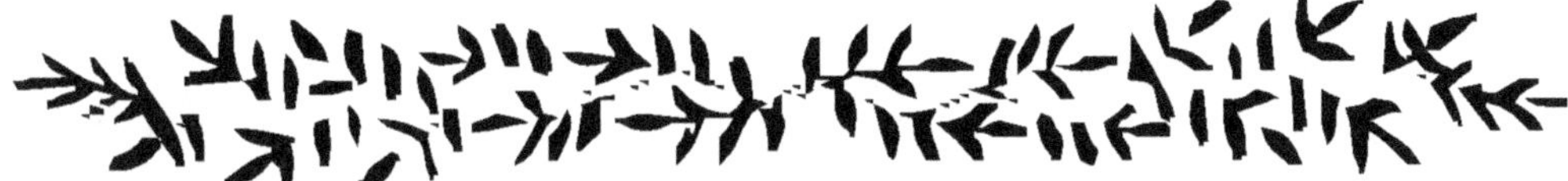

WISDOM TIP 180

Idleness is a living man's tomb.

"Lazy people sleep soundly, but idleness leaves them hungry."
PROVERBS 19:15 (NLT)

"Life collapses on loafers; lazybones go hungry."
PROVERBS 19:15 (THE MESSAGE)

Ever notice that after a few hours of sitting around doing absolutely nothing, you start to feel more tired than rejuvenated. Now imagine if your entire lifestyle was that of slothfulness. You would virtually feel drained all the time. Recall Newton's first law of motion, even if you didn't take physics, I'm sure you've heard this stated a few times: "An object at rest stays at rest and an object in motion stays in motion." This applies to your life as well. The people who are classified as the "shakers and movers" are in constant motion and we see the results of their actions. Developing a habit of slothfulness will bring about the visible results of slothfulness-hunger within and around you. Laziness will literally zap your entire zeal for life and productivity. Idleness is a living man's tomb.

Reference:

Proverbs 6:9–10, 20:13, 24:33, 31:27

WISDOM TIP 181

Careless living will destroy you little by little.

"Obey the Lord's teachings and you will live—disobey and you will die."

Proverbs 19:16 (CEV)

"Keep the rules and keep your life; careless living kills."

Proverbs 19:16 (THE MESSAGE)

Careless living kills! The message is clear—follow God's way of living and you will enjoy a good life; if not, you will eventually shrivel up and die. Just as living is unique to each individual, death also comes in various forms. There's nothing like being dead to life amongst the living. Let that sink into your mind for a minute. You can be alive and be a walking zombie with no peace, no hope, and no foreseeable future. That's what dying spiritually feels like. Careless living will kill you little by little, spiritually, physically, socially, mentally, financially, and relationally. Keep the rules and enjoy an abundance of life!

Reference:

Proverbs 13:13, 16:17

WISDOM TIP 182

The love and charity you give in this world will be repaid in ways beyond your imagination.

"If you help the poor, you are lending to the Lord—and he will repay you!"

Proverbs 19:17 (NLT)

"Mercy to the needy is a loan to God, and God pays back those loans in full."

Proverbs 19:17 (THE MESSAGE)

Let's quantify who the needy are because some like to confuse needs with wants. They also like to confuse a moment of being needy because of poor choices with poverty. True poverty has no recourse outside of God. Not many in the United States truly know poverty. We may know of American citizens who live in deplorable conditions; however, it is likely that the meekest shack in America is equipped with clean running water and indoor plumbing. Let's look at this verse in terms of those who have no access to government assistance to feed, shelter, or assist with basic living necessities such as clean drinking water … that's true poverty. Find a missionary in your church and spend a few minutes talking to them; better yet, find an immigrant from a less established country and I'm sure they can provide you with a firsthand account of what poverty truly is. Let us not forget about the poor in spirit. You may be sitting next to someone who can be classified as poor in spirit and not even know it until they open their mouth. Words will give you away every time. We should be just as zealous about showing mercy and giving assistance to the poor in spirit as we are about building wells for clean water and providing shoes for the shoeless. Whatever it is that God may be calling you to do in the area of helping the poor and needy, know that He sees every deed, every dollar, and hears every word of encouragement. He will repay with dividends that are out of this world. Be His hands and feet knowing that your labor is not in vain and not without recognition. Store up for yourselves treasure in heaven where thieves cannot break in and steal and where it will not rot or decay. The love and charity you give in this world will be repaid in ways beyond your imagination. It will leave your hand but it will never leave your life.

Reference:

Matthew 10:42, 25:40; Deuteronomy 15:7–8; Ecclesiastes 11:1

WISDOM TIP 183

Discipline your children early and promptly.

"Discipline your children while there is hope. Otherwise you will ruin their lives."

PROVERBS 19:18 (NLT)

"Discipline your children while you still have the chance; indulging them destroys them."

PROVERBS 19:18 (THE MESSAGE)

Parents, aunties, uncles, grandparents, and otherwise concerned adults. We are not doing the next generation any favors by pacifying bad behavior. There are many forms of discipline, so be sure to apply your chosen forms of discipline as early as possible and as promptly as possible. It may be cute at the age of two for little Johnny to tell you "NO," but at twelve, it will be a destructive pattern that will lead to trouble. Indulgence of our children is not true love, true love points out wrong behaviors with the purpose of correction and training in the right way. Indulgence destroys our children and causes them to live in an unrealistic bubble, but when that bubble pops, they are left with an inability to function appropriately. While our children are still young and impressionable, you and I have the hearty task of lovingly correcting them, so they develop good habits at an early age instead of trying to break bad habits during the adolescent stages when parental impression is less influential. A German saying, "It is better that the child weep than the father." Let little Johnny weep now so he does not have to weep later at a far greater cost.

Reference:

Proverbs 13:24, 19:19, 23:13, 29:15, 29:17

WISDOM TIP 184

It is better to stand back and allow the intervention of consequences to help soothe the temperament of the angry.

> "Hot-tempered people must pay the penalty. If you rescue them once, you will have to do it again."
>
> Proverbs 19:19 (NLT)

> "Let angry people endure the backlash of their own anger; if you try to make it better, you'll only make it worse."
>
> Proverbs 19:19 (THE MESSAGE)

Listen closely, you cannot shield hotheaded people from the consequences of their lack of self-control. I know they are remorseful the day after, but you have to allow that remorse to turn into true repentance that results in thinking before reacting. For a hot-tempered person, often this change in behavior only comes when the pain of consequences has been invoked. All your efforts to help someone who has not sought help for the core problem of a bad temper is useless. You know what will happen, he will be back into another broil the next day or very soon after until he deals with the unresolved issues that are contributing to an out of control temperament. Pray for them and love them from a distance, but do not bail them out, figuratively and literally.

Reference:

Proverbs 22:24–25, 25:28, 29:22

WISDOM TIP 185

Take good counsel and accept correction —that's the way to live wisely and well.

"Listen to advice and accept discipline, and at the end you will be counted among the wise."

PROVERBS 19:20 (NIV)

Ideally, wisdom gathered and digested in your youth will compound and build upon each principle as you enter adulthood and further into old age. However, I have had the unpleasant experience of running into some old fools in my lifetime. No matter your age or standing in life, having an ear that is open to receive good counsel along with the acceptance of correction will guarantee an expansion of wisdom that leads to a more excellent way of right living. That's what this is all about—right living. Right living can only be found in the One who is the *way*, the *truth*, and the *life*! Ultimately, right living can only be attained in Jesus Christ by heeding the instruction of His Word, learning from Him, and committing the affairs of your life to to His Lordship.

Reference:

Proverbs 1:3, 4:1, 8:33–35, 12:15

WISDOM TIP 186

Stay true to God, yourself, and others.

"Loyalty makes a person attractive. It is better to be poor than dishonest."

PROVERBS 19:22 (NLT)

"It's only human to want to make a buck, but it's better to be poor than a liar."

PROVERBS 19:22 (THE MESSAGE)

If cash rules everything around you, then you have the potential to fall into the trap of doing whatever it takes to serve the almighty dollar bill. Loyalty, trustworthiness, and kindness are some of the wealthiest attributes a person can possess. A backstabbing, dishonorable liar may gain money, but how many riches did he have to pass up to get it? The richness of relationships, the richness of a clear conscience, the richness of honor all equate to wealth that far surpasses the almighty dollar. Not all money is good money, so in all you're getting, get the wisdom that teaches the power of kindness and loyalty. Stay true to God, yourself, and others and your amassed wealth will be countless.

Reference:

Proverbs 19:1

WISDOM TIP 187

Grow all the wiser by heeding the mistakes of others.

"If you punish a mocker, the simpleminded will learn a lesson; if you correct the wise, they will be all the wiser."

PROVERBS 19:25 (NLT)

"Punish the insolent—make an example of them. Who knows? Somebody might learn a good lesson."

PROVERBS 19:25 (THE MESSAGE)

If you recall from previous Wisdom Tips, a mocker, aka a fool, will not learn from lectures. He may not even learn from punishment the first, second, or tenth time around. Your words and efforts of discipline will not be completely in vain because he will serve as an example to others of what not to do. The simpleminded are the young and impressionable who are still figuring things out. The fool can serve the purpose of helping others reflect on how to make better choices when faced with the same or similar situation. The key here is making a personal decision to be counted amongst the wise who grow all the wiser by reflecting upon the mistakes of others and learning from them.

Reference:

Psalm 141:5; Proverbs 9:7–8, 21:11

WISDOM TIP 188

You are never "one and done," instead, be "one and reaching."

"If you stop listening to instruction, my child, you will turn your back on knowledge."

Proverbs 19:27 (NLT)

"Cease to hear instruction, my son, and you will stray from the words of knowledge."

Proverbs 19:27 (ESV)

"If you quit listening, dear child, and strike off on your own, you'll soon be out of your depth."

Proverbs 19:27 (THE MESSAGE)

Wisdom is never "one and done," meaning you got a little taste, so now you can "drop the mic" and handle your life on your own terms. No, no, no! Not only are you never done with your pursuit of wisdom, but you should be ever striving for greater revelation of what it means to live your life wisely. Can you recall being tested in school and the horror that gripped your heart when you saw a question that contained information you did not recall covering in class? After some brave soul makes his way to the teacher, she realizes she didn't cover the material and announces to the class that everyone can skip that problem. A sigh of relief normally echoes across the classroom. But if the material was covered and you simply didn't apply the material properly by studying it and completing the assignments then it's all on you for not applying the knowledge you received properly before the test day. Basically, you turned your back on knowledge by not listening to the instruction of completing the homework assignment that mirrors the problem at hand. Don't get caught slipping by dropping the mic on wisdom when you should be following through by applying it to your daily life in greater degrees as you grow wiser still. None of us have ever arrived to the point of ceasing to pursue wise instruction.

Reference:

Mark 4:24, 1 Timothy 4:7, 1 Timothy 6:3–5

WISDOM TIP 189

Not all things that are legal are permissible, and not all things that are permissible are acceptable for you.

"Wine produces mockers; alcohol leads to brawls. Those led astray by drink cannot be wise."

PROVERBS 20:1 (NLT)

"Drinking too much makes you loud and foolish. It's stupid to get drunk."

PROVERBS 20:1 (GNT)

I once heard someone call alcoholic beverages "liquid courage." When you've had too much to drink, you become courageous in all the wrong ways. When alcohol becomes your master, you are unrestrained morally and many times legally, thus the mockery that alcohol produces and the brawls that it helps to incite. Getting drunk, wasted, lifted, inebriated, or any other term you choose to use is foolish because you are allowing something else to control your actions and your emotions; you are literally out of your right mind when you are under the control of alcohol. A wise person remains in control of their temperament and their surroundings. Alcohol is a deceiver; you think you have it under control and poof, you are overcome by its controls before you are even aware of its crafty devices that are slowly taking over your bloodstream. Although drinking is legal at age twenty-one, the wise will ask themselves, "Although it is permissible, is it good for me?" You be the judge prior to the morning after hangover.

Reference:

Ephesians 5:18; Leviticus 10:9; Proverbs 23:20, 29–30

WISDOM TIP 190

For the sake of peace, acknowledge when it is time to yield and walk away.

"Avoiding a fight is a mark of honor; only fools insist on quarreling."

PROVERBS 20:3 (NLT)

"It's a mark of good character to avert quarrels, but fools love to pick fights."

PROVERBS 20:3 (THE MESSAGE)

"You win some and you lose some" goes the cliché, but you can win them all when you choose to yield in a matter before a fight breaks out. This is where the wise and foolish are truly separated. When you can yield for the sake of peace even when you feel that your arguments are justified and your dignity is at stake, then you have officially joined the "Wiseman's Club." This concept is not second nature, especially in this day and age when putting some "respect on my name" is the sentiment of the day. It comes down to long-term or short-term pleasure. Yes, you will feel some pleasure for giving them a piece of your foolish mind and all the venomous emotions that come with it. What will the consequences be? A broken relationship, a fight, loss of respect, or perhaps legal troubles. For those who have mastered this concept, you understand that there is nothing like remaining in control and walking away when a quarrelsome fool attempts to make you "come out of yourself." That's old school for "go plum off" on somebody. In the end, it is more honorable to be known as a person of peace than a person of wrath.

Reference:

Proverbs 17:14, 14:29, 16:32, 17:14, 19:11, 25:8–10

WISDOM TIP 191

There is a season for everything in life. Know your season and adjust accordingly.

"Sluggards do not plow in season; so at harvest time they look but find nothing."

PROVERBS 20:4 (NIV)

"Those too lazy to plow in the right season will have no food at the harvest."

PROVERBS 20:4 (NLT)

What is the right season for you? Let's explore some examples. I want to go on vacation this summer, so the seasons for saving toward that vacation should be in the winter, fall, and spring. If I do not remain motivated to work my savings plan during those months, then I can only be mad at myself if my vacation fails to harvest.

How about this one. My best friend is getting married in four months and I want to shed ten vanity pounds. I come home from work and flop down on the couch with my normal bag of potato chips coupled with an ice cold Dr. Pepper. In four months, not only have I not lost a pound, but I've gained a few more and my dress shows every bulge to prove it. I didn't plow the gym and local farmers market for healthy food choices and now I will not harvest a more sculpted body. A lack of discipline in one season will show up in the next season. When it's time to work, work. When it's time to play, play. If you are having trouble identifying what season you are in, ask someone close to you or seek the counsel of an expert in the area where you are planning to harvest. Set realistic goals and work the plan until the crops are blooming and waiting for you to haul it in.

Reference:

Proverbs 6:6, 13:4, 21:25, 10:4, 19:15, 24, 6:10–11

WISDOM TIP 192

Allow the steady hand of equality to guide you rather than the shiftiness of inequality.

"False weights and unequal measures—the Lord detests double standards of every kind."
Proverbs 20:10 (NLT)

"Switching price tags and padding the expense account are two things God hates."
Proverbs 20:10 (THE MESSAGE)

Unequal measures or double standards are weaved into the fabric of our institutions. Name one and we could hold an hour-long conversation, reciting all the injustices and unequal measures found within. Whatever the case, God hates double standards of every kind. Double standards in wages earned between men and women doing the exact job. Double standards in the distribution of discipline in our school systems based on gender and race. Double standards in our judicial system based on your ability to pay a well-qualified lawyer. As well as double standards in the market place. The corner store sells a loaf of bread in a poor community for $5 solely because the people in the community lack the transportation to access a better grocery store and the same item is sold in the suburban grocery chains for $1 due to competition. You name it, double standards and unequal measures are all around us. Be known as a person of fairness and equality in every arena of your life. When you base your actions and decisions on fairness, there will be no need to switch price tags when someone else enters your presence and no need to recall which policy you changed to suit whom. It's much easier to let the steady hand of equality guide you instead of the shiftiness of inequality.

Reference:

Leviticus 19:36; Proverbs 11:1, 20:23; Deuteronomy 25:13

WISDOM TIP 193

You will know a tree by its fruit.

"Young people eventually reveal by their actions if their motives are on the up and up."

PROVERBS 20:11 (THE MESSAGE)

"Even a child makes himself known by his acts, by whether his conduct is pure and upright."

PROVERBS 20:11 (ESV)

I love the pureness of children. For the most part, they are open books. Children are often the most open and straightforward individuals to talk to because they normally do not have a hidden agenda. One conversation and you will be able to easily identify their character traits and personal dispositions. As adults, we tend to be a little murkier. We often say one thing and do another. However, one truth remains—your actions reveal who you really are. You are the tree and your actions and deeds are the fruit. Jesus said it's impossible for a good tree to produce bad fruit and it's impossible for a bad tree to produce good fruit. The goodness of the tree reveals the condition of your heart. Good heart, good motives, good fruit, and good outcomes. Bad heart, bad motives, bad fruit, and bad outcomes. If you do not like the outcomes you have experienced thus far in life, you have the ability to change the heart that produces the motives that causes the fruit to bud and grow on your tree. Likewise, closely examine the fruit you see in the lives of others before you add them to your inner circle.

Reference:

Proverbs 21:8, Matthew 7:16, Luke 6:43–44

WISDOM TIP 194

#StayWoke

"Don't be too fond of sleep; you'll end up in the poorhouse. Wake up and get up; then there'll be food on the table."

PROVERBS 20:13 (THE MESSAGE)

"If you love sleep, you will end in poverty. Keep your eyes open, and there will be plenty to eat!"

PROVERBS 20:13 (NLT)

"Stay woke" is a popular term that has nothing to do with being fond of sleep, it has everything to do with being slothfully complacent to the point of losing sight of what is going on around you. It's a call to wake up spiritually in order to become alert to the times in which you live and your surroundings, so you are equipped and prepared to make the most of the opportunities to impact the lives of those around you. As Solomon once said, "There is nothing new under the sun." The gnomist of the eighteenth century urged others with this worthwhile saying that still holds true today, "Do not slumber at your post, or sit downwardly waiting; but be up and doing, be wakeful and diligent, and then you shall prosper." While sleep is required to rejuvenate the body, wokeness is required to rejuvenate the soul and provision of the body. Don't think only in terms of physical provision, but also spiritual provision that your activity will provide to you and others. According to one of ATL's finest poets, the group OutKast, get up, get out, and do something; don't let the days pass your life by.

Reference:

Proverbs 6:9–10, 19:15, 24:33, 28:19, 10:4, 12:11, 13:4

WISDOM TIP 195

Distinguish yourself from the rest with the rare beauty of wise knowledge.

"Gold there is, and rubies in abundance, but lips that speak knowledge are a rare jewel."

PROVERBS 20:15 (NIV)

"Drinking from the beautiful chalice of knowledge is better than adorning oneself with gold and rare gems."

PROVERBS 20:15 (THE MESSAGE)

If I were to take a poll, I believe most people would say that they prefer the rare jewel of true wisdom and knowledge over all the bling money can buy. I say most, because we will always have some exceptions to the rule. However, if we really believed this truth, the Word of God and the priceless treasures it provides would be valued above all else in our daily lives. The cultural norms and societal influences that are in direct opposition to the Word of God would lose attractiveness and allure. People would be running to the church by the masses. Although we find this overflow played out in some churches around the nation, by far, many churches are not experiencing the overflow of seekers of the rare jewels of knowledge presented in the Word of God. The Message translation mentions drinking from a chalice, a word that is not commonly used in our modern times. A chalice is a storage vessel of some kind, a big golden goblet spewing over with choice prizes like those found in raided tombs of Egyptian pharaohs. The lips of the wise are compared to a storage vessel that pours out rare knowledge. When you find such a vessel, do whatever it takes to drink as much of their knowledge, so you too can be a rare treasure filled to overflowing, equipped to impart spiritual wisdom to others.

Reference:

Job 28:18; Proverbs 3:15, 8:11, 10:20, 16:16

WISDOM TIP 196

What tastes sweet going down can be bitter for your digestive system.

"Stolen bread tastes sweet, but soon your mouth is full of gravel."

PROVERBS 20:17 (THE MESSAGE)

Oh, the allures of deceit and sin! It tastes so good at first, but its true nature is revealed once it has seeped into the taste buds of your mouth. Very similar to that trick candy that has a layer of sweetness followed by a burning mix of spice that hits you like a ton of bricks with surprise. "What is sweet at first but afterwards like sand in the mouth?" Anything gained by falsehood and deceit. The sweet taste of casual sex can end with the gravel of a sexually transmitted disease. The sweet taste of that stolen credit card and all the items you were able to purchase can end with a felony charge of identity theft that follows you for ten years into the future. The sweet taste of getting the answers to the test from a friend who took it in an earlier class period could end in an F in the class when it is discovered that the two of you missed all of the same questions. It all tastes sweet at first, but trying to spew out the remains of the gravel of consequences can be a very grievous task.

Reference:

Proverbs 9:17, Job 20:14

WISDOM TIP 197

Count the cost before you build.

"Plans succeed through good counsel; don't go to war without wise advice."

PROVERBS 20:18 (NLT)

"Form your purpose by asking for counsel, then carry it out using all the help you can get."

PROVERBS 20:18 (THE MESSAGE)

My wise husband has a saying he has repeatedly quoted when we sit down to discuss important matters, "Count the cost before you build." What he is wisely communicating is the need to be careful and cautious to weigh all the pros and cons before making a final decision. Taking the time to seek counsel will guard against making a hasty decision that you may later regret. Good counsel can come through a litany of options at our disposal in the twenty-first century. However, seeking the counsel of God Almighty and other godly sources are at the heart of wisdom. The key is to actually get advice, ponder the advice, and make the best decision possible based on the guidance you receive from your sources of "good counsel." The Talmud says, "Even the most prudent of men needs friends' counsels" and none but the most conceited would deem himself superior to advice. When you have given due diligence upfront, you can move forward with confidence in the successful outcome of your plans.

Reference:

Proverbs 11:14, 15:22, 24:6

WISDOM TIP 198

Be careful not to share the flavor of your "tea" with a blabbermouth.

"A gossip goes around telling secrets, so don't hang around with chatterers."

PROVERBS 20:19 (NLT)

"Gossips can't keep secrets, so never confide in blabbermouths."

PROVERBS 20:19 (THE MESSAGE)

A gossiper is sure to let out any secret he knows so do not "spill your tea" in his presence. You can be sure that the flavor of the day may be Sussie's business, but with a little slip of the tongue, you will be the main flavor served tomorrow. The best advice is to stay clear of people who thrive on telling everybody's business. When they come to you with their flattery, attempting to engage you in conversation, know that the design of their scheme is to get you comfortable so you can add a new flavor of tea to their gossip party. Keep your lips zipped because there is no regret attached to having kept silent in the presence of a gossiper. A little slip of the tongue has the potential to ignite flames that will burn down the entire neighborhood!

Reference:

Leviticus 19:16; Proverbs 11:13, 13:3, 26:20–22

WISDOM TIP 199

Anything worth having is worth working for and waiting for.

"An inheritance obtained too early in life is not a blessing in the end."

PROVERBS 20:21 (NLT)

"Getting rich quick may turn out to be a curse."

PROVERBS 20:21 (CEV)

What is gained too easily has the potential to be taken for granted. There is no feeling that can compare to the satisfaction you feel when you have worked for something meaningful to you. Not to mention the magnitude of gratitude that accompanies that possession. If you have to work hard to earn a B in algebra, then you will have a greater appreciation for that B than you will for the A you earned in a subject that comes easy to you. If you have to save up for the down payment on your first home for a few years, then you have a greater appreciation for homeownership. If you have to pursue the girl of your dreams versus being hawked down and given exactly what your unrenewed mind wanted on the first date, then you will value your bride as you see her walking down the aisle because you understand the pursuit behind the veil. Anything acquired too quickly can give you a false sense of entitlement and devalue the worth of the possession. Do not be in a hurry to gain anything in life. Anything worth having is worth working for and waiting for. Take the time to gain a sense of appreciation and value for the things you desire, so when they arrive, they will not be just another possession to add to your collection, but a valued treasure that comes with a healthy respect of ownership.

Reference:

Proverbs 21:6, 28:20

WISDOM TIP 200

Evil for evil leaves evil.

"Don't ever say, 'I'll get you for that!' Wait for God; he'll settle the score."

PROVERBS 20:22 (THE MESSAGE)

"Don't take it on yourself to repay a wrong. Trust the LORD and he will make it right."

PROVERBS 20:22 (GNT)

I will be the first to admit that I am still working on this one. By nature, I am a "don't start none, won't be none" around the way girl from Houston, TX. My look may say "prim and proper," but if you push the wrong button, you will experience the "Don't Mess with Texas" slogan up close and personal. I have to fight this nature and submit my will to God when it comes to defending myself or my family when I feel we have been wronged. God ain't done with me yet y'all! (in my best Texas accent). I will be the first to admit that every time I pounce and take matters into my own hands, it ends badly, very badly. I have to ask God to forgive me and humble myself and go to the other person whether I feel that I was in the wrong or not. Fighting evil with evil or wrong with wrong only produces more of its kind—more evil and more wrong. There's a Chinese proverb that states, "Water does not remain on the mountain, or vengeance in a great mind." Allow me to rephrase the Chinese proverb to read, "Vengeance does not remain on the wise mind." God has a way of setting things in order when we allow him to argue our case and defend our cause. Proverbs says, "When your ways please the Lord, he will make even your enemies be at peace with you." When confronted with the opportunity to avenge ourselves, we back down because we want our ways to please the Lord. The only way your way of handling things will please the Lord is when you act and react in accordance with His wisdom. Wait on the Lord and He will settle the score! Not only will He settle the score, but He will give you the wisdom to bear the wrong so that vengeful thoughts will not dominate your mind.

Reference:

Romans 12:17–19, 1 Thessalonians 5:15, 1 Peter 3:9, Proverbs 24:29, Deuteronomy 32:35

WISDOM TIP 201

Be careful not to make rash vows!

"An impulsive vow is a trap; later you'll wish you could get out of it."

PROVERBS 20:25 (THE MESSAGE)

"It is a trap to dedicate something rashly and only later to consider one's vows."

PROVERBS 20:25 (NIV)

A shotgun wedding in Las Vegas at 2:00 a.m. with a person you just met in the casino at 10:00 p.m. would be considered an impulsive vow. What happens in Vegas will follow you home if you make a rash vow. Online shopping in the middle of the day when you are bored, tired, or hungry could result in impulsive vows that you attempt to reconsider after you receive your monthly credit card bill. Most decisions arrived at impulsively lead to destruction. Unfortunately, many impulsive decisions cannot be fixed with an annulment of your vows or the return of merchandise. Do you recall the wisdom tips that urged you to seek sound counsel prior to moving forward with your plans? Well, now is the appointed time to execute that wisdom tip before you make an impulsive decision that has long-term repercussions. Before committing to a vow, first determine if you are willing and able to fulfill that vow come what may. It is better not to vow than to make a vow and not fulfill your end of the bargain.

Reference:

Ecclesiastes 5:5, Matthew 5:33

WISDOM TIP 202

Clear corrupting cancer out of the camp before it spreads like wildfire!

"After careful scrutiny, a wise leader makes a clean sweep of rebels and dolts."

PROVERBS 20:26 (THE MESSAGE)

It is wise to locate dissension in the ranks and to quickly identify and remove the source of the dissension. As a leader, this is probably one of the hardest parts about leading. Not only are you a guide, but you are a protector. As a protector, you must stop the cancerous corrupting influence of troublemakers before it spreads and brings ruin upon the entire organization. The additional portion about being a guide and protector is executing punishment. Punishment is required to set an example as well as precedence of your leadership and authority. Whether you are leading a family, a team, or an organization, you must be both a guider and protector to those entrusted to your care. This will require you to establish your authority when it is challenged. There is a time to back down and there is a time to assert yourself and your authority. When you have been entrusted with leadership, you have full reign to assert yourself against anyone or any idea that tries to infiltrate your camp with commotion and chaos.

Reference:

Proverbs 20:8, Matthew 3:12

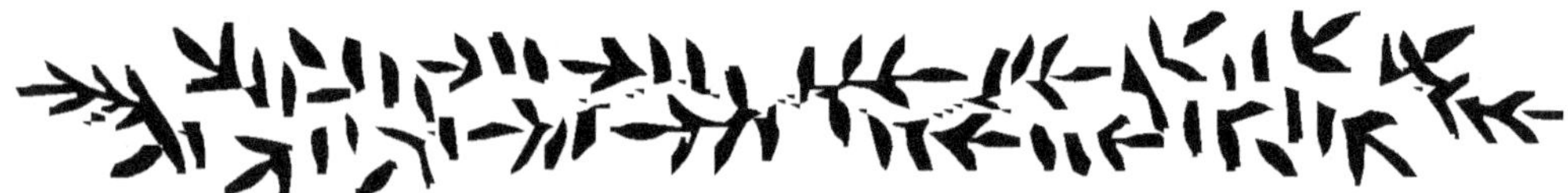

WISDOM TIP 203

Leaders, you will reproduce your own kind. Be careful to set a standard by which others can follow.

"Love and truth form a good leader; sound leadership is founded on loving integrity."

PROVERBS 20:28 (THE MESSAGE)

Integrity and character are what form the qualities of a good leader. As a leader, what you give is what you will get in return because you set the atmosphere and the standard by which others follow. When you display qualities such as integrity, truthful dealings, love, and compassion, then those who follow you will in turn follow your lead. If the goal of leadership is to replicate yourself in the efforts of your followers, then you will reproduce your own kind. Just as any other law of reproduction, input equals output. What you input into the minds and hearts of those who seek your guidance and protection as a leader will find you in return. We have already established the role that structure, respect, and retribution play in leadership with those who are disloyal. However, with those who are supportive and loyal to your leadership, your integrity and compassionate dealings toward them will uphold their commitment to your leadership over the long run, and reproduce the same qualities in the future leaders who will follow in your footsteps for generations to come.

Reference:

Proverbs 3:3; 16:6, 12

WISDOM TIP 204

Slow and steady wins the race while quick and hasty cannot keep up the pace.

"Good planning and hard work lead to prosperity, but hasty shortcuts lead to poverty."

PROVERBS 21:5 (NLT)

"Careful planning puts you ahead in the long run; hurry and scurry puts you further behind."

PROVERBS 21:5 (THE MESSAGE)

Diligence and consistency are where winners thrive. When hurry and scurry drive us, we tend to make mistakes and poor decisions not backed by sound judgment. The result is loss of time, loss of energy, loss of effort, and a loss of lots of money. Sometimes the damages are more permanent than others and involve more intangible goods, such as friendships and future opportunities. Be wise and slow down. Adopt a thoughtful and studious mindset that can be diligently and consistently followed over the long run. Cutting out all carbs, sugar, and running three miles a day may work for two weeks, but a more realistic and effective plan for most of us would be to choose to reduce carbs, be more conscious about our daily sugar intake, and aim to incorporate more movement in our daily routine. You may not lose twenty pounds in a week that way, but you will adopt a healthy lifestyle that will eventually lead to the loss of pounds and inches. Slow and steady wins the race while quick and hasty cannot keep up the pace.

Reference:

Proverbs 10:4, 13:4

WISDOM TIP 205

Dirty money is here today and gone tomorrow.

"A fortune made by a lying tongue is a fleeting vapor and a deadly snare."

PROVERBS 21:6 (NIV)

"Wealth created by a lying tongue is a vanishing mist and a deadly trap."

PROVERBS 21:6 (NLT)

Mist is a form of water vapor that cannot be grasped in your hand. Mist is visible to the human eye, but it cannot be contained. Likewise, "ill-gotten" gain. It is visible to the eye, but it can never be properly grasped. For one, you must continue to lie to keep it. Secondly, you are so paranoid about it that it cannot be truly enjoyed. Like mist, money gained from any type of scheme will quickly vanish. The lyrics of a Christian rap song stopped me in my tracks as the artist recited his conversation with a convicted drug dealer who longed to trade in the $5000 a week business he once heralded for his freedom. The song went on to describe how the dealer could have earned more money working a minimum wage job over the course of his 25 year sentence with the ability to improve his economic standing with hard work and ingenuity. You do the math. What amount is worth your freedom, your life? 52 × $5000 = $260,000 vs 40 hours a week × $9/hour × 52 weeks a year for 25 years = $468,000.

Reference:

Proverbs 8:36, 10:2, 13:11

WISDOM TIP 206

Wives, nag less and pray more!

"Better to live alone in a tumbledown shack than share a mansion with a nagging spouse."

PROVERBS 21:9 (THE MESSAGE)

"It's better to live alone in the corner of an attic than with a quarrelsome wife in a lovely home."

PROVERBS 21:9 (NLT)

Hear ye! Hear ye! Calling all wives to attention this day. Calling myself twice. It is better for your husband to make residence in a tumbledown shack or in the corner of an attic than to live in a lovely HGTV designer decorated home with a nagging and quarrelsome wife. Ladies, we can make or break the atmosphere in our homes with our mouths. If the tone is not right, then we are tearing our lovely homes down and our husbands in tow with our own hands. I have been guilty of this exact folly so I am no expert on this matter. Maya Angelou once said, "When you know better, do better. When you learn, teach." Hearken to the word of the kings' edict and tone it down with the nagging and quareling. Ladies, I get it and I'm sure I have personally experienced or heard over the years from other women almost all of the reasons why we tend to go that route, but the end result is never what we hoped to accomplish. Not to mention, the wedge nagging drives in our relationships can be detrimental.

Reference:

Proverbs 21:19, 25:24

WISDOM TIP 207

Ponder the consequences of the foolish decisions of others.

"Simpletons only learn the hard way, but the wise learn by listening."

PROVERBS 21:11 (THE MESSAGE)

"If you punish a mocker, the simpleminded become wise; if you instruct the wise, they will be all the wiser."

PROVERBS 21:11 (NLT)

A wise person uses every opportunity and takes advantage of every circumstance and event to increase his knowledge and experience. As for the simplemided, those easily persuaded by the wrong influences, they gain bits of wisdom when they witness the consequences of those wrong influences. The simpleminded have a knack of hanging with the wrong crowd, yet in the back of their minds, they ponder the chaos found in their surroundings as well as the negativity that encompasses the consequences of their selected peer group. Simpletons do not speedily make their home amongst the wise, yet they gain insightful tidbits of wisdom by analyzing the consequences of the foolish mistakes of others. Simpletons eventually make the decision to undergo a 180-degree lifestyle change by making steps toward the direction of wisdom or they are given over to full blown mocker status as a result of pondering wisdom, but never applying wisdom in order to see changes in their own lives. Those who make steps toward wisdom will inevitably take a seat at the table of the wise and one day serve as an example to others based on the good outcomes the application of wisdom has produced for their lives. Every wisdom tip within this book is designed to provide you with instruction that will produce good outcomes so you can grow all the wiser.

Reference:

Proverbs 1:5, 9:9, 19:25

WISDOM TIP 208

When you know better do better!

"The person who strays from common sense will end up in the company of the dead."

PROVERBS 21:16 (NLT)

"A person who wanders from the way of wise behavior will rest in the assembly of the dead."

PROVERBS 21:16 (GW)

I can recall hearing this phrase over and over again growing up as a child, "You know better than that." My parents would belt that out confidently because they knew the instruction and teaching they had provided me and my siblings. Now, as a mother of three, I find myself using that same phrase because I am also confident of the good godly instruction my husband and I have given our children. However, every now and then, they make a choice to wander from the example of "wise behavior" they have been taught and seen modeled before them. When they choose this route, they encounter a series of consequences. When you know better, you are expected to do better. When you know better and make the choice to stray from the right path, then you find yourself in unfamiliar territory. Similar to an honor student landing herself in detention. Culture shock! Likewise, this proverb is describing a person who had a good life, two-story house with the white picket fence, but began to wander from the right path only to look up and find the house in foreclosure, family gone, with roaches crawling around in the cheapest motel in town. The assembly of the dead can be various situations that are outside of the confines of the good life that God has planned for each of us. When you know the right way and make the choice to reject the right way, you are headed down a dead-end road straight into a scene that resembles *Night of the Living Dead*. When you know better, you have got to act on the better you know, or life as you have known it will be ripped away from you slowly but surely.

Reference:

Proverbs 11:19, 13:20; Psalm 125:5; Hebrews 6:4–6; 2 Peter 2:21–22

WISDOM TIP 209

Look up, look around, and use your affluence to influence.

"You're addicted to thrills? What an empty life! The pursuit of pleasure is never satisfied."

PROVERBS 21:17 (THE MESSAGE)

"Those who love pleasure become poor; those who love wine and luxury will never be rich."

PROVERBS 21:17 (NLT)

When you are in constant pursuit of thrills, spending all your time, energy, and money on things that bring you pleasure, when do you work? When do you sleep? When do you create? When do you give back to the lives of others? This proverb is warning against the self-centered mindset produced when your life is out of balance. The proverb is not saying do not have a good time, it is warning against anything in excess that leads to a selfishly unfulfilled life. When you live a lifestyle of pursuing only that which gives you comfort and pleasure, then you are no longer growing as a person. On the financial side, you may find that you are spending money faster than you are making it, which will eventually lead to impoverishment. Affluence and luxury are two different concepts. The most affluent people I know are also amongst the most giving and influential people I know because they seek to live a life of purpose. However, I also know people who like to flaunt every bit of luxury they can afford to charge on a credit card, living paycheck-to-paycheck as they chase after the lifestyle of the rich and infamous characters from the latest reality television show. These luxury seekers are too focused on themselves and how they appear to the world around them to understand what it means to really live in the fullness of life. I encourage you to use the measure of affluence you have been entrusted with to influence the lives of others.

Reference:

Proverbs 23:21, 1 Timothy 5:6

WISDOM TIP 210

Don’t allow money to burn a hole in your pocket.

“The wise have wealth and luxury, but fools spend whatever they get.

Proverbs 21:20 (NTL)

“Valuables are safe in a wise person’s home; fools put it all out for yard sales.”

Proverbs 21:20 (THE MESSAGE)

In our modern-day times, we have seen the headlines that announce the latest celebrity filing for bankruptcy. If you are like me, you may have wondered how in the world can you make fifty million dollars and not have enough to pay your debts. The answer is foolishness! A fool will swallow up, run through, and exhaust every cent he has earned. If you do not have the wisdom to manage your money properly, or the wise discernment to hire the right people with integrity to do it for you, then you will find yourself filing for bankruptcy, and in some cases, more than once. The wise have wealth and valuables that are safe because they are wise managers of their possessions. My motto is, “Just because you can afford it, doesn’t mean you should have it.” Do not allow what you do have to have you. Give your money an assignment so you can enjoy it later in life. Once you spend money, it leaves your life. On the flip side, if you learn to manage your money and assign it well, then your lifestyle will be safely sustained over the long run. Be wise with your money, and little by little, it will continue to grow.

Reference:

Psalm 112:3; Proverbs 8:21, 22:4, 15:6; Ecclesiastes 7:11

WISDOM TIP 211

A wise act will yield more territory than brute force.

“A wise person went up against a city of warriors and brought down its secure fortress.”

Proverbs 21:22 (HSCB)

More can be accomplished when battles of life are won by prudence and wisdom, artistic expression and strategy, than by power and brute force. It is my opinion that force should be the last resort after all efforts to strategize and diplomatically resolve problems have been deployed, especially in military affairs. I can force you to act in a certain way physically while your mind is conniving every strategy and scheme possible to launch your next attack. However, I'll be more successful if I can turn an enemy into an ally and an ally into a close friend and put to rest the dissension planned for the future. Wisdom has the ability to handle and squash disputes far better than force, which tends to lead to more force and conflict. Make a decision to apply wisdom to your arsenal of weaponry so that your strength may be reserved for planning the offense required to secure the fortresses of your life against future conflict.

Reference:

Proverbs 24:5; Ecclesiastes 7:19, 9:15–16

WISDOM TIP 212

Speech is silver, but silence is golden!

"Watch your tongue and keep your mouth shut, and you will stay out of trouble."

PROVERBS 21:23 (NLT)

"Watch your words and hold your tongue; you'll save yourself a lot of grief."

PROVERBS 21:23 (THE MESSAGE)

Knowing when to speak and when to be silent is wisdom in action. The wise person keeps his mouth shut until he has considered the words he will speak. The times when I have gotten myself into the biggest trouble, my mouth was involved. I spoke when I should have been quiet, and when I did speak, it was with venom. Oh yes, I am personally in an ongoing recovery group for "put you in your place" verbiage, so this proverb hits me where it hurts. Our words can cause strife like no other. Words have destroyed more relationships, opportunities, and possibilities than anything else in our lives. Watch what you say. Guard your tongue and guard your life. Think before you speak. Yeah, all of that!

Reference:

James 3:2; Psalm 141:3; Proverbs 13:3, 18:21, 10:19

WISDOM TIP 213

The higher your ego causes you to float, the greater the possibility of a crash landing.

"Show me a conceited person and I will show you someone who is arrogant, proud, and inconsiderate."

PROVERBS 21:24 (GNT)

"You know their names—Brash, Impudent, Blasphemer—intemperate hotheads, every one."

PROVERBS 21:24 (THE MESSAGE)

When you think you know it all, have it all, and will figure it all out on your own, you tend to shut out others and any benefits they are able to bring to the table. In this case, the proud fool is so blinded by his own worth that his arrogance is expressed contemptuously upon others. Unfortunately, we see this type of foolish pride displayed in the lives of people in positions of authority from the controlling father in the home to the CEO who treats all of his employees with contempt, ruling the organization with a closed iron fist. However, we also see this type of conceited, smirk of the nose behavior on our high school and college campuses across this nation. Brash … rude … hotheaded … conceited ... arrogant … inconsiderate. You can't tell them nothing! They foolishly walk around "smelling themselves" as if they own the school and everyone in it. Unfortunately, this behavior is tolerated if the person happens to be a star athlete or if their parents happen to be large alumni donors. The higher your ego causes you to float in the sky, the greater the possibility of a crash landing. The moral of the story is to be a person who lives by the Golden Rule, "Treat others the way you would want to be treated." Be a person who sees the value in every human being and treat them accordingly.

Reference:

Proverbs 24:9; Proverbs 6:16–17, 16:18, 18:12

WISDOM TIP 214

The dream is free, but the hustle is real.

"Despite their desires, the lazy will come to ruin, for their hands refuse to work."

PROVERBS 21:25 (NLT)

"Lazy people finally die of hunger because they won't get up and go to work."

PROVERBS 21:25 (THE MESSAGE)

Here lies the undoing of the "lazynaire," they refuse to work for an honest day's pay, yet their hearts crave all the perks that can only come from working. You know, perks like food, shelter, clothing, self-respect, and Starbucks white chocolate mochas to name a few. I was in a local home improvement store, shopping for a remodeling project, when the gentleman assisting me started talking about his daughter. He casually told me he is a retired Air Force member who now works for the Civil Service, but moonlights at this home improvement store because his college-educated daughter will not wake up before 2:00 p.m. to look for a job and, in his words, even if she did find a job, "She wouldn't have it long because she can't get out of the bed before noon." It took all the wisdom in me to keep my mouth shut, mind my own business, and muster up a smile instead of uttering, "Fool, what you talkin' 'bout? She lives in your house!" This example is not the extreme, nor is it the exception these days. Young and old alike have been zapped of something called "work ethic." Something for nothing is their motto and society has normalized this behavior with a new psychological disorder. I'm sure you have heard of the new psychoanalysis study that discovered the cells that produce "lazyology disorder"! Ha! The diligent rule and advance sometimes out of their sheer resolve to simply be diligent in their pursuit. Ten minutes a day of doing anything equates to one hour and ten minutes a week, multiply that by fifty-two weeks a year and you will accomplish something on accident just because you diligently applied yourself to a consistent task, also known as work. Put some action behind your desires. The dream is free, but the hustle is real.

Reference:

Proverbs 13:4, 20:4, 6:6–11, 12:24, 24:30–34

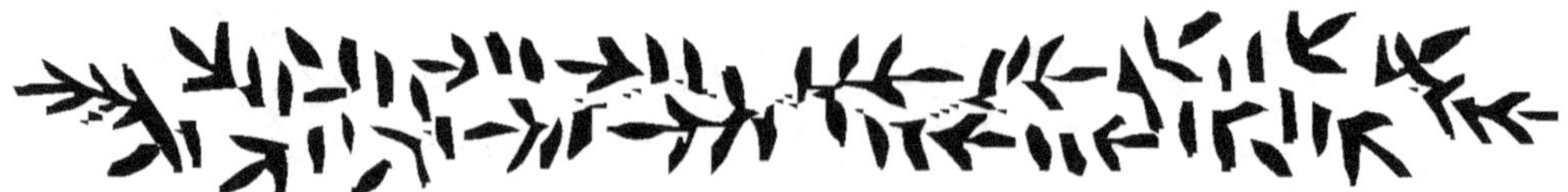

WISDOM TIP 215

Make it, so there will be no need to fake it!

"The wicked bluff their way through, but the virtuous think before they act."

PROVERBS 21:29 (NLT)

"Unscrupulous people fake it a lot; honest people are sure of their steps."

PROVERBS 21:29 (THE MESSAGE)

While my wiser readers have grown wiser still by learning to give proper thought and consideration to their words and actions before making a move, some are still struggling with their attempts to "fake it until they make it." I have never liked that phrase. I do not want to be fake and exactly who, what, when, and where do the fake finally make it? Fake people have no clear concept of who they are or where they are headed, so they mock behaviors, styles, and actions of others in a fake attempt to mask their insecurities. The wise, virtuous person is sure of their steps, in other words, they know exactly who they are, what they want to make, have the recipe in hand, and are headed in the direction of the kitchen to whip it up. The confidence that comes with the wise, virtuous person comes as a result of careful and considerate thought that aligns with truth, wisdom, and wise counsel. When he heads toward the kitchen, he is very sure that his recipe of success will go as planned. Now that's what I call SWAG! Go head, with yo bad self! ("Bad" is good y'all, LOL!)

Reference:

Proverbs 11:5, Ecclesiastes 8:1

WISDOM TIP 216

Preparation is necessary and diligence is required, but God brings the victory.

"Do your best, prepare for the worst—then trust God to bring victory."

PROVERBS 21:31 (THE MESSAGE)

In all your getting, get understanding. You must understand that preparation is necessary, diligence is required, and wisdom is the momentum behind the action of your diligent preparation. However, the victory that you are looking for after you have wisely exercised diligent preparation comes from the Lord alone. Your trust can never be in your own efforts and abilities. Your confident trust must be in the Lord who gives you the ability to prosper in all things. When we start to believe our "own hype," pride sets in followed by the crash landing. Surely, in the Lord our God lies the victory you desire! If you have not allowed Him to be your confident trust, then I invite you to ask Jesus to come into your life; ask Him to give you the ultimate victory that His death won for all people.

Reference:

1 Corinthians 15:57; Psalm 20:7, 33:17; Isaiah 31:1; Ecclesiastes 9:11

WISDOM TIP 217

A good name is priceless.

"A sterling reputation is better than striking it rich; a gracious spirit is better than money in the bank."

Proverbs 22:1 (THE MESSAGE)

"Choose a good reputation over great riches; being held in high esteem is better than silver or gold."

Proverbs 22:1 (NLT)

What people think of when your name is mentioned is the basis of your reputation. Yes, you cannot please everybody and, yes, some people will dislike you for absolutely no reason, but can those same people say you are a liar, a cheater, a scandalous fraud without being put in check by the majority? A good name that causes your reputation to precede you is better than money, because money cannot earn respect. Money cannot cause the hearts of people to flutter when you are in their presence. Heck, money can't even make people genuinely like you. A good name is more valuable because it has the ability to win affections, favors, and friendships that produce intangible treasures. Sometimes a good name comes with tangible treasures as well. I'll never forget the time I entered a large stadium-size building for an event. The seating was first come, first served. I stood in the back and looked around for a seat when an attendant came up, greeted me, and ushered me to an empty seat on the second row. She did it because she recognized me as Mrs. Williams; she knew my husband who had a good reputation for being humble and kind to people no matter their position. I later found out that she felt the same about me and wanted to show her gratitude by finding a good seat for me in the midst of the crowded arena. Money bought all of the attendees the same ticket, but a good name, a good reputation bought me a seat on the second row instead of the balcony.

Reference:

Proverbs 10:7, Ecclesiastes 7:1

WISDOM TIP 218

Wisdom is an internal GPS that provides directions to alternate routes when danger lies ahead.

"A prudent person foresees danger and takes precautions. The simpleton goes blindly on and suffers the consequences."

PROVERBS 22:3 (NLT)

"A prudent person sees trouble coming and ducks; a simpleton walks in blindly and is clobbered."

PROVERBS 22:3 (THE MESSAGE)

There's a Spanish proverb that states, "That in which the fool does in the end, the wise man does at the beginning." This Spanish proverb gives light to the discernment offered by wisdom. Wisdom can see with the internal eye of foresight and act or react accordingly. Wisdom will look around and take note of observations that the human eye cannot see in order to take cover and prepare for what she can see coming in the not so distant future. A person without wisdom will be completely unaware of the danger lurking ahead and continue down the same path, right dab into the eye of the storm. In some cases, a person without wisdom may even be aware of danger that could possibly present itself, but because of a foolish heart, will press forward anyway with the faulty belief that they can somehow avoid the trouble. Whatever the case, wisdom will shield and guard you so that your path will be free of danger. She will be your internal GPS directing you toward an alternate route that avoids the clamor of traffic and construction zones that delay those traveling without her.

Reference:

Proverbs 14:6, 27:12

WISDOM TIP 219

Value your life by avoiding the roads that are clearly marked, "Danger, keep out!"

"Corrupt people walk a thorny, treacherous road; whoever values life will avoid it."

PROVERBS 22:5 (NLT)

"The perverse travel a dangerous road, potholed and mud-slick; if you know what's good for you, stay clear of it."

PROVERBS 22:5 (THE MESSAGE)

Thorny and treacherous are descriptive words that sound excruciatingly painful. Who in their right mind would want to walk on a thorny path? I can picture the stalks of rose bushes with the thorns sticking up, cutting into the soles of my feet with every step. The thought of it sends pain down my spine. What about treacherous? Treacherous sounds criminal to me. The mental picture I see is that of a biker gang dressed in all black leather. Treacherous is not for me either. I want no part of thorny or treacherous, and those of you who value constructing a life that looks more like roses than thorny branches will join me in staying far away from the roads of treacherous hardships. Some of you are well aware of what a treacherous road looks like because you've seen the examples all around your neighborhood, your family, or even in your own life. Others may need to watch the evening news; either way, roads of treachery can be easily identified when observed. Value your life and your destiny by avoiding the thorny and treacherous roads that are clearly marked, "Danger, keep out!"

Reference:

Proverbs 13:15, 16:17; Psalm 1:1; Job 18:8

WISDOM TIP 220

Parents, your direction pointer should be clearly aligned to best benefit the personal nature, temperament, and abilities of each individual child.

"Point your kids in the right direction—when they're old they won't be lost."
PROVERBS 22:6 (THE MESSAGE)

"Direct your children onto the right path, and when they are older, they will not leave it."
PROVERBS 22:6 (NLT)

Point literally means to direct in a certain direction, K-Dub definition. When we think about pointing, you can only direct someone in a certain direction if you know the way yourself, have traveled down that path, and are familiar with the way. As parents, aunts, uncles, grandparents, and others that make up the village of child-rearing, we are called to direct our children in the right direction. It is up to that child to take the direction and arrive at the final destination smoothly. However, we all know of some children who will hear the direction and make the decision that another way is faster or better, only to aggravate themselves and their parents along the way. For this reason, we have to be very careful to direct or point in a way that benefits the personal nature, temperament, and abilities of each individual child. For instance, I am a landmark type of girl. If you start talking to me in terms of cardinal directions, go east on Greenmount and north on Lincoln Trail, I will be lost all day every day. But if you tell me to go to the corner of Greenmount by the Circle K and make a left then a right onto Lincoln Trail by Barnes & Noble, I will find my way to my final destination in no time. This is where wisdom comes into play for parents and their village of child-rearers. We must be keenly aware of what will work for each child and fashion our pointing accordingly. Only then will your pointing turn into directions that are etched into their hearts and becomes a part of who they are and the decisions they make in life. As Christian parents, we have the task of praying for our children, modeling before them what it looks like to study the Word of God, and love the Lord our God with all our hearts, minds, and souls in very practical day-to-day efforts. Also, modeling before them principles, such as how to love others as ourselves, how to be a committed and loving spouse, and how to work toward a goal and see it completed until the end. When we properly point these principles, they will become habits in the lives of our children that are not easily broken.

Reference:

Ephesians 6:4; Deuteronomy 4:9, 11:19, 6:7

WISDOM TIP 221

Keep out of debt!

"Just as the rich rule the poor, so the borrower is servant to the lender."

PROVERBS 22:7 (NTL)

"The poor are always ruled over by the rich, so don't borrow and put yourself under their power."

PROVERBS 22:7 (THE MESSAGE)

Off to work I go because I owe, I owe, I owe! I am in no way diminishing the importance of working, nor the importance of paying debts. What I am attempting to bring to light is that many people rise early only to arrive at a job that they have no passion for because they are servant to their creditors. Working just to pay the bills is not what God had in mind when He said, "Be fruitful and replenish the earth." I often wonder what percentage of the American workforce would opt to find employment with an organization with a mission that fuels the passions of their hearts, but earns less money if it were not for their servitude to creditors. Also, how many would pursue their artistic and creative giftings or business ideas if they were not under the power of debt? How about you? What do you have a passion for that you are not able to pursue because of student loans, car notes, credit card payments, and last year's Christmas presents? This wisdom tip is all about making wise money choices. The only thing you want to owe someone is your beautiful smile and love. As much as you can, pay cash for your purchases. When you find that you cannot pay cash, put a little aside until you have enough to purchase with cash. In instances of very large purchases, if you must borrow money, get the best interest rate possible and only borrow the amount that you will be able to pay back comfortably. Invite wisdom to help guide you in your purchases and to help you understand your purchasing power when it comes to using credit wisely. I'm not a financial advisor, but I do know by the wisdom of God's Word and from my own life experience that you should never spend more than you make, nor have every hard-earned dollar leave your hands because the credit master came calling for his purse. This week, sit down and conduct an in-depth analysis of your finances and make a commitment to do whatever it takes to free yourself from the servitude of debt. Allow wisdom to guide you along the way. She may lead you to a financial advisor, a credit repair organization, or a money wise family member who can help you budget and serve as an accountability partner for your purchases.

Reference:

Matthew 18:25, Nehemiah 5:4–5, 2 Kings 4:1

WISDOM TIP 222

You will reap what you sow!

"Those who plant injustice will harvest disaster, and their reign of terror will come to an end."

Proverbs 22:8 (NLT)

"If you plant the seeds of injustice, disaster will spring up, and your oppression of others will end."

Proverbs 22:8 (GNT)

"Troublemakers get in trouble, and their terrible anger will get them nowhere."

Proverbs 22:8 (CEV)

This wisdom tip is twofold. Not only will the trouble you stir up come back to you, but if you are abusing the little power you have been entrusted with, it will be snatched from you when the harvest of trouble you produced comes calling your name. In the end, you will be left hanging with nothing but a bad reputation and the stench attached to all the mess you stirred up along the way. You will get exactly what you hoped would fall upon those whom you tried to "do wrong," and the injustices you were scheming up in the backdrop will fall right into your front yard. The takeaway is to take note of your actions and your motives. If you don't want to see it fall back on you, then make sure you are not plotting and scheming against others.

Reference:

Job 4:8, Proverbs 1:31, Galatians 6:7–8

WISDOM TIP 223

Your motivation to give should spring from a heart of generosity and not obligation.

"Generous hands are blessed hands because they give bread to the poor."

PROVERBS 22:9 (THE MESSAGE)

"Blessed are those who are generous, because they feed the poor."

PROVERBS 22:9 (NLT)

I attended a church that would sing the same song every Sunday during offering time, "If you want to be blessed, pay your tithes and your offerings. If you want more, give unto the poor. And the Lord will give it back to you." The song had a nice P-Funk beat that made you rock and sway as you passed the offering basket. I would find myself singing the words during the week, so the purpose behind the song actually took root in my heart. You will be blessed in more ways than one when you are generous. Generosity does not mean gullibility. Wisdom will not allow you to be taken advantage of. In fact, wisdom will allow you to sniff out a "user" before they can get the words "I need" out of their mouths. When legitimate needs are presented before you, your eyes of wisdom will respond with generosity, seeing it as an opportunity to bless someone and not an obligation.

Reference:

Proverbs 11:25, 19:17, 31:20

WISDOM TIP 224

Be careful with the company you keep.

"Throw out the mocker, and fighting goes, too. Quarrels and insults will disappear."

PROVERBS 22:10 (NLT)

"Kick out the troublemakers and things will quiet down; you need a break from bickering and griping!"

PROVERBS 22:10 (THE MESSAGE)

Calling all instigators, this one is for you! We all know them, they egg on fights and quarrels as a form of entertainment. Peace is not a part of their vocabulary. As Michael Jackson would say, "You want to be starting something, got to be starting something" all the time! When you rid your life of instigators, you will have peace in your crew of friends, in your home, and most importantly in your life. "Where no wood is, the fire goes out" (Proverbs 26:20). Kyna translation, "Where the instigator once stood, peace has taken his place!"

Reference:

Proverbs 26:20–21, Psalm 101:5

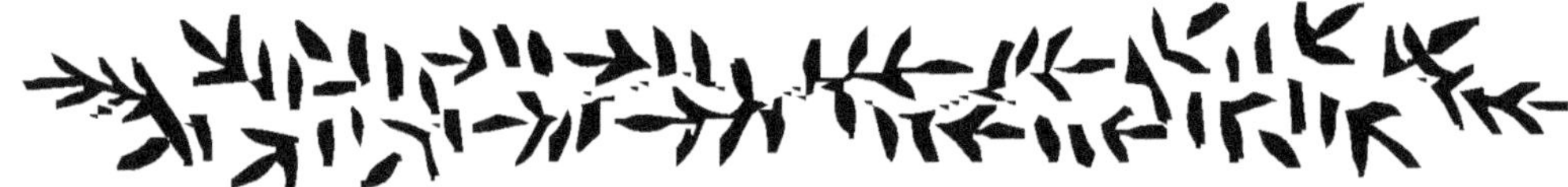

WISDOM TIP 225

Children need correction in order to thrive and survive.

"Young people are prone to foolishness and fads; the cure comes through tough-minded discipline."

PROVERBS 22:15 (THE MESSAGE)

"All children are foolish, but firm correction will make them change."

PROVERBS 22:15 (CEV)

"Children just naturally do silly, careless things, but a good spanking will teach them how to behave."

PROVERBS 22:15 (GNT)

Public Service Announcement (PSA): All children are mischievous at one point or another! If children came into this world perfectly capable of fending for themselves, they would not need parents, they would only need friends. As parents, part of our position description is correction. I'm not here to instruct you on what type of correction you should administer to your child or the children you have a hand in raising, but please note that there must be some type of correction for the mischief that will eventually stroll across their path. I know some of you have little angels so you may believe that Prince Blake and Princess Brooke cannot possibly do anything that will require correction, but the Bible has decided otherwise, so I'm going with the Bible on this one.

Correction needs to be applied early in life and promptly. Don't put off correction like my parents and so many others would do with phrases such as, "I'm going to get you when we get home." Twelve hours later, I had forgotten what I did and so did they on many occasions. Turn correction into teachable moments so your little angels will begin to grow in their ability to make wise choices. If you employ wisdom in the area of administering correction, it will show you how to be creative and fair with the correction you administer, so your child will learn the lesson and bring to mind for the rest of his natural life exactly what not to do, or ELSE!

Reference:

Proverbs 13:24, 23:14, 29:15, 19:18

WISDOM TIP 226

You become who you closely associate with.

> "Don't hang out with angry people; don't keep company with hotheads. Bad temper is contagious—don't get infected."
>
> PROVERBS 22:24–25 (THE MESSAGE)

> "Don't befriend angry people or associate with hot-tempered people, or you will learn to be like them and endanger your soul."
>
> PROVERBS 22:24–25 (NLT)

There's an African proverb that says, "Show me your friends and I will show you yourself." Basically, you become who you closely associate with. Hang with wise people and eventually you will be wise. Hang with fools and eventually you will start making foolish choices. Hang with a quick-tempered hothead and you will learn his methods and start acting just like him. You need to be very careful who you allow into your inner circle. You cannot be "bosom buddies" with people you already know are a little on the "cray cray" side. Do not invite that type of danger into your life. Choose your friends wisely.

Reference:

1 Corinthians 15:33, Proverbs 13:20

WISDOM TIP 227

Robbing Peter to pay Paul is a gamble against financial security.

"Don't gamble on the pot of gold at the end of the rainbow, hocking your house against a lucky chance. The time will come when you have to pay up; you'll be left with nothing but the shirt on your back."

PROVERBS 22:26-27 (THE MESSAGE)

"Don't agree to guarantee another person's debt or put up security for someone else. If you can't pay it, even your bed will be snatched from under you."

PROVERBS 22:26-27 (NLT)

We've already explored the danger of cosigning for the debts of others, so let's flip the script for this proverb and explore another taboo subject—"Robbing Peter to pay Paul." You know how it goes, taking the money you owe for rent to let someone "hold it" for a few days until they can pay you back. The money designated for rent so you can have a roof over your head, technically does not belong to you, it is no longer yours to give unless you somehow want to find "your bed snatched from under you" if the money is not returned to you as promptly as promised. In this case, you did not sign your name on the dotted line, but you still put up security, your security, for someone else. Bad boy, bad boy, what you gonna do, what you gonna do when the landlord comes for you! To the tune of the *Cops* theme song. Be responsible with the funds you are entrusted with and definitely don't make the foolish decision to back the irresponsibility of others. If you owe it in rent, lights, gas, water, tuition, or otherwise, then it is no longer yours to gamble with. The rightful owner is the electric company, mortgage company, or whomever, take your pick. Likewise, do not take out a loan that you have no intention of paying back. Let me rephrase that, you may have honorable intentions, but you realistically know that it will take divine intervention for you to pay it back, but you secure the loan on a "hope and a prayer" that maybe, just maybe, "God will come through" and you will be able to pay it back one day. Word to the wise, where God guides, He also provides.

Reference:

Proverbs 6:1–5, 11:15, 27:13

WISDOM TIP 228

Honor agreements promoting peace and harmony that have been in place for generations before you.

"Don't stealthily move back the boundary lines staked out long ago by your ancestors."

PROVERBS 22:28 (THE MESSAGE)

"Don't cheat your neighbor by moving the ancient boundary markers set up by previous generations."

PROVERBS 22:28 (NLT)

Most of us are aware of generational feuds like that of the Hathfield and McCoy families, but what about generational peace agreements? Some agreements are informal such as the property line marked by the tree in your grandparent's backyard. Others carry more weight like the Geneva Convention that guarantees safety to all modes of transportation and buildings bearing the Red Cross symbol signifying medical professionals during times of war. It is wise to honor generational peace agreements for the sake of maintaining peace. In many cases, no written evidence can be found, only a handshake and an honorable word were required. As long as it depends on you, honor those peaceful agreements and thereby honor those who came before you.

Reference:

Deuteronomy 19:14, 27:17; Job 24:2; Proverbs 23:10

WISDOM TIP 229

Success is the reward of diligence.

"Observe people who are good at their work—skilled workers are always in demand and admired; they don't take a back seat to anyone."

PROVERBS 22:29 (THE MESSAGE)

Those who are good at what they do did not get there by accident. Becoming good requires effort, long hours of practice, going the extra mile, making mistakes, and learning from those mistakes in the process. Whatever skill God has graced you with must be developed in order to go from good to great. Whatever you develop will eventually leave the good category and cross over to extraordinary with diligent effort. Often, people believe the fallacy that because God has naturally gifted a person, that talent is completely tweaked and polished upon delivery. Wrong, diligence and hard work must be applied in order to develop and produce the full manifestation of the fruits of that gift or skill. It is also important to note that mere diligence will not automatically produce success with a desired skill set. There are some skills that can be developed, but there are some that no matter how diligently you practice, you will never develop. That's why it is important to seek God for the skills that you decide to pursue in life. You are naturally bent toward certain subjects and interests for a reason.

> "In the business of his calling, be it what it will, whether for himself or his master; constant in it, swift, ready, and expeditious at it; who industriously pursues it, cheerfully attends it, makes quick dispatch of it; does it off of hand, at once, and is not slothful in it, nor weary of it; when you have observed and taken notice of such a man, which is not very common, you may, without a spirit of prophecy, foresee that such a man will rise in the world."
>
> (*John Gill's Exposition*)

Reference:

Proverbs 10:4, 21:5; Ecclesiastes 9:10

WISDOM TIP 230

Moderation is a friend that avoids the trappings of gluttony.

> "When you go out to dinner with an influential person, mind your manners: Don't gobble your food, don't talk with your mouth full. And don't stuff yourself; bridle your appetite."
>
> PROVERBS 23:1–3 (THE MESSAGE)

> "When you sit to dine with a ruler, note well what is before you, and put a knife to your throat if you are given to gluttony. Do not crave his delicacies, for that food is deceptive."
>
> PROVERBS 23:1–3 (NIV)

In order to avoid the dangers of gluttony, you must first recognize that gluttony does not merely pertain to overindulging in the food delicacy of your choice. Gluttony has the potential to appear under the guises of business deals, lustful desires, promises of position and prestige, and all the attention that comes along with those things. When I was a kid, I could always tell when we were going somewhere important or if someone important was coming to us because we would hear the inevitable line, "Act like you have some sense," or "Act like you have some home training." I believe I may have more than a few witnesses! It's less about acting and more about using discretion that leads to moderation in conversation, appetite, and conduct. In this wisdom tip, the warning to avoid gluttony extends beyond the dinner table of an influential person. You can be a glutton for things like attention, recognition, or respect. Oh yes, gluttony comes in all shapes, forms, and sizes. The issue with gluttony is the sneakiness in which it disguises itself. It shows up as a little fox, but once you feed it, your appetite for that thing increases until full blown gluttony takes over. The deceptive food described in this proverb pertains to things that may be permissible, but when overindulged in will ruin your life. To bridle your appetite for something that is permissible and enjoyable will require the wisdom to exercise moderation. For example, video games are permissible in my household, but only on the weekends. If I were to allow my son to pursue his desire for video games seven days a week, then school work, chores, or face-to-face time with another human would never happen. His appetite for video games would take over and trump his appetite for food or any other bodily function required to thrive. However, there is nothing inherently wrong with video games, they are permissible and enjoyable when moderation is enforced.

The second tip that can be obtained from this verse is to beware of what is being offered to you as a form of appeasement. When others are aware of what you crave or your gluttonous tendencies, then they have the ability to attempt to trap you based on your craving. You may be offered more wine because you have a tendency to overindulge and begin to share private information that was meant for your ears only. The local Casanova has been studying your craving for male attention, so he begins to overindulge in compliments and public admiration in order to find a quicker route to get you to agree to a sexual relationship once you are hypnotized by all the attention and flattery you receive from him. Beware that people will prey upon the gluttonous habits that show up in your life with deceptive purposes that are meant to trap you and expose a weakness in your character. The examples are limitless, so keep in mind that moderation and discretion will preserve you from falling prey to the dangerous traps brought on by gluttony.

Reference:

Proverbs 23:19–20, Philippians 3:19, Psalm 141:4, Proverbs 23:6

WISDOM TIP 231

You will wear yourself out chasing after riches.

"Don't wear yourself out trying to get rich; restrain yourself! Riches disappear in the blink of an eye; wealth sprouts wings and flies off into the wild blue yonder."

PROVERBS 23:4–5 (THE MESSAGE)

"Don't wear yourself out trying to get rich. Be wise enough to know when to quit. In the blink of an eye wealth disappears, for it will sprout wings and fly away like an eagle."

PROVERBS 23:4–5 (NLT)

An unhealthy eagerness for wealth leads to the neglect of all else in life including your integrity. Money is a wonderful servant, but a terrible master. Money is also temporary, meaning it can be in your account today but gone tomorrow. You have to put money in its proper place in order to thrive in life. Most people have a false security attached to money. They believe that if they can just make enough, save enough, or invest enough, then all their worries will be over. While you are overworking to get "enough," what happens to your health, your relationships, and your joy for life? Be wise enough to know when to quit your pursuit of wealth in exchange for your pursuit of life. That old phrase, "the best things in life are free", is true. Money can buy you a house, but not a home. It is the love of family that makes a house a home. Money can buy you a bed, but not sleep. Money can buy you a clock, but not the time to stop and enjoy your life. Money can buy you a book, but not the knowledge that brings understanding. Money can buy you food, but not an appetite. Money can buy you friends, but not mutually beneficial relationships. It's time to open your eyes to the difference so you can pursue those things that will remain in your life beyond the fleeting security of money. What took you twenty years to acquire can be gone in twenty months or, in some cases, twenty minutes, so fix your mind on acquiring the true riches of life. Wear yourself out for the sake of love, service to others, and righteous causes. These, my friend, will last beyond your lifetime and leave enduring satisfaction in your heart and the hearts of others.

Reference:

1 Timothy 6:9, 17; Hebrews 13:5; Proverbs 28:20; 1 John 2:16

WISDOM TIP 232

Extend courtesies from the kindness of your heart or not at all.

"Don't accept a meal from a tightwad; don't expect anything special. He'll be as stingy with you as he is with himself; he'll say, 'Eat! Drink!' but won't mean a word of it. His miserly serving will turn your stomach when you realize the meal's a sham."

PROVERBS 23:6-8 (THE MESSAGE)

"Don't eat with people who are stingy; don't desire their delicacies. They are always thinking about how much it costs. 'Eat and drink,' they say, but they don't mean it. You will throw up what little you've eaten, and your compliments will be wasted."

PROVERBS 23:6-8 (NLT)

While it is beneficial to be able to detect a person who extends bogus invitations and vain compliments, it is also important to ensure you are not the stingy tightwad described here. Whatever you decide to offer someone, be certain that you have first decided within your heart to do it cheerfully and not out of obligation. If it does not come from the heart, please do not extend the courtesy or invitation. Some hostesses watch every morsel of food their guests eat while they internally grudge over every item they appear to offer so liberally. While their words are saying, "You are welcome to whatever you see. Yes, help yourself!" Their hearts are far from the flattering invitation. Steer clear of invitations that come from stingy tightwads, their motive will be made clear by the empty flattering words thrown your way as an attempt to cover up their true intentions.

Reference:

Psalm 12:2, 55:21

WISDOM TIP 233

Don't bother talking sense to fools; they'll only poke fun at your words.

"Don't waste your breath on fools, for they will despise the wisest advice."

Proverbs 23:9 (NLT)

"Don't bother talking sense to fools; they'll only poke fun at your words."

Proverbs 23:9 (THE MESSAGE)

Here is another case in which "sweet words" are spoken in vain. Your words will ricochet in full effect when attempting to speak wisdom to a foolish-minded person. Before you make an attempt to convey advice that will not be heard nor appreciated, wisdom will forewarn you to zip your upper lip. Wisdom has an edge to it that this upside-down culture of ours does not always easily grasp or even want to obtain. Mainly because wisdom, true godly wisdom, is holy advice that can only be properly digested by seekers of God. Fools don't even have an appetite for the menu that wisdom offers. Save your delicacies for those who will partake with gratefulness.

Reference:

Matthew 7:6; Proverbs 1:7, 9:7–8

WISDOM TIP 234

Put a little "tough love" in your rod of discipline.

"Don't be afraid to correct your young ones; a spanking won't kill them. A good spanking, in fact, might save them from something worse than death."

Proverbs 23:13–14 (THE MESSAGE)

"Don't fail to discipline your children. The rod of punishment won't kill them. Physical discipline may well save them from death."

PROVERBS 23:13–14 (NLT)

With a resounding megaphone I solemnly make this announcement to all twenty-first century parents: You will not injure your child's self-esteem, self-worth, or identity if you pop them on the hinny when they need it. In fact, you just may be teaching Prince Robert and Princess Pfalin that consequences will revolve around their inappropriate behavior. The quicker a child learns this truth, the better off he and his kindergarten teacher will be. Disciplining a child early in life is for their greater good as well as the greater good of your family and society at large. Proverbs is not advocating abusive discipline. This proverb, however, is not shying away from a nice little pop or two that stings just enough to cause a child to think twice about repeating an inappropriate act in the future. This proverb is also identifying that true affection in parenting is found when applying loving correction that may require a suitable swat here or there in order to preserve the life of your child from a repeated pattern of behavior that could prove to be detrimental in the future. I'm a living witness that a few pops on the backside saved me and my parents from excessive therapy fees, bail money, and legal fees. Parents, discipline is a terrible thing to waste, so let the mind of your child be transformed into considering discipline before they act and the world will be a better place for you and me, just wait and see … put a little love in your rod.

Reference:

Proverbs 13:24, 19:18, 22:15, 29:15 and 17

WISDOM TIP 235

Don't for a minute envy the fun others are appearing to have while you follow God's leading for your life.

"Don't for a minute envy careless rebels; soak yourself in the Fear-of-GOD—*That's* where your future lies. *Then* you won't be left with an armload of nothing."

PROVERBS 23:17–18 (THE MESSAGE)

Social media constantly bombards us with images of glamorous lifestyles that seemingly depicts the fabulous life we should all aspire to attain. Funny how the posts rarely show the trauma of the day after once reality sets in. Often, we look with envy even when we dare not pierce our lips to express the envious words our hearts may feel at that moment. We think thoughts such as, "I'm around here picking up five people every Sunday for church and my car is on its last leg, meanwhile Ray Ray in da club every weekend and just got "blessed" with a new S Class Mercedes. Lord, what's up with that?" What's up with that is the fact that you are sowing seeds into your future with the Word of God, honoring God by serving in your local church, and faithfully blessing the lives of others in preparation for something far greater than a new Mercedes. Not to mention Ray Ray's Mercedes is one car payment away from repossession, he still lives with his mother, and all of those Saturday night extracurriculars just landed him eighteen years of child support payments. The fast life is only pleasurable for a season. In the end, you give more than you ever dreamed, and pay more than you ever imagined. The benefits of Ray Ray's seemingly fabulous life are temporary and deceptive, while godly principles are accompanied with long-term dividends. Relationships are here today and gone tomorrow while your marriage remains intact. Finances are abundant and lavish for a few years, while your 401(k) is steadily increasing. Fun and laughter with all the sex, drugs, and alcohol leads to long-term health problems while you age gracefully looking at least ten years younger than your chronological. You are winning even when it appears that you are limping.

Reference:

Psalm 37:1–2; Psalm 73:16–19; Proverbs 3:31, 24:1 and 19–20

WISDOM TIP 236

Watch out for the socially acceptable vices that will slow leak your potential and bring ruin to your life.

> "Don't drink too much wine and get drunk; don't eat too much food and get fat. Drunks and gluttons will end up on skid row, in a stupor and dressed in rags."
>
> Proverbs 23:20-21 (THE MESSAGE)

> "Do not join those who drink too much wine or gorge themselves on meat, for drunkards and gluttons become poor, and drowsiness clothes them in rags."
>
> Proverbs 23:20-21 (NIV)

Isn't it ironic that both food and wine (alcoholic beverages) are huge denominators in most social settings, yet they both have the potential to bring a person to ruin. Consider that statement for a moment. There are more commercials advertising alcoholic beverages and weight loss products than any other industry that I can pinpoint at this moment. The wisdom tip to take away from this proverb is moderation in all things. I personally do not enjoy the taste of wine or any other alcoholic beverage. As I normally state, it is not pleasing to my palate. Yet, this proverb does not advocate for complete abstinence, only the overindulgence that leads to forming a habit that will eventually bring a person to ruin. Likewise with food. For some of you, food is your alcohol of choice. The wrong food choices can bring just as much harm to your body as alcohol. Both excessive eating (gluttony) and drinking can send you to the poor house due to the negative physical, emotional, and social effects on your life. Practice moderation in all things, and in some cases, completely abstain from socially acceptable vices that will slow leak your potential and ultimately bring ruin to your life.

Reference:

Matthew 24:49; Ephesians 5:18; Proverbs 20:1, 21:17, 23:2, 29–30, 31:6–7; Isaiah 5:11, 22; 1 Corinthians 5:11; Philippians 3:19

WISDOM TIP 237

It is easy to be led down the path of seduction, but much more difficult to rise out of its grips.

> "A prostitute is a dangerous trap; a promiscuous woman is as dangerous as falling into a narrow well. She hides and waits like a robber, eager to make more men unfaithful." (Even unfaithful to yourself, your plans, your dreams, your body.)
>
> PROVERBS 23:27–28 (NLT)

> "A whore is a bottomless pit; a loose woman can get you in deep trouble fast. She'll take you for all you've got; she's worse than a pack of thieves."
>
> PROVERBS 23:27–28 (THE MESSAGE)

It is my opinion that no vice known to man has the potential to stupefy a man faster than an addiction to a woman. While this proverb warns against a whore or a promiscuous woman, let it be known that a man can also fill this role. What is it about the male-female sexual relationship that makes us lose our minds, up in here, up in here! Sex will cause you to lose every ounce of good sense and act a complete fool. How easy it is to be led down the path of seduction, but how difficult it is to rise out of its grips. The New Living Translation eloquently explains that the "whore" you lust for will make you unfaithful to yourself! Forget about a spouse, what about the faithlessness that comes as a result of your reckless abandon of your own plans, dreams, and body.

Ultimately, your faithlessness to the laws of God. Somebody help me get this point across. You will find yourself in a bottomless pit, swimming for your life, yet sinking deeper and deeper if you hook up with the wrong person at the wrong time. Speaking of timing, it's always the wrong person if you are A-L-R-E-A-D-Y married. You don't even need wisdom for that decision nor a bolt of lightning to crack the sky as a sign from heaven. Just pull out your marriage license and if her name does not match the name written, then poof! Wrong person and wrong time because you are already taken, my brother. For my singles, you may meet the right person at the wrong time. They may not be ready to settle down or their walk with God may not be where it should be so they are still given to seduction, lust, and using their sexual nature to manipulate and prey upon the opposite sex. Singles, it is imperative that you have your wisdom guard up and intact in order to remain faithful to yourself.

Reference

Proverbs 2:26, 5:20, 22:14, 6:26, 7:12; Ecclesiastes 7:26; Proverbs 7:12, 22–27, 9:18

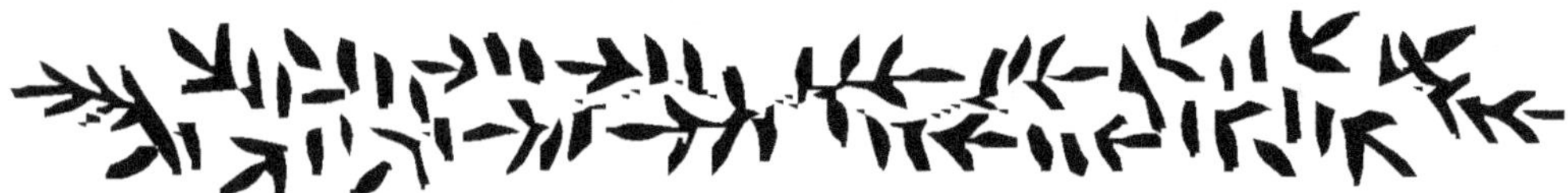

WISDOM TIP 238

Side effects tell you what's really going on.

> "Who are the people who are always crying the blues? Who do you know who reeks of self-pity? Who keeps getting beat up for no reason at all? Whose eyes are bleary and bloodshot? It's those who spend the night with a bottle, for whom drinking is serious business. Don't judge wine by its label, or its bouquet, or its full-bodied flavor. Judge it rather by the hangover it leaves you with—the splitting headache, the queasy stomach. Do you really prefer seeing double, with your speech all slurred, reeling and seasick, drunk as a sailor? 'They hit me,' you'll say, 'but it didn't hurt; they beat on me, but I didn't feel a thing. When I'm sober enough to manage it, bring me another drink!'"
>
> Proverbs 23:29–35 (THE MESSAGE)

Drunk and falling for a whore usually go in the same sentence. Once again, the side effects of overindulgence in alcoholic beverages are brought to your attention. Don't think about what it tastes like, how prestigious you think it makes you look, or your "liquor holding" bragging rights. Rather, let's explore the side effects. Splitting headache—check. Queasy stomach followed by vomiting—check. Passed out and can't remember the night before—check. Walking around seeing other people with double heads or bodies—check. Slurred speech, or in some cases no speech because your brain is so impaired that words will not form properly—check. Liquid courage that leads to fights and violence—check. These side effects are not written in small print nor spoken so fast at the end of an advertisement that they can barely be understood. These side effects are tangibly real, with vulturous pains and shrills. The warning alert has been given, now take heed.

WISDOM TIP 239

Your mind is the house for your body.

"It takes wisdom to build a house, and understanding to set it on a firm foundation; it takes knowledge to furnish its rooms with fine furniture and beautiful draperies."

PROVERBS 24:3–4 (THE MESSAGE)

"A house is built by wisdom and becomes strong through good sense. Through knowledge its rooms are filled with all sorts of precious riches and valuables."

PROVERBS 24:3–4 (NLT)

Your spiritual and emotional dwellings are housed within the confines of your mind. Wisdom will strengthen your mind and expand your ability to make sound decisions steeped in good sense. Through knowledge, the rooms of your mind will be filled with precious, rich, and valuable thoughts that convert to words, that convert to actions, that convert to results. Think of your imagination as fine furniture and your inner dreams as beautiful draperies that make up the value of your transformed mind. How is your home looking—rich or destitute? Just as a home is built up, furnished, and supplied with the necessities and conveniences of life by wise and diligent management, so does you mind require the same diligent and wise application in order for your body and your life to flourish.

Reference:

Proverbs 9:1, 14:1, 8:21, 15:6, 21:20

WISDOM TIP 240

With knowledge comes staying power!

"It's better to be wise than strong; intelligence outranks muscle any day."

PROVERBS 24:5 (THE MESSAGE)

"The wise are mightier than the strong, and those with knowledge grow stronger and stronger."

PROVERBS 24:5 (NLT)

A person of brute strength may be useful for a season, but a person of wisdom will be useful for a lifetime. Most athletes are at the top of their game during their early twenties, few continue in their sport of choice into their thirties, and even less into their forties. However, a judge in her sixties is considered well-seasoned, experienced, and shrewd. A business man in his seventies is respected and revered for his business acumen and sought after for mentorship. I think you get the picture. At the end of a war when all the troops have given all of their physical force, you have what some would term a meeting of the minds to work out diplomatic peace agreements. The strength of wisdom outranks and outlasts physical strength. When your physical stature has lost its form, the strength of the wisdom you spoke, lived, and radiated will remain.

Reference:

Proverbs 21:22, 8:14; Ecclesiastes 7:19; Colossians 1:11

WISDOM TIP 241

Adversity is a reality of life, "man up" so you can discover what you are made of!

"If you fall to pieces in a crisis, there wasn't much to you in the first place."

PROVERBS 24:10 (THE MESSAGE)

"If you fail under pressure, your strength is too small."
PROVERBS 24:10 (NLT)

Each of us will face an adverse situation that forces the reality of fight or flight. My prayer for you is that you will make the choice to fight, so the strength that rests dormant within you will have the ability to emerge in full force. The option of "flight" is really no option at all. Choosing to flee when you should stay and fight will bring great remorse, compounded by multiple feelings of failure. I am in no way advocating physical violence when I declare to you to stand and fight. Remember, wisdom is much stronger than brute force and the results of the meeting of the minds will outlast the bloodshed of the battlefield. When you make the decision to fight the adversity that comes to shake the very foundation in which your life is built upon, the weapons in your arsenal will have names like Prayer, the Word of God, Faith, Perseverance, Living Hope, Steadfastness, and Wisdom. When applying weapons such as these, you will receive guidance and action steps that will break adversity in half, not to mention a supernatural force that will contend against every foe that dares to contend against you. I urge you to stand your ground and fight for what you believe in. Fight for your marriage. Fight for the well-being of your children. Take up the righteous cause that has been assigned to you and fight!

Reference:

Deuteronomy 20:8, Jeremiah 51:46, Job 4:5, 2 Corinthians 4:1

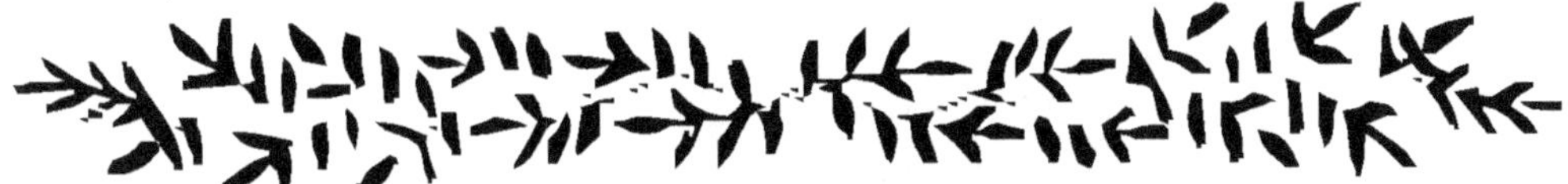

WISDOM TIP 242

Vindictiveness is not a good look for you!

"Don't laugh when your enemy falls; don't crow over his collapse."
PROVERBS 24:17 (THE MESSAGE)

"Do not gloat when your enemy falls; when they stumble, do not let your heart rejoice."
PROVERBS 24:17 (NIV)

I know you knew and even their mother may have known that they had it coming, but we are not to gloat over someone's downfall. Vindictiveness and vengefulness are not a good look on anyone. A person who will walk in the way of wisdom will also understand the power of forgiveness. Forgiveness allows you to acknowledge the wrong committed yet make the choice to move forward, and in some cases, have pity on the state of the person who wronged you. This type of wisdom will not allow you to gloat when the person who wronged you begins to experience the consequences of the chaos they may have sown. The exact opposite will often occur, which is empathy. From your own hurtful experiences and rock bottom moments, you can respond with empathy because the hurt that comes as a result of regret, failure, public exposure, and heartache is universal. As the old saying goes, "I wouldn't wish this on my worst enemy." When you've been there, you cannot bask in the downfall of another human being, you may even be moved to reach out to the person who betrayed you or whisper prayers from a distance. Either way, vindictiveness and its toxic emotions will not be found lingering in your heart.

Reference:

Obadiah 1:12, Micah 7:8

WISDOM TIP 243

Respectful rebels help bring about lasting change.

"Respect your leaders; don't be defiant or mutinous."
PROVERBS 24:21 (THE MESSAGE)

"Don't associate with rebels."
PROVERBS 24:21 (NLT)

Respect for authority will save your life! You may not agree with that authority figure, but respecting the position that person holds or the authority that comes with that position is paramount. I know there are some who abuse their authority, but sooner rather than later, the public downfall of corrupt leaders are exposed in just about every media outlet known to man. Until that day comes, no matter how we feel about the person, we need to practice respectful exchanges. Wisdom will give you the ability to respect authority in the moments of disagreement. When you encounter a person who is unbecoming of the authority they are currently entrusted with, an act of defiance will not be the best route in the heat of the moment. In most cases, respect will allow you to get past the situation and live to tell your story so you can pursue other avenues of justice. A rebel without respect will cease to be a rebel. On the other hand, rebels who respect authority will live to present causes that will shatter the axis of corruption found in immoral authority figures in order to make room for the right leaders. This wisdom tip can be applied to your dealings with police officers, teachers, parents, elected officials, you name it. Learn to respectfully communicate with and handle anyone in a position of authority over you; there is power in a respectful approach.

Reference:

Romans 13:1–2

WISDOM TIP 244

Lady Justice ought to be competent in wisdom.

"It's wrong, very wrong, to go along with injustice."
PROVERBS 24:23 (THE MESSAGE)

"It is wrong to show favoritism when passing judgment."
PROVERBS 24:23 (NLT)

I do not support the notion of blind justice. I prefer Lady Justice to have eyes all around her head so she can wisely discern the facts of a matter and judge appropriately, not blindly. Call wrong "wrong" in the face of the rich or poor, relative or stranger, friend or foe. That's the result of wisdom combined with justice. Decide to be a person who will not stand on the side of partiality and injustice, but one who will stand on the side of righteousness and truth no matter who presents it and what package they may appear in. If that means your son will be called to the carpet because of wrongdoing, so be it. If that means your best friend will be held accountable for her actions, so be it. If that means you have to stand on the side of a person of a different race when your entire family has turned their back on you as a result, so be it. A competency of wisdom steeped in justice will provide you with the tools to refuse the impartial and unfair treatment unjustly applied in any spectrum of influence you encompass. In the words of Dr. Martin Luther King Jr., "Injustice anywhere is injustice everywhere." Be one of Lady Justice's eyes and wisely discern so you can justly act.

Reference:

Deuteronomy 1:17, 16:19; Proverbs 18:5, 28:21; Leviticus 19:15; John 7:24; 1 Peter 1:17

WISDOM TIP 245

Genuine truth matters, loving truth matters, and saving truth matters.

"An honest answer is like a warm hug."
Proverbs 24:26 (THE MESSAGE)

"An honest answer is like a kiss on the lips."
Proverbs 24:26 (NIV)

Imagine a warm, snuggly hug accompanied by a fat, juicy kiss right on your cheek after walking through the doors of your grandmother's home. Once you can feel your grandmother's hug and the wetness on your cheek from her kiss then you can understand the warmth of an honest answer spoken at just the right time. It is likened to receiving an affectionate kiss on the lips, not romantic affection, but you are deeply and genuinely loved and cared for type of affection. Genuine truth matters, loving truth matters, and saving truth matters. We all need versions of these types of honesty at different junctures of our lives, covering various situations. Likewise, we can all give the gift of genuine, loving, and saving honesty to others when needed. I don't necessarily want you kissing me on the lips, but your honest words in the right situation can provide all the affection I could ever hope for in my moment of need.

Reference:
Proverbs 15:23, 16:1, 25:11–12

WISDOM TIP 246

The key to precision in execution is proper planning and preparation.

"Do your planning and prepare your fields before building your house."
Proverbs 24:27 (NLT)

General contractors and homebuilders will attest to the fact that prior to the building of a physical structure the architectural plans must be drawn. Good architectural plans include the drawings for each phase of construction and end with the final completed structure. Once the plans are drawn up and approved, then the preparation for bringing the plans to life begins. Preparation may include the proper building permits, hiring adequate construction staff, gathering the building materials, and finally, the labor that goes into clearing the land that will serve as the foundation for the home. What goals do you have for your life? They deserve to be honored with the proper planning and preparation, so they can one day become the reality of the final completed structure you have envisioned. Planning allows you to aim your efforts in the appropriate direction and preparation sets those efforts in correct alignment for the action that will move you closer to your desired outcome. When you take the time to first plan and prepare, you can act and react with the certainty of the sufficiency to see your goals accomplished.

Reference:

Luke 14:28–30

WISDOM TIP 247

Thou shall not tear others to pieces with your lips.

"Don't talk about your neighbors behind their backs—no slander or gossip, please."

PROVERBS 24:28 (THE MESSAGE)

"Do not be a false witness against your neighbor and do not tear him to pieces with your lips."

PROVERBS 24:28 (ARAMAIC BIBLE)

Your neighbor is not just the person who lives within the confines of your street or your community. Your neighbors are those whom you share close space and contact with. In a work setting, your neighbors are your coworkers and those whom you work amongst. In a school setting, your neighbors are your classmates and collective student body. When it comes to sharing space with other humans, there will be some kind of conflict sooner or later. Someone will get mad at someone else and attempt to turn the entire group against the other person with gossip that is one-sided. This is what I term "murder by mouth," slowly attempting to tear the other person to pieces with lips that drip with slander and gossip. Guess what, even if it is true, you should not speak your truth needlessly against someone else just to make yourself look good by calling it a "prayer request," or the legendary "just so you are aware," "for your own good" type of gossip.

Just in case no one has ever told you this, allow me to be the first, those "prayer requests" and "just so you knows" are still gossip. Allow wisdom to be the filter for your words. Think before you speak, especially when it can damage the reputation of someone else.

Reference:

Proverbs 25:18, Leviticus 19:11, Exodus 20:6, Exodus 23:1, Ephesians 4:25, Colossians 3:9

WISDOM TIP 248

Even Stevens are double losers.

"And don't say, 'Now I can pay them back for what they've done to me! I'll get even with them!'"

PROVERBS 24:29 (NLT)

For some of us, the first reaction is one of retaliation when we are wronged. Some prefer immediate wrath, while others like long planned out, thoughtful retaliation. Either way, a person of wisdom understands that retaliation of any kind will only add fuel to the fire and cause more harm to everyone involved. Not to mention, for those of us who want to follow the teachings of Christ, vengeance belongs to the Lord and our part involves forgiving wrongs and offenses no matter how egregious they may be. Suppose God decided to retaliate against you for every wrong you have committed against Him? Your power lies in forgiveness, moving forward, and enjoying a prosperous life despite the harm maliciously planned against you. Living your best life is the best retaliation in the world.

Reference:

Matthew 5:39; Romans 12:17, 12:19; Proverbs 20:22, 25:21–22; 1 Thessalonians 5:15

WISDOM TIP 249

Slothfulness today produces the lack of tomorrow.

"One day I walked by the field of an old lazybones, and then passed the vineyard of a lout; they were overgrown with weeds, thick with thistles, all the fences broken down. I took a long look and pondered what I saw; the fields preached me a sermon and I listened: 'A nap here, a nap there, a day off here, a day off there, sit back, take it easy—do you know what comes next? Just this: You can look forward to a dirt-poor life, with poverty as your permanent houseguest!'"

PROVERBS 24:30–34 (THE MESSAGE)

"To pass by the field of the slothful, and by the vineyard of the man void of understanding, is to look into the life of any careless liver, and to take a view of his deeds."

Oh, what wisdom to allow the overgrown weeds in someone else's field to preach a sermon by which you learn a valuable lesson. Look long and hard and receive instruction so you don't walk away and forget what you just saw! Turn around and look again to get a view from a different angle and learn something from the overgrown weeds. In this proverb, Solomon is explaining the instruction he received from viewing the overgrown field of a slothful man. If Solomon lived in the twenty-first century, he would have most likely explained what he learned in these phrases:

No sweat, no sweet.
No money, no honey.
No pain, no gain.
If you have the nut in your hand, you must crack it to eat.

The moral of the story is that you can gain insight from the failure of others. If their failure was brought on by laziness, then do just the opposite to get different results. Look at the life of someone who has lived unwisely and make a decision that you will study his deeds, not for the purpose of replicating them, but from the point of eliminating from your life what you have discovered in his.

WISDOM TIP 250

Real diamonds sparkle without an announcement and glisten without drawing attention.

"Don't work yourself into the spotlight; don't push your way into the place of prominence. It's better to be promoted to a place of honor than face humiliation by being demoted."

Proverbs 25:6–7 (THE MESSAGE)

Pride is fostered and encouraged by every act of self-assertion. Therefore, this wisdom tip warns against arrogance and presumption by promoting humility. When you pull yourself into a place of prominence, you may find that you are not ready to play with the big dogs. When it is time for the spotlight to shine upon you, no one will be able to dim your light, but do not allow pride to place you in a place that will tear you down when humility would have exalted you in due time. Real diamonds sparkle without an announcement and glisten on any finger they find themselves adorning. Be like the diamond—radiate and shine, but do it behind the locked glass door until someone points you out and says, "Can you please bring that one to the forefront for my viewing?"

Reference:

Luke 14:7–10; Proverbs 16:19, 27:2

WISDOM TIP 251

Respect what is shared with you in confidence.

"In the heat of an argument, don't betray confidences. Word is sure to get around, and no one will trust you."

Proverbs 25:9–10 (THE MESSAGE)

"When arguing with your neighbor, don't betray another person's secret. Others may accuse you of gossip, and you will never regain your good reputation."

Proverbs 25:9–10 (NLT)

This scenario has been played out time and time again. Betty and Connie are best friends. Betty and Connie get into a disagreement and their friendship is now compromised. Betty begins to tell every secret Connie ever told her out of anger to defend her case against Connie. "I knew I should not have trusted you, you scandalous, backstabbing, two-timing on your husband, cheating on your taxes, with your illegitimate child fathered by the lawn man." Betty has just spilled the tea on every secret Connie ever entrusted to her, guaranteeing this friendship will not be restored nor replaced by any other woman in the neighborhood. With so-called friends like Betty, who needs enemies? If someone disclosed something to you in confidence, whether it happens to be as scandalous or reproachful as described above or not, do not divulge of it when a dispute breaks out. In the end, you will be the person who is most harshly judged. Respect what is shared with you in confidence. Just as that moment of sharing was limited to the two of you, the secret was told in order to stay between the two of you.

Reference:

Proverbs 11:13, 20:19, 25:9

WISDOM TIP 252

The right words spoken at the right time will custom fit your life like a tailor-made suit fits your physique.

"The right word at the right time is like a custom-made piece of jewelry, and a wise friend's timely reprimand is like a gold ring slipped on your finger."

Proverbs 25:11–12 (THE MESSAGE)

"Timely advice is lovely, like golden apples in a silver basket. To one who listens, valid criticism is like a gold earring or other gold jewelry."

Proverbs 25:11–12 (NLT)

Think of how you would gladly receive a custom-made piece of bling to add to your jewelry collection or a diamond ring designed just for you to perfection. That's exactly how excited you should be to receive a timely word of advice, sprinkled with loving correction from those who have your best interest at heart. Their godly counsel should be just as valuable to you, if not more, than any piece of jewelry or other prized possession you may currently own. In fact, their timely counsel has the potential to move you further along the customized path God has ordained for your life. When stuck in a rut or when you simply find yourself at the crossroads of life, possibly about to make the wrong turn, wisely consider the words of those who love you enough to bestow upon you the kiss of truth when you need it most.

Reference:

Proverbs 15:2, 31, 24:26; Ecclesiastes 7:5

WISDOM TIP 253

Don't talk about it, be about it!

> "A person who promises a gift but doesn't give it is like clouds and wind that bring no rain."
>
> PROVERBS 25:14 (NLT)

> "Like billowing clouds that bring no rain is the person who talks big but never produces."
>
> PROVERBS 25:14 (THE MESSAGE)

To under promise and over deliver is much better than to overpromise and under deliver. A fool will boast about what he plans to do knowing full well he doesn't have the ability or the heart to make it happen. This proverb warns of such behavior. The wise at heart will not talk about it without first "being about it." Now that's an old phrase, but it still holds weight. The proof is in the pudding, not empty promises. Further, if you do make a promise do everything within your power to keep your word. The Word of God tells us it is better not to vow (promise) than to vow and not pay.

Reference:

2 Peter 2:17, Jude 1:12

WISDOM TIP 254

Gentle words and persuasive language are the dynamic duo that makes for successful mediation.

"Patience can persuade a prince, and soft speech can break bones."
PROVERBS 25:15 (NLT)

"Patient persistence pierces through indifference; gentle speech breaks down rigid defenses."
PROVERBS 25:15 (THE MESSAGE)

Gentle and kind words have the power to overcome the most rigidly stubborn hearts. A modern Greek gnome says, "The tongue has no bones, yet it breaks bones." Gentle speech has the power to soften the bones of the "boneheaded". A calm and composed demeanor will overcome opposition and disarm the most determined enemy. During my time in the Air Force, we practiced "military bearing" in order to perfect the art of functioning with professionalism and clarity during extremely high stress situations. Military bearing was required above all, even above your personal discomfort. For instance, if you were standing at attention in formation and a bee began to buzz around your face, you cannot swat it away due to the discomfort of its presence or you would break "military bearing" for yourself and your entire formation. Wisdom is the spiritual bearing that empowers you to rise beyond your physical senses in moments of great opposition and react constructively with words that gently persuade opponents. The calmness that radiates from the spiritual bearing enforced by wisdom will allow you to control the situation at hand and react in accordance with the good of all involved. Your calmness will thwart your opponent, causing him to be disarmed when he would otherwise take it up a notch to match or outmatch your reaction. Gentle speech allows you to become a mediator of influence instead of an instrument of wrath.

Reference:

Proverbs 15:1, Ecclesiastes 10:4

WISDOM TIP 255

Be careful not to wear out your welcome.

"Don't visit your neighbors too often, or you will wear out your welcome."

PROVERBS 25:17 (NLT)

Just about every American neighborhood has the kid who goes from door to door bright and early in the morning in search of someone to play with. This particular kid does not perform this ritual a few times a week but every day of the week, especially in the summer, earning him the reputation of the neighborhood nuisance. He has worn out his welcome with his frequent breakfast-to-dinner playdates. Even the most welcoming of parents set boundaries on how often and how long this particular kid can come over because the welcome mat is worn completely out by the middle of the summer. I was always taught not to visit someone before 10:00 a.m. and definitely not to attempt to visit on a regular basis. However, this concept is not necessarily widely taught today. While you may have great friends who welcome you over like a member of the family, it is still very wise to maintain a healthy balance and respect for their home and their need for periodic privacy. Too much of anything or anyone, no matter how good, can have negative consequences. Don't show up so much that your neighbor, best friend, or family members are "filled with thy company to a loathing of it, as the stomach with eating too much honey."

WISDOM TIP 256

Where you find gossip, you are sure to find lies.

"Telling lies about others is as harmful as hitting them with an ax, wounding them with a sword, or shooting them with a sharp arrow."

PROVERBS 25:18 (NLT)

A person who spreads slanderous lies about someone causes as much destruction to their reputation as an ax or sword would to their body. Lies have sent men to their graves prematurely, broken up relationships, imprisoned the innocent, and destroyed reputations that took decades to build. Often, the root of the lie is envy, jealousy, revenge, or plain hatred. Again, this type of wisdom tip is replayed throughout this book because the tongue is a powerful weapon that, if not tamed, will destroy lives. The constant reminders of the importance of speaking truth and the importance of watching what you say not only produces measures of wisdom in you, but also warns you of the dangers of developing friendships with people who practice gossiping like a competitive sport. Where you find gossip, you are sure to find lies. Tame your tongue and keep those who will not make an effort to tame their tongue at arm's length.

Reference:

Exodus 20:16; Psalm 57:4, 52:2; Proverbs 24:28; Jeremiah 9:8; Proverbs 12:18; James 3:6

WISDOM TIP 257

Faithfulness is being reliable, dependable, and consistent.

"Putting confidence in an unreliable person in times of trouble is like chewing with a broken tooth or walking on a lame foot."

PROVERBS 25:19 (NLT)

"Trusting a double-crosser when you're in trouble is like biting down on an abscessed tooth."

PROVERBS 25:19 (THE MESSAGE)

Trusting an unreliable person in a time of need is like having a broken tooth and a foot injury at the same time. You cannot bite or chew your food properly with broken teeth and you cannot walk with an injured foot. No food and no way of getting around is the same feeling of disgust you will have in the pit of your stomach if you trust a no-good, unreliable, wishy-washy person to come through for you when you are really in need. This wisdom tip goes back to the development of character in yourself as well as the type of characters you want to surround yourself with on a consistent basis. If your best friend from high school cannot pick up his kids on time from school because he is too busy hanging with the boys, take heed. If your girlfriend can show up on time for her weekly beauty salon appointment, but she is thirty minutes late picking you up for your doctor's appointment, take heed. Faithfulness is not just a character trait reserved for marriage or church. Faithfulness is modeling long-term consistency and reliability in the little things of life day after day, week after week, month after month, and year after year.

Reference:

Isaiah 36:6

WISDOM TIP 258

Punish your enemy by helping him.

"If you see your enemy hungry, go buy him lunch; if he's thirsty, bring him a drink. Your generosity will surprise him with goodness, and God will look after you."

PROVERBS 25:21–22 (THE MESSAGE)

As metals are melted by fire, so is the heart softened by kindness. Please understand that wisdom is the direct opposite of what your personal opinion or comfort level may be because wisdom comes from the Kingdom of God, therefore, it is reflective of how things should be. The forgiveness and kindness you offer to someone who has intentionally sought to hurt you will bring shame upon them with the intention of having them consider the error of their ways. To show your enemy clemency, you are reserving yourself from the resentment and sorrow that comes with unforgiveness and vengefulness. When we attempt revenge, we are attempting to play the role of God who has already instructed us that "Vengeance is mine," "Love those who hate you," and "Pray for those who spitefully misuse you." Finally, paying back evil for evil will only serve to harden the heart of your enemy and increase his hostility toward you, leading to more retaliation. It is a never-ending cycle of negativity. Doing good to someone will eventually cause them to deal with the internal pain of regret for every wrong thing they have ever said or done to you. Nothing you could offer in terms of payback has the power to match the pain of regret. When you follow God's way of dealing with your enemies, God will bless you and cause your enemies to be at peace with you.

Reference:

Matthew 5:44; Romans 12:20; Exodus 23:4–5; 1 Samuel 24:17 and 19, 26:21

WISDOM TIP 259

Compliments piled upon compliments when overconsumed will topple you.

"It's not good to eat too much honey, and it's not good to seek honors for yourself."

PROVERBS 25:27 (NLT)

"It's not smart to stuff yourself with sweets, nor is glory piled on glory good for you."

PROVERBS 25:27 (THE MESSAGE)

Glory piled on glory is the same as compliments piled upon compliments. When someone is constantly told how wonderful they are, they start to believe all the fanfare to their own detriment. We see it in athletes, the super beautiful, and hugely successful individuals. They have a constant barrage of compliments that brings about the "bighead" of conceit. We all need at least one person in our lives who will speak the truth to us, put us in our place, and bring us down off our high horse a couple of notches when needed. Just as honey is sweet to taste and accompanied with many health benefits, it can have a dual negative effect when overconsumed. We all need to be praised and admired, it's a part of the human growth experience, but when overconsumed, it can also become a part of the human downfall experience. Pride comes before the fall; crash and burn! Whatever you are good at, whatever others admire most about you should be viewed as a gift from God. Treat it as such so you know when to sit down and be humble!

Reference:

Proverbs 27:2, Luke 14:11

WISDOM TIP 260

Never come down to the level of a fool.

"Don't respond to the stupidity of a fool; you'll only look foolish yourself."

PROVERBS 26:4 (THE MESSAGE)

"Don't answer the foolish arguments of fools, or you will become as foolish as they are."

Proverbs 26:4 (NLT)

When you make an attempt to answer the silly questions of a fool that are designed to persuade you toward his foolish viewpoints, you will make yourself look as foolish as the fool. Further, to attempt to engage in a productive debate by defending your point with someone you know is lacking in good sense is a pure waste of your valuable time. In fact, some people should not even be dignified with a response from you. Don't fall for the fool or his tactics to make you look like a fool. If you follow this simple wisdom tip, you will save yourself from engaging in many disputes and unfruitful discussions. Learn how to smile and keep it moving.

Reference:

Proverbs 23:9, 29:9

WISDOM TIP 261

Be careful who you allow to represent you.

"Hire a fool or a drunk and you shoot yourself in the foot."

Proverbs 26:10 (THE MESSAGE)

"Like an archer who wounds at random is one who hires a fool or any passer-by."

Proverbs 26:10 (NIV)

Your reputation is a part of your brand, therefore, whoever represents your brand is a representation of you. If you are blessed to be in a position to supply job opportunities for others through entrepreneurship or as a hiring manager, take your position seriously. Look for those who have a proven track record of professionalism that duplicates your own qualities or better. Most people will not knowingly hire a person who is considered a drunk or a drug addict. Likewise, most people will not knowingly hire a fool. However, when the F bomb is dropped, we are often guilted into bringing family, friends, and a friend of a friend on board. Yes, those gut-wrenching F bombs—Family, Friend, or Friend of a Friend. To employ anyone who is incapable of representing your brand in skill and character will cause your business to suffer in reputation and eventually profit. Be careful who you hire because incompetence will eventually come back to bite you.

WISDOM TIP 262

Recycle trash not foolishness.

"As a dog returns to its vomit, so a fool repeats his foolishness."
PROVERBS 26:11 (NLT)

"So a fool returneth to his folly."
PROVERBS 26:11 (KJV)

"Though he knows it to be folly, and ruinous to him: but vice has become to him a second nature, and he cannot, even if he would, escape from it."

A fool recycles foolishness over and over again to the point of habit. A fool never frees himself from the hindrances brought on by his foolishness, and like any other addict, the hindrance will show up and the fool will return to his trappings. For some, the trapping may be wrong relationships; for others, overspending. Whatever your personal trapping might be, you must first come to terms with the hindrances they bring to your life; recognize them and their trigger points, so you are aware of the trappings when they appear. Some people will feel temporary regret and make the brave attempt to cast off the monkey of foolishness that's riding their back, but their character, words, mindset, and environment often remains exactly the same. If nothing changes, then nothing changes! The trap becomes a second nature that results in relapse after relapse right back into the same old bad habit. Take note of the man who has multiple baby mamas after saying he wouldn't put himself in that position again. What about the person addicted to porn who refuses to turn the television commercial showing what I have termed "soft porn" with everything hanging out necessary to arouse the imagination? You better take a note from Michael Jackson and "Remember the Time"! A foolish person will forget the uneasiness and discomfort of the situation and return to his old course of life. Gamblers, sex addicts, gossipers, name your trap and know that if you do nothing to recognize the hindrance it brings to your life and absolutely nothing to change your mindset, your environment, or your identification with that thing, then you too will fall into the category of a fool who will recycle his foolishness until death do you part. That's tight, but it's right! Real talk.

Reference:

2 Peter 2:22, Proverbs 27:22

WISDOM TIP 263

The self-conceited are met with more difficulty than the stupid.

"See that man who thinks he's so smart? You can expect far more from a fool than from him."

PROVERBS 26:12 (THE MESSAGE)

"Do you see a person wise in their own eyes? There is more hope for a fool than for them."

PROVERBS 26:12 (NIV)

There is not a fool who recycles his foolishness faster than the self-proclaimed "know-it-all." They know it all so they repeat it all over again and again. Self-improvement and self-conceit are like oil and water; they do not mix, not even a little bit. The oil will eventually rise to the top and the water will sink below it. In this analogy, oil is your conceit and the improvement of your life is the water that continues to sink to the bottom, unable to rise above that big blob of oil called your ego. The Asian culture speaks of the fox finding his shadow very large, and of the wolf when alone thinking himself a lion. This is the only case where it is better to be a fool because a fool has the potential of receiving wisdom that can cure him of his foolishness. But if you don't even believe that you need wise instruction, then you are lost to your own way of doing things that will lead straight to your demise. When you arrive, the tombstone will read, "Here lies one worse than a fool, he knew it all except how to dig himself out of this hole!" The litany test to the road of self-discovery is to ask at least three people whom you trust if you are open and willing to listen to the constructive criticism of others. Heed their honest response and humbly make the needed adjustments required to start digging yourself out of the hole of ego and conceit.

Reference:

John 9:41; Proverbs 3:7, 26:5

WISDOM TIP 264

The quarrels of others are none of your business.

"You grab a mad dog by the ears when you butt into a quarrel that's none of your business."
PROVERBS 26:17 (THE MESSAGE)

"Interfering in someone else's argument is as foolish as yanking a dog's ears."
PROVERBS 26:17 (NLT)

If you walk up to a dog and yank him by the ears, you are sure to feel the wrath of that dog. Heck, if you yank a cat by the ears, you are inviting a scratch-a-thon. That's the same effect created by getting in the middle of someone else's mess! If Aaron and Aiden have beef with each other, then let them have it unless you are acting as a peacemaker. If Chase and Lexy just had a spat, then their spat does not give cause for your interference. Most of us want to come to the aid of family and friends whom we hold near and dear, but when you come with wrath that will add greater flames to the burning fire instead of in the spirit of mediation and peace, when 5–0 rolls up, be prepared with your bail money. Parents, hear me out, when your little princess has a disagreement with my little princess, please let it stay between the little princesses. I've learned that the two little princesses will draw up a peace treaty and not tell either of us while we are still acting out the War of the Roses in real time. As long as it depends on you, stay clear of the quarreling dog's ears. Family, let husbands and wives handle their own disputes unless the dispute has become abusive. Allow siblings to work out disagreements amongst each other. Your dearly beloved politicians know how to use the law of the land to defend themselves, they don't need you going from fist to cuffs at the family Thanksgiving gathering. I know the quarreling dog's ears look perky and inviting as they stand at attention, but trust me when I advise you to walk away while you still have two good hands and your reputation intact. Meddling in the disagreements of others will write a check that you may not be prepared to cash.

Reference:

Proverbs 3:30

WISDOM TIP 265

Contention is like a fire that is blown up by the detonation of gossip.

"Fire goes out without wood, and quarrels disappear when gossip stops."

PROVERBS 26:20 (NLT)

When I was a kid, we would call it "instigating" when someone would come back and tell you "such and such was talking about you" in a very conniving manner, trying to get something started. Proverbs refers to this person as a talebearer. They come every day about the same time to add the fuel of gossip as they relay the latest insults rallied against you, your mama, and your crew. I can't even begin to count the number of friendships I have seen broken up this way, and the number of physical fights that erupted after weeks of this type of slow burning flame. To the instigator, get some business of your own so you don't have time to focus on others. To the hearer, don't listen to the instigating gossiper who secretly wants to see your friendship destroyed. When the gossip ceases, so does the strife. When you ignore the instigators, they will get out of your ear and the road to peace can begin, even if that road does not include the person you were at odds with.

Reference:

Proverbs 16:28, 22:10

WISDOM TIP 266

Jaded kisses attempt to hide true intentions.

"Smooth words may hide a wicked heart, just as a pretty glaze covers a clay pot."

PROVERBS 26:23 (NLT)

I have one word for you on this one—Judas. Yes honey, the same Judas who betrayed Jesus with a jaded kiss. In Middle Eastern culture, it is very common to greet with a kiss. For this reason,

Judas chose the one thing that represented brotherly love to be the source of his betrayal. When words are dripping with affection and kisses are glowing with love, but the heart is filled with envy and hatred, then jaded kisses and words of friendship are only masking the evil intents that lurk within. Like Jesus, you need the discernment of wisdom to recognize who is kissing you and why. All that flattery just may be covering an evil intent. All those kisses may be hiding the promise she made to herself to never let another man get over on her. He may just be seeking payback for the last relationship he was in and you just happened to be the first unsuspecting prey to walk his way. How about this one—someone in your inner circle has had haterism written all over their face for years now and only sticks around to flatter you in person while secretly wishing for your demise. You better learn how to discern who the Judas amongst you may be, so the kiss will not bite when it is revealed. As Jesus has already warned, "You will be like sheep amongst the wolves so be as shrewd (wise) as a snake, but innocent as a dove" (Matthew 10:16, author's paraphrase); so you recognize yet cautiously handle the devious wolves of the world. Two cannot play this game without both getting burned, so guard your heart while staying alert to cunning devices.

Reference:

Matthew 23:27, Luke 11:39, Proverbs 26:25

WISDOM TIP 267

The snake in the grass yesterday is the same snake in the grass today.

> "Your enemy shakes hands and greets you like an old friend, all the while conniving against you. When he speaks warmly to you, don't believe him for a minute; he's just waiting for the chance to rip you off. No matter how cunningly he conceals his malice, eventually his evil will be exposed in public."
>
> Proverbs 26:24–26 (THE MESSAGE)

When someone shows you who they are, believe them the first time. For instance, Miss Thang could not stand the ground you walked on last week. What changed this week? You may be apt to believe that your good looks and charming personality coupled with Christ-like forgiveness will cause anyone to pursue a meaningful friendship with you. Unfortunately, this fallen world in which we live comes with a lot of fallen souls who will not like you for something as simple as the color of your hair, or even hate you for something as divine as the color of your skin. This wisdom tip is a warning against gullibility and naïveté of the world in which you currently live. Enemies will lurk, some will even lurk in the midst of your camp, disguised as a fan, a supportive coworker, or a newly converted friend. This is not a call to stoop to their level, but to readily recognize them for what they really represent. Hatred can be covered by deceit to the unsuspecting and cloaked in sugarcoated promises of peace and prosperity. It may even come in the form of a once-in-a-lifetime opportunity, a romantic relationship, a signing bonus, or a smooth-talking college recruiter. Be careful and consider all the ins and outs. That recording contract may be the enemy shaking hands with you and greeting you like an old friend only to reveal its financial and moral malice at the least opportune time. Some relationships and opportunities have attachments and loopholes that cunningly conceal malice. Wisely discern the purposes, schemes, and designs of cunning devices that secretly await the opportunity to divulge their true colors.

Reference:

Psalm 41:6, 28:3; Proverbs 10:18 and 9, 23:7, 26:23; Luke 8:17; Matthew 23:28

WISDOM TIP 268

Do not plot against others lest you injure yourself.

"If you set a trap for others, you will get caught in it yourself. If you roll a boulder down on others, it will crush you instead."

Proverbs 26:27 (NLT)

"Malice backfires; spite boomerangs."
Proverbs 26:27 (THE MESSAGE)

When you dig a grave for someone else, first dig one for yourself.
When you point the finger at me, there are four pointing back at you.
Malice backfires; spite boomerangs.

Plotting, scheming, and blaming will only cause the harm you meant for others to come upon you instead. Even if at first your scheme appears to be successful, it will eventually come to light publicly or play out in your life privately with public repercussions. For instance, you may not be completely exposed in the public, but your private and inward guilt may show up in other self-destructive behaviors such as anger, irritability, and restlessness to name a few. The times in which we live, we have seen presidents, senators, priests, principals, police officers, preachers, and the soccer mom exposed publicly because of malicious plans and plots that backfired and exposed their devious intentions. Before you plan your own form of retribution, ask yourself, "If this were exposed, how would my closest relatives and friends feel about this?" Better yet, "How would I feel if someone attempted to carry this plot out on one of my closest relatives or friends?" Clear your heart of malice and your intentions of harm will melt away.

Reference:

Psalm 57:6, 7:15, 9:15; Ecclesiastes 10:8

WISDOM TIP 269

Seize the day for tomorrow is not promised.

"Don't brashly announce what you're going to do tomorrow; you don't know the first thing about tomorrow."

PROVERBS 27:1 (THE MESSAGE)

Take heed of any arrogance you have for future plans that have not been vetted by the One who knows the end from the beginning. Likewise, when making plans for tomorrow and all the tomorrows yet to come, ask God for instructions and leave space in your plans for flexibility in accordance with His needs and His will. When I was active duty in the Air Force, there was a saying called "Air Force needs," meaning the Air Force had the right to relocate you based on their need for your AFSC (Air Force Specialty Code) at a certain location. The Air Force also had a right to send you back to school in order to retrain you in a certain career field if "Air Force needs" dictated a shortage in one career field and an overflux in your current career field. Why should God Almighty receive anything short of this same level of commitment and flexibility? Listen to the guidance of the voice of wisdom today and make the call, take your wife out to that fine restaurant, finish that project, take the trip, write the letter, make the correction, stop the habit that's killing you slowly, make amends. Most importantly, seek God for your tomorrows so His blessing can cause your plans to flourish.

Reference:

James 4:14, 1 Kings 20:11

WISDOM TIP 270

Sit down and be humble!

"Don't call attention to yourself; let others do that for you."
PROVERBS 27:2 (THE MESSAGE)

"Let someone else praise you, and not your own mouth; an outsider, and not your own lips."

PROVERBS 27:2 (NIV)

The avoidance of self-praise is not the same as the development of confidence. Arrogance and confidence are vastly different concepts that are adorned in vastly different aromas. An old English saying announces, "He who praises himself is a debtor to others." You owe others the debt of having to stand the stench of your arrogance while in their presence. Arrogance boasts of conceit, superiority, pride, and egotism. Learn to recognize that stench, so you can detect it in yourself. On the other hand, confidence exudes poise, assurance, and safety. Less talk about who you are and what you can do and more action of displaying the poise, assurance, and safety of who you are and what you can do on behalf of others. The latter guarantees that your praise will be multiplied in the mouths of others.

Reference:
2 Corinthians 10:12, 10:18; Proverbs 25:27

WISDOM TIP 271

Jealousy is not love nor does love abide in jealousy.

"Anger is cruel, and wrath is like a flood, but jealousy is even more dangerous."

PROVERBS 27:4 (NLT)

"We're blasted by anger and swamped by rage, but who can survive jealousy?"

PROVERBS 27:4 (THE MESSAGE)

Jealousy submits to nothing, but total control. When you become angry, your anger will eventually subside. When you act upon your anger in what the Bible terms as "wrath," you will have some damaging consequences. Oh, but jealousy is not so easily overcome! Jealousy doesn't have a sudden outburst of anger or the wrath that follows. Jealousy sits and simmers, it feeds upon itself until it demands total control or total destruction of the object of its affection. I use the word affection loosely because so many have fallen to the grips of jealousy by confusing it with affection and love. If only I had a dollar for every time I heard a woman say, "He acts that way because he loves me so much." Wrong, he acts that way because you are the object of his jealousy and the only way his jealousy will be subsided is through complete control of you or total destruction of you. Song of Solomon 8:6 (KJV) reads, "Love is strong as death; jealousy is cruel as the grave." If you are still not convinced that jealousy is cruel as the grave, recall the murderous jealousy of Cain against his brother, Abel; the jealousy of Joseph's brothers that sold him into slavery; and the jealousy of the religious leaders that caused them to conspire to set a trap against Jesus. These are all biblical accounts of acts driven by jealousy, but you need only to scroll the internet, watch the evening news, or ask a family member to get a current example of how jealousy has ruined lives and sent others to an early grave. Take heed if you are the one given to jealousy or if you are the object of someone's jealous passion. Jealousy does not blaze a trail and suddenly vanish, it lives and breeds and feeds itself hourly with fresh twisted fantasies. Jealousy will act and react at any moment, often when least expected, sacrificing without mercy its victim. I plead with you to not be fooled and mistakenly confuse jealousy with love or affection. 1 Corinthians 13:4–7 gives the greatest account of what love looks like, what it feels like, and how it is displayed in its purest form.

"Love is kind and patient, never jealous, boastful, proud, or rude. Love isn't selfish or quick tempered. It doesn't keep a record of wrongs that others do. Love rejoices in the truth, but not in evil. Love is always supportive, loyal, hopeful, and trusting."

1 CORINTHIANS 13:4–7 (CEV)

Reference:

Proverbs 6:34; Job 5:2; Acts 7:9, 17:5; James 3:14–16

WISDOM TIP 272

An open rebuke is better than hidden love!

"An open rebuke is better than hidden love! Wounds from a sincere friend are better than many kisses from an enemy."

Proverbs 27:5–6 (NLT)

"A truly good friend will openly correct you. You can trust a friend who corrects you, but kisses from an enemy are nothing but lies."

Proverbs 27:5–6 (CEV)

Everyone needs at least one person in their life who will tell them the truth whether they like it or not. A person who will call right "right" and wrong "wrong" no matter what side of the line you may currently stand on. I've come to value these relationships in my life. Ephesians 4:15 urges us to "speak the truth in love." An open rebuke does not mean that your friend will put you on blast in the middle of the courtyard for all to see and hear. An open rebuke means they have the boldness and freedom to pull you aside and openly communicate just how wrong you are, speaking the truth in love. Cicero wrote, "When a man's ears are shut against the truth, so that he cannot hear the truth from a friend, the welfare of such a one is hopeless." Now if you have an entourage of what I call "yes men" surrounding you, kissing your gluteus maximus with all the good things that you want to hear about yourself right, wrong, or indifferent, then you are surrounded by enemies. Ask yourself, why are they afraid to tell me the truth? Why do they agree with everything I say and do? A note to those who have ears to hear and a heart to receive this hard truth: A real and faithful friend will not praise everything you say or do, on the contrary, they will celebrate you when you are right and they will rebuke you when you are wrong. If you don't have this type of friendships in your camp then I recommend a camp evaluation. This is for the grown and mature. It's tight, but it's completely right.

Reference:

Proverbs 28:23, Matthew 18:15, Psalm 141:5, Proverbs 20:30, Revelation 3:19, Job 5:17–18

WISDOM TIP 273

Comfort is often the enemy of greatness.

"A person who is full refuses honey, but even bitter food tastes sweet to the hungry."
PROVERBS 27:7 (NLT)

One of the worst enemies to productivity and success is comfort. A person who is full is so comfortable that he sits on the couch with the remote in hand and prepares himself for a nap. His refusal of honey is not based on necessity, but on comfort. He is too comfortable to get up and get the honey or to even recognize that at some point in the near future, he may need the honey to sweeten some tea, ward off seasonal allergies, or attract busy bee employees. Whatever the case may be, he is no longer hungry for improvement, advancement, or what some have termed "the come up"! An eager person filled with hunger for improvement and advancement will take something as bitter as vinegar, mix it with the sweet sauce of hard work, and an unrelenting persistent drive until the vinegar has evaporated, leaving room for the honey that is sure to follow. Now I want you to recall when you first began your career, first got married, first committed your life to Jesus, or first had the desire to learn something. Recall that hunger and thirst to be "on point," to be good, to strive to be the best and to give it your all. Stay hungry in the pursuit of your dreams. Stay hungry for knowledge. Stay hungry in your marriage. Stay hungry in your desire for the things of God. Stay hungry in your pursuit of the wisdom to live your daily life honorably. Stay hungry so the sweetness of the honey that drips from the hand of God in the form of love, provision, and advancement will never lose its sweetness.

WISDOM TIP 274

There is safety in your set place.

"People who won't settle down, wandering hither and yon, are like restless birds, flitting to and fro."

PROVERBS 27:8 (THE MESSAGE)

"As a bird wandering from her nest, so is a man wandering from his place."

PROVERBS 27:8 (YLT)

When I consider the word wander, I think of a person walking aimlessly without a sense of direction or purpose. However, wandering here takes my idea to a different level. Here, a person, man or woman, who wanders from his place does so at great cost. The wanderer is lured away by some external reason or internal battle exposing his life to undo discomfort and danger that would not otherwise happen if he had remained at home in the safe place God has provided for him. Think of it this way, a mother bird leaves the nest with a clear sense of purpose—to locate food or other materials for the nest and her children. However, every now and then while the mother is away, a baby bird will stray from the nest before she is properly prepared. The baby left before her time and exposed herself to great danger. The danger of predators or simply the danger of being ill-prepared to deal with the realities of the world outside of the nest. She lacks feathers to protect her fragile body from the elements of weather and fully developed wings to assist with fleeing to safety when predators appear. We can learn so much from this proverb. First, there is safety in the place where God has planted you. Husbands, there is safety in your home. Wives, there is safety in your home. Children, there is safety in your home. Do not allow external forces or internal lusts to lure you away from the safety and provision God has provided for your family. I do understand that not every person can affirm this as their reality, but for those who have it, do not take this nest of safety for granted and do not leave before your time. Secondly, you must be quick to recognize the luring enticement of external or internal forces that will attempt to steer you away from you set place. This can be true of a job that God has blessed you with, a college scholarship, a church home, a friendship, or a marriage covenant. Be on guard against anything or anyone that attempts to persuade you that the grass is greener somewhere else when God is saying, "Stay, bloom where you are planted, and enjoy the safety net of this safe environment I've given you." Lastly, if you make the decision to step outside of the safety net of your set place, are you prepared and equipped to deal with the dangers and predators that await you on the other side? Not to mention the consequences of leaving before your time. Learn to abide in the safety of your set place. When or if the time comes for you to move on, remember that where God guides, He will also provide safety and provision.

Reference:

Job 39:14–16, Isaiah 16:2, Proverbs 21:16, 1 Corinthians 7:20

WISDOM TIP 275

The sweet aroma of a good friend will add a distinctive fragrance to your life.

> "Perfume and incense bring joy to the heart, and the pleasantness of a friend springs from their heartfelt advice."
>
> Proverbs 27:9 (NIV)

Have you ever walked passed someone who smelled so good you wanted to double back to enjoy the fragrance? I know I'm not the only one who will admit to doing this at least once. There is something about a nice aroma that brings joy. When you walk into a home and smell something sweet baking, you immediately get happy. For a Texas girl with Louisiana roots, when I walk into a home and smell Gumbo or fish frying, it brings a rush of fond memories that make me leap with joy on the inside, not to mention my taste buds begin to do the happy dance. Moving on to how this relates to a friend who provides heartfelt advice. When a friend provides you with heartfelt loving and wise advice, your ears perk with joy as does your heart because you are able to recognize both the truth of their words and the love behind the words they have spoken to you. Sweet and loving words coming from someone who gives you hearty and wise counsel will gladden your heart, provide direction, and make you grateful to have such a friend in your life. You will want to double back and enjoy the fragrance of the presence of a friend like this. Just as the fragrance of perfume or your favorite food delights your senses and brings joy, so does a good friend.

Reference:

Proverbs 7:16, 21:17; Daniel 2:46

WISDOM TIP 276

Caution is a gift, prompting you to exit stage right before the curtain falls.

> "A prudent person foresees danger and takes precautions. The simpleton goes blindly on and suffers the consequences."
>
> PROVERBS 27:12 (NLT)

> "A prudent person sees trouble coming and ducks; a simpleton walks in blindly and is clobbered."
>
> PROVERBS 27:12 (THE MESSAGE)

During the summer my kids and I will venture to our neighborhood pool to enjoy some fun in the sun. Well, they enjoy the pool while I relax under the umbrella in a pool chair drowning out the background noise with my favorite '90s tunes. I know what you are thinking, but my kids are teens and preteens, excellent swimmers, and still seem to find something to argue about even in the pool, so I take the time to zone out and transport myself back to the times when things were simple. Don't judge, I highly recommend Pandora therapy for all mothers and fathers especially during the summer months. How about that for a prudent person who foresees trouble and takes precautions? Ha! Back to the subject matter at hand—when you see a bad situation twirling up like a tornado tunnel, take it as a warning alert and duck, run, turn around, and seek shelter. Only a simpleminded fool will see trouble coming and head toward the trouble, ignoring all warning alerts and signs. Caution is an emotion that is often not addressed in our society or validated. When you sense caution, follow that God-given internal prompting and do something different. Today, you may be cautious about going on a date with a certain person, so call and cancel. You may be cautious about a certain business deal, back out of it. You may simply be cautious because you hear thunder while you are at the pool. Since thunder and lightning travel in packs, get out of the pool ahead of time and go home. Never discount your internal cautious meter that's guiding you to stop, leave, get out the car, change jobs, find new friends, or leave the party. Whatever the case may be, allow wisdom to guide you to safety.

Reference:

Proverbs 22:3

WISDOM TIP 277

When iron collides with iron, sparks begin to fly!

"As iron sharpens iron, so one person sharpens another."
Proverbs 27:17 (NIV)

"Iron sharpens iron; so a man sharpens the countenance of his friend [to show rage or worthy purpose]."

Proverbs 27:17 (AMPC)

Who you are connected with matters. Show me your friends and I will show you your future. The people you choose to allow into your inner circle will influence your character, sharpen you mentally, influence your conduct, and brighten your demeanor. Bottom line, good friendships will add to your life and sharpen you spiritually, mentally, physically, and emotionally in preparation for a worthy purpose. If you don't see this in your inner circle, then you are not being sharpened and should seek precautions now to find a new inner circle that will pull the best out of you as you, in turn, pull the best out of them. When iron collides with iron, sparks begin to fly. When you combine your wisdom with the wisdom of friends, you have a meeting of the minds that turns into the meeting of the hearts that turns into a meeting of the spirit. It's this final stage—a meeting of the spirit—that ignites purpose, momentum, and accountability that is not found outside of bonding with others who are of the same mind and spirit, yet uniquely gifted and driven for a worthy purpose. I love the true story of three young African American boys who made a pact to get out of their crime-ridden, impoverished neighborhood in New Jersey. They made a pact to help keep each other in school, to graduate, and to stay out of trouble on their journey to and through medical school. They sharpened the worthy purpose of one another the day they made the pact, and during the years when they had to be accountable to one another to fulfill that pact. They had to encourage one another along the way, help one another with their studies, and probably talk some sense into one another a time or two when they noticed one heading the wrong way. Today Dr. Rameck Hunt, Dr. Sampson Davis, and Dr. George Jenkins are medical doctors and dentist because of the pact they made in high school to sharpen one another toward their worthy purpose.

Reference:

Hebrews 10:24, 1 Samuel 13:21

WISDOM TIP 278

You can never lose with a work ethic that is honorable and diligent.

> "As workers who tend a fig tree are allowed to eat the fruit, so workers who protect their employer's interests will be rewarded."
>
> Proverbs 27:18 (NLT)

> "If you care for your orchard, you'll enjoy its fruit; if you honor your boss, you'll be honored."
>
> Proverbs 27:18 (THE MESSAGE)

Calling all employees, calling all employees! This right here is the way to success. The employee who carefully watches over, tends, and cultivates the job, position, and organization that she is currently employed with will in time enjoy the fruit of her labor. Do not hang out with the buzzards who complain, show up late, and halfway work when they get there. Diligence, thoughtfulness, and stewardship over the job in which you are paid to accomplish will reward you one day. You better believe that producers and those who have been diligent in their employment efforts will be rewarded even with nothing more than the skill set to find another job or a better job when the time comes. Not to mention, if you really believe the verse that says, "We should work as unto the Lord," then you know God will not forget your diligent labor. Your service will be honored and will never go to waste; one way or another, you will be recognized. Ask Joseph how he went from prison to slavery to the palace as second in command, answering to no one but Pharaoh himself, pinky ring and all! You know you got it going on if you have the power of the pinky ring working in your favor. Not only will your employer become acquainted with the excellence of your work, but the clients of your employer and oftentimes competing organizations. You can never lose with a work ethic that is honorable and diligent.

Reference:

Luke 12:42; 1 Corinthians 3:8, 9:7; 2 Timothy 2:6; Colossians 3:22; 1 Peter 2:18, 21; Matthew 25:21–22; 1 Samuel 2:30

WISDOM TIP 279

What you reflect from your heart is what you attract into your life.

"As water reflects the face, so one's life reflects the heart."
PROVERBS 27:19 (NIV)

"Just as water mirrors your face, so your face mirrors your heart."
PROVERBS 27:19 (THE MESSAGE)

Water mirrors your face; your face mirrors your heart; your heart mirrors your life; your life mirrors what and who you attract based on the mirror of your heart; your attractions mirror the environment and circumstances you currently see in your life. That was a mouthful. Everything in life mirrors what is going on inside your heart. Just as in the physical body or the world of science, the heart is the center of all other systems; in the spiritual sense, your heart houses the reality of who you are, your mind, intellect, imagination, and will. That's why Proverbs 4:23 tells us to "guard your heart with all diligence," for out of your heart flows your life, your very existence. Let's back up and deal with reflections for a moment. What you reflect from your heart is what you attract into your life. What is in you will attract that same characteristic in others. Money attracts more money. Lust attracts more lust. Grace attracts more grace. Love attracts more love. Fill in the blank and you will have mastered the Law of Attraction. What is reflected from your heart will find harmony in the similar disposition found in others. If you do not like what or who you see around you, then go back and do a heart test to determine how it was attracted to your life. That wisdom tip alone is worth the price of this book. What is in your heart influences your actions and the attractions that will create more of what you currently see. How can you overcome this water cycle of heart-life reflections? I'm glad you asked. The most powerful force known to man is the Gospel of Jesus Christ, the good news, the reflection shaper. The gospel is a glass, a mirror that will help you rightly identify where your heart stands. That's what this book of wisdom is all about. Identifying how your life lines up with the principles found in the Word of God versus the ever-changing morals of society. Time to dive into the water of truth so you can identify how to correctly reflect the image of greatness that lives inside of you, begging to be released.

Reference:

James 1:22–25, Psalm 33:15, Mark 7:21

WISDOM TIP 280

Gratification grows as it is fed.

"Just as Death and Destruction are never satisfied, so human desire is never satisfied."
PROVERBS 27:20 (NLT)

What you desire is never satisfied because when that desire is gratified, it naturally desires more gratification. I've been told that the drug addict becomes addicted to the first high, and every high afterwards is an attempt to gratify what they first felt. Sex, alcohol, shopping, porn, eating, power, attention, money, whatever your personal vice may be, it will always require more and more in order to be gratified. Let's flip that to the positive. Knowledge yearns for more knowledge, wisdom for more wisdom, love for more love. A giver wants to be able to give more, just like a taker will create ways to take as much as he can from anyone who is willing to comply. This wisdom principle is important because it allows you to identify desires that are consuming your life. I'm not an expert on how to overcome each and every human desire known to man, but I do know someone who is. If you find that you have something in your life that continues to require more and more of you in order to be satisfied, then it's time to name it, attempt to locate the source of the desire, and take it to Jesus for a divine elimination plan. Some of you may need professional assistance, some of you may need personal accountability, and others may simply require an encounter with God that will cause your desires to become agreeable with His desires, so that you develop an unquenchable desire to satisfy God and God alone.

Reference:

1 John 2:16; Proverbs 30:15; Ecclesiastes 1:8, 2:10–11, 4:8, 5:10–11; Jeremiah 22:17; 1 Corinthians 2:9; Psalm 36:8–9

WISDOM TIP 281

Vain men seek praise, weak men are inflated by praise, and wise men disregard the praise that comes from public opinion.

"The purity of silver and gold is tested by putting them in the fire; The purity of human hearts is tested by giving them a little fame."

PROVERBS 27:21 (THE MESSAGE)

"Fire tests the purity of silver and gold, but a person is tested by being praised."

PROVERBS 27:21 (NLT)

Popularity and praises garnered by the regards of public opinion will test the character of a person like fire tests the purity of gold and silver. How a person deals with the praise that comes from public opinion shows a great deal of who they are. Thus, as it has been explained, vain men seek praise, weak men are inflated by praise, and wise men disregard the praise that comes from public opinion. While precious metals are refined when placed in fire, people tend to show their "true colors" when placed in the fire of public opinion and popularity. This can be seen when the growing consensus of public regard is that you are the greatest thing since sliced bread, as well as when public opinion begins to sway and you are suddenly faced with the decision to stand your ground or go with the sway of the public for the sake of remaining in their good graces. Students face this dilemma, parents, church members, and celebrities alike. No one escapes this trial by fire no matter how great or how small the platform. The litany test comes in the face of making the right decision and doing the right thing when the overwhelming majority call right "wrong" and wrong "right." Will you befriend the nerdy kid who's being bullied? Will you join in the gossip session about the mom who is going through a divorce and shun her to remain a part of the Thursday playgroup? Will you take the steroids to keep that number one running back position because everyone else is doing it to remain competitive? Will you compromise your integrity and fudge the numbers in order to keep your company's largest client happy? Will you change your position on abortion to be elected to public office? All of these are simply examples of how people, Christians even, sell out to popularity on a daily basis. We know what is right in our hearts, but when put to the test under the fire of public opinion, oftentimes we have a tendency to forget that our ultimate audience of One has the highest approval rating in the galaxy. Do not allow the temporary comforts of being liked, popular, praised, or famous to cause you to lose sight of doing and/or saying what you know to be right before God in your heart. If you change for people today, you will have to change for them again tomorrow. Soon, you will be a chameleon who changes faces with every wind of public opinion until you no longer recognize yourself. Stay true to you and stay true to the God in you!

Reference:

Proverbs 17:3, 25:4; Psalm 12:6, 66:10; Malachi 3:3

WISDOM TIP 282

A guilty conscience will be written all over your demeanor.

> "The wicked are edgy with guilt, ready to run off even when no one's after them; Honest people are relaxed and confident, bold as lions."
>
> Proverbs 28:1 (THE MESSAGE)

There is an edginess brought on by guilt and a jumpiness that occurs when you believe you may be found out at any moment. An uneasy conscience will not allow you to rest during the day and will make you paranoid during the night hours. It has been said that a guilty conscience betrays while no one finds fault, and condemns while no one accuses. On the contrary, honesty allows you to breathe deeply with a sigh of relief even when honesty comes with consequences. Honesty leaves you with a clear conscience, nothing to confess, and a pep in your step because you have the internal joy of knowing that you did the right thing even if it would have been easier to do wrong. When I was a teenager, we had a term called "riding dirty." That meant you were operating a vehicle without a driver's license, car insurance, proper registration, or some other legality that could get you into big trouble if you were stopped by the police. Before I received my driver's license, I would flinch every time I heard a police siren while I was driving. That's what a guilty conscience will do. Some of you are still flinching, so go get all your papers right so you can ride your "whip" in peace. Now as a middle-aged, minivan-driving suburbanite, I have no fear of police sirens. I've been licensed in several states, had the same auto insurance coverage for about twenty years, vehicles are registered in accordance with state law, and have absolutely no other legalities to be concerned about. When I see a police officer, I wave and pray for their protection and their ability to make righteous decisions with those they encounter. That's an example of the righteous being relaxed, confident, and as bold as a lion. While this is a mild example, it portrays the difference doing things the right way will make in your life. Stop operating that daycare in your home without a license, get your car registered in your own name and out of your nephew's name. You better not claim anyone else's kids on your taxes this year! Study for your exam so you don't have to ask your friend who took the test in first hour to screenshot the test and send it to you. All of these contribute to the uneasy jumpiness that comes with doing wrong. Relaxed, confident, and bold look so much better on you.

Reference:

Psalm 112:7, Proverbs 14:26, Psalm 27:1

WISDOM TIP 283

Pray for your nation and its leaders.

> "When the country is in chaos, everybody has a plan to fix it—But it takes a leader of real understanding to straighten things out."
>
> PROVERBS 28:2 (THE MESSAGE)

> "When there is moral rot within a nation, its government topples easily. But wise and knowledgeable leaders bring stability."
>
> PROVERBS 28:2 (NLT)

If you know how to pray, then why are you not praying for the chaos you see in this nation? We are living in a day where moral rot is in full effect from the highest office in the land to the corruption in our local counties. This proverb is a wisdom principle that must be adhered to, because your government plays a large part in the freedoms you enjoy in your daily life as a citizen. I mentioned praying for our nation, government, and elected officials. However, we cannot stop with a prayer, we must also vote for those who have a proven track record of integrity and substance that aligns with godly wisdom. In fact, some of you may actually need to step up and submit a bid for office because you have what it takes to be a wise, knowledgeable, and stable leader. We cannot sit idly by with the mindset that someone else will come along and straighten out the mess our government may find itself in. We must be actively engaged in prayer, voting, volunteering, donating, and in some cases, public service. Otherwise, you have no say in your government affairs, and by default, contribute to the chaos that will eventually show up on your doorstep.

WISDOM TIP 284

A poor man walking in truth is better than a rich liar.

"Better to be poor and honest than to be dishonest and rich."
PROVERBS 28:6 (NLT)

You cannot serve both God and money! However, money can be an excellent servant when you have a godly purpose for its usage and the wisdom to carry it out. The phrase "it is better to be poor and honest" does not mean you have to be poor to be honest, or that every rich person is dishonest. When faced with the choice of financial gain based on some dishonest act, it is better to take the big "L" (lose) than to live with the money that comes from dishonest gain. Remember, not all money is good money. Allow godly wisdom to guide your life and your choices for provision. Many people prefer to separate God from their money, but the truth is He wants to guide you in the financial arena so you can gain something far beyond a fat bank account. Don't believe the hype; a mind improvised by guilt leaves you in poverty even while you rest in luxuries.

Reference:
Proverbs 19:1, 16:8; James 1:8; Ecclesiastes 2:12

WISDOM TIP 285

Consider your family's reputation before you act; your actions have the potential to add to the family name or detract from it.

"Practice God's law—get a reputation for wisdom; hang out with a loose crowd—embarrass your family."

PROVERBS 28:7 (THE MESSAGE)

"Young people who obey the law are wise; those with wild friends bring shame to their parents."

Proverbs 28:7 (NLT)

Let's deal with the aspect of embarrassing your family and bringing shame on your parents as a result of making the choice to hang with the wrong crowd. When I was a teenager, it was embarrassing for a parent to come to school for any reason whatsoever. I had pretty cool parents, they kept themselves in shape and wore the latest fashion so it was not their outer appearance that created the embarrassment; it was their actions that could make me squirm and want to sink into oblivion. If you know that feeling, then you understand the concept of this proverb. Your actions can either make your parents want to squirm and sink into the oblivion of disgust, or your actions can cause them to beam with pride and gratitude. Young people, the easiest way to get your parents off your back and cause them to consider and possibly agree with almost anything you desire is to be a wise and compliant child. If your parents are not wasting time or money dealing with your foolish choices, they will have just that much more time and money to contribute to your law-abiding activities. Skipping school may not land you a spot in the county jail, but it is breaking the law, and guess who gets the call at work when you are caught? Ding-dong ditching your neighbor's house at midnight may not be technically illegal, but guess who has to apologize on your behalf and deal with the whispers in the neighborhood every time something suspicious occurs? You decided to sneak out the house to attend a party, the party was raided by the police who discovered illegal drugs and underage drinking, so everybody was escorted into the paddy wagon and taken to jail. Guess who just spent their time and money to get your backside out of the jail cell? Think about your actions and how they will reflect back on your family's reputation.

Reference:

Proverbs 29:3, 3:1, 19:26, 23:19–22, 6:10, 10:5; Ephesians 6:1; Deuteronomy 4:6

WISDOM TIP 286

Don't get caught up in a system that is designed to keep you financially dependent; check your interest rates, pay off the higher interest accounts first, and free yourself from the clutches of debt.

"Whoever increases wealth by taking interest or profit from the poor amasses it for another, who will be kind to the poor."

PROVERBS 28:8 (NIV)

"Get as rich as you want through cheating and extortion, but eventually some friend of the poor is going to give it all back to them."

PROVERBS 28:8 (THE MESSAGE)

Payday loan organizations collect anywhere from 200%–300% interest on each loan transaction. This, my friend, is an example of modern-day extortion by way of interest. While it takes two to rumble in the payday loan exchange, most people who frequent the establishments are either poor in finances, credit, or knowledge of how to obtain a loan directly through a bank. Either way, the poor are getting poorer and those who have are getting 200%–300% richer with each transaction. The moral of this lesson is threefold. First, exercise wisdom in the conditions by which you receive a loan. Don't allow a system that is designed to keep you indebted to their system to trap you. Get knowledge on other organizations, including nonprofits, that will loan money at a lower interest rate or even with no interest. Secondly, be leary of businesses that take advantage of the poor and vulnerable. Be a part of the solution by helping to educate and enlighten your friends and family members. Employ the "each one, teach one" philosophy in order to do your part toward eliminating the vicious cycle created by a lack of knowledge and poor financial choices. Further, if you are a business owner who charges exorbitant interest rates, take heed of your business practices and the latter part of this verse if you plan to have long-term success. Finally, some of you reading this right now have ideas of how to be a financial friend to the poor. Take a step of faith, write that business plan, open a nonprofit, do what God has placed on your heart to be of assistance to people who are being cheated and extorted. Allow wisdom to be your guide and take action.

Reference:

Exodus 22:25; Leviticus 25:36, Job 27:27; Proverbs 13:22, 14:31; Ezekiel 18:8, 13, 17

WISDOM TIP 287

If you are bad enough to do it, own up to it!

"You can't whitewash your sins and get by with it; you find mercy by admitting and leaving them."

PROVERBS 28:13 (THE MESSAGE)

"He who conceals his transgressions will not prosper, but he who confesses and forsakes them will find compassion."

PROVERBS 28:13 (NASB)

I'm a mother of three distinctively different personalities. All three have done something wrong and made attempts to cover it up in some fashion. It's funny how children learn to lie in an attempt to cover-up when they have done something wrong. As a result, I have repeatedly informed my children of my policy on honesty. It's not what you do wrong that will garner the most punishment, it's lying about what you did wrong that will earn harsher punishment. It is better to openly and honestly confess so that mercy may be extended rather than lie, cover up, and omit truth in an effort to conceal wrongdoing. This truth applies to adults as well. Come clean and you will be respected for your honesty and admittance of guilt. Not to mention the disappointment and betrayal that occurs when those who trusted you are intentionally deceived. Remember Bill Clinton's "I did not have sexual relations with that woman!" It was like a stab in the heart when the evidence was produced to prove otherwise. The public, his cabinet, and his family would have been able to bear it a little better if he had just told the truth, so we could have absorbed the truth and mulled it over. Instead, we had to absorb the lie along with the wrong committed by our leader simultaneously. Grasp this wisdom principle and come clean. Here's a notion—if you will need to lie about it or cover it up in some way, then just don't do it!

Reference:

1 John 1:9, Leviticus 5:5, Psalm 32:3, 5

WISDOM TIP 288

When you do not know the purpose of a thing, you will abuse it.

"Among leaders who lack insight, abuse abounds, but for one who hates corruption, the future is bright."

PROVERBS 28:16 (THE MESSAGE)

Power in the wrong hands results in the cruel extraction of more power from the very people they have been entrusted to serve and protect. Leaders who do not possess the wisdom and prudence necessary to serve their constituents will ultimately abuse them. If you do not know the purpose of your leadership, the purpose of the power entrusted to you, or the purpose of your authority, then you will eventually abuse it and those under it. We see corruption in government, law enforcement, school districts, churches, and even in homes because of corrupt leaders who have allowed their position of power and authority to turn them into monsters. Do not step into a position of leadership lightly. Husbands, parents, public servants, political appointees, pastors, teachers, police officers, entrepreneurs, and industry leaders of all types. You have a great responsibility to serve and protect those who are under your authority. Aspiring leaders, I encourage you to follow the path of those who have fulfilled their duties with integrity and wisdom if you desire longevity.

Reference:

Jeremiah 22:13–19, Proverbs 15:27

WISDOM TIP 289

A murderer will never go "scot free"!

"A murderer haunted by guilt is doomed—there's no helping him."

PROVERBS 28:17 (THE MESSAGE)

"A murderer's tormented conscience will drive him into the grave. Don't protect him!"
PROVERBS 28:17 (NLT)

Murder is a heinous crime that has become a staple on our evening news reports across this country. Murders are committed across racial, socioeconomic, and religious lines. From the quiet kid who grew tired of bullying, to the jealously enraged boyfriend, to the suburban mother who wanted her daughter to secure the top cheerleading spot for the upcoming school year, to the executive who pays a hit man to eliminate his wife in hopes of being free to marry his mistress. These are only the tip of the iceberg of the murderous plots that have been unfolded on *48 hours*, *20/20*, and *Dateline*. The violence in our society has caused us to become slightly desensitized to its effects. No community and no group of people are above experiencing the heinous crime, which is the exact reason why this proverbial warning should be sounded from the mountain top and the valleys below. The whole snitches get stitches mind frame or covering for a loved one will land you in the pit of a tormented and haunted conscience until the day you die. Even if you have enough money to pay off judges, buy the best legal defense money can afford you, or simply pay someone to take the downfall for you, you will never escape the internal judgment that will torment you for the rest of your life. Murder is never the answer nor the escape that the enemy of your soul tries to convince you of. Murder takes the life of the victim as well as the perpetrator's and adversely affects the lives of everyone connected to them. If you've had thoughts of murder or suicide, I plea with you to seek help and professional counseling. You can bounce back from the thought of hurting someone or yourself, but the action will change your life forever.

Reference:

Genesis 4:14, 9:6; Isaiah 14, 19, 38:14; Psalm 28:1; Proverbs 24:11

WISDOM TIP 290

Maintain the dream and the hustle.

"A hard worker has plenty of food, but a person who chases fantasies ends up in poverty."
PROVERBS 28:19 (NLT)

"Work your garden—you'll end up with plenty of food; play and party—you'll end up with an empty plate."
PROVERBS 28:19 (THE MESSAGE)

I once heard someone say, "The dream is free, but the hustle will cost you something." The dream is planted in your heart at absolutely no cost to you, but the hard work required to make that dream a reality will cost you time, effort, social events, sleep, and money. However, it is well worth it because the alternative is an empty plate. That's where we get the term "stay hungry." Stay hungry with the appetite to work your dream, to hustle for the next level, to stay motivated to fill your plate with seed-producing efforts that will roll in harvest for the next season. Those with a dream and no hustle to back the dream are simply daydreaming and chasing fantasies that will keep them empty-handed, empty-minded, and empty-pocketed. Hold on to your dream and back it up with hustle. Take flight!

Reference:

Proverbs 12:11, 20:13, 10:4, 20:4; Psalm 26:4

WISDOM TIP 291

Faithful commitment and persistence are the substances by which a dream is fulfilled.

"Committed and persistent work pays off; get-rich-quick schemes are ripoffs."

Proverbs 28:20 (THE MESSAGE)

"A faithful person will be richly blessed, but one eager to get rich will not go unpunished."

Proverbs 28:20 (NIV)

Now that you have "taken flight" with your dream, you must remain committed and persistent over the long run. After the glimmer of the dream has faded, consistent and committed efforts will eventually pay off. I often hear celebrities say, "I am not an overnight success." When it appears that someone has come on the scene suddenly, I invite you to take a sneak peek into the years of consistent and committed efforts that finally brought about the "big break" that landed them in the spotlight of public recognition. Faithfulness is a big word for commitment that trumps feelings. Your feelings may change; however, commitment will keep you faithful until that book is published, that degree is completed, the grand opening of that business, or the closing date on your new home. Whatever your dream may be, faithful commitment and persistence will cause you to press on toward the prize of a dream fulfilled. Along the way, avoid the schemes that promise the easy route to accomplish your goals. For instance, taking one pill per day that guarantees you will lose twenty pounds in a month, while maintaining improper eating habits and absolutely no physical activity is a scheme and a rip-off. Don't be surprised when at the end of the month, your scale still tips the same weight if not more. How about the website that promises to double your money if you will act as a mail courier on their behalf? This screams scheme and rip-off. The agent who promises meetings with the major leaders of your industry for a hefty upfront cost along with a small print contractual obligation. Do not make haste to fulfill your dreams to the point of pursuing any and every method presented before you that makes promises with hidden repercussions.

Reference:

1 Timothy 6:9; Proverbs 20:21, 23:4, 28:22, 13:11

WISDOM TIP 292

Do me no favors, do me no harm.

"Playing favorites is always a bad thing; you can do great harm in seemingly harmless ways."

Proverbs 28:21 (THE MESSAGE)

"Showing partiality is never good, yet some will do wrong for a mere piece of bread."

Proverbs 28:21 (NLT)

Favoritism that originates as a direct result of a bribe can produce great harm to the recipient. Think in terms of a judge presiding over a highly publicized case who accepts a hefty monetary payoff to rule in favor of a defendant who would otherwise be found guilty as all the evidence is revealed. Politicians can compromise their political positions in favor of powerful lobbyist who make promises of back end kickback payments and future campaign financial backing. Some people will even compromise for sexual favors, guaranteed admissions for their children in certain elite schools and colleges, and others will compromise for favors of far less significance. The point that should be taken is that compromise initiated as a result of a favor or a bribe will do more harm than good.

Reference:

Proverbs 18:5, 24:23; Ezekiel 13:19; Romans 16:18; 2 Peter 2:3

WISDOM TIP 293

Flattery is deceit dressed up in a designer suit, do not be deceived by its looks.

"In the end, people appreciate honest criticism far more than flattery."

PROVERBS 28:23 (NLT)

"In the end, serious reprimand is appreciated far more than bootlicking flattery."

PROVERBS 28:23 (THE MESSAGE)

It is possible to do great harm in a seemingly harmless way. Flattering someone who needs truth will always cause more harm than good. A person who will tell someone about their faults and "check" them when they are headed down the wrong path will be more respected in the end. A person in the middle of foolishness may not initially accept your honest feedback, but trust that your words will ring in their ears long after you have spoken them. When the fog is lifted, the flattery will be seen for the misguided deceit that it is, while the truth spoken in love from a place of affection and concern will prevail. Upon reflection, most will have a greater degree of respect for someone who offers honest criticism and correction than a bootlicking, kiss-up flatterer. Show yourself to be a true friend by speaking truth when it is required instead of a fleeting foe that flatters for the sake of going along just to get along.

WISDOM TIP 294

Honor your parents by handling their possessions honorably.

"Anyone who steals from his father and mother and says, 'What's wrong with that?' is no better than a murderer."

PROVERBS 28:24 (NLT)

If there's one thing I cannot tolerate, it is a thief. This is one of the exceptions to the "what's mine is yours" concept in the parent-child relationship. You can share my DNA, my blood type, a room in my home, and sometimes my clothing, but you do not have free-range access to my possessions. The mindset of a thief is to take something that does not rightfully belong to him. Usually, that "something" has been earned through a great deal of effort on the part of the owner. I view stealing as a violation of my possessions, my time, my efforts, and my trust all in one package. This proverb states that someone who will steal from his own parents is "no better than a murderer." Shut your mouth! How can stealing something be compared to killing someone? In this case, you kill trust, you kill aspects of your relationship with your parents or loved one, you kill the truth, you kill with the deceitfulness attached to the act of stealing. Most of all, you kill the simplest duty of giving honor to the people who are responsible for your debut in the world. Most parents will freely give to their children under the right circumstances and conditions. I do say most because I understand that not all parents are created equal in my ideology of what parenting should look like. Look at it this way, if all your parents did was provide the sperm and egg donation that brought you into this world, then they deserve the honor of not suffering loss due to a theft committed by your hands or masterminded by your planning. Whatever they may have in this world does not automatically make you the beneficiary to dispose of as you see fit, when you see fit. Honor your parents by dealing with their possessions honorably. If you did not work for it, pay taxes on it, or retrieve it by honest means on your own terms, then it does not belong to you so keep your paws off.

Reference:

Proverbs 19:26, Matthew 15:4–6

WISDOM TIP 295

The emptiness of grasping greedily after things gives birth to more emptiness.

"Greed causes fighting; trusting the LORD leads to prosperity."

Proverbs 28:25 (NLT)

"A grasping person stirs up trouble, but trust in God brings a sense of well-being."

Proverbs 28:25 (THE MESSAGE)

Graspers suck the air out of the room. We all have known and experienced a "Greedy Grasper" who dominates the conversation, the platform, the discussion, and any activity they participate in because of their greedy nature to consume every ounce of attention, every word of praise, every opportunity to be had, and every dollar to be made. A "Greedy Grasper" will deplete all your energy as soon as they walk in the room because they suck the life, joy, and peace out of everyone and everything they encounter. The sad part is that all the things they are greedily grasping for will never fulfill their lives because we, humans, were not created to be fulfilled by anything other than the fullness of God. His fullness gives us a sense of well-being and success that a six- or seven-figure salary will never achieve. A Greedy Grasper is so full of himself that he has no room for the fullness of God and therefore continues on the same empty path that produces the same empty feeling day after day. Whereas, the one who trusts in the Lord can also rest in His lavish green pastures of grace and feast on the abundance of His glorious provision that brings an untouchable peace that quietly whispers, "It is well with my soul in any situation I may encounter today." I invite you to step over to the side of God's gracious pastures where grasping turns into giving and greed turns into sharing from a place of fullness.

Reference:

1 Timothy 6:6; Proverbs 11:25, 15:18, 29:22

WISDOM TIP 296

Forget about self-confidence; it's useless. Cultivate God-confidence!

"If you think you know it all, you're a fool for sure; real survivors learn wisdom from others."

Proverbs 28:26 (THE MESSAGE)

"It is foolish to follow your own opinions. Be safe, and follow the teachings of wiser people."

Proverbs 28:26 (GNT)

Blind self-confidence that prevents you from seeing the value in the wise counsel of others is a tripping hazard waiting to happen. You will get tripped up on your pride, arrogance, lack of perspective, and limited experience that all prevent you from considering the "big picture" shown from an eagle's sky view versus your kitchen window vantage point. Your own opinion, when not steeped and marinated in the universal truths that permeate wisdom, will land you in the dumps trying to figure out how to get the stench off your life. Some trouble is completely avoidable if only you had ears to hear, eyes to see, and a teachable heart! "Let him that thinketh he standeth take heed lest he fail" (1 Corinthians 10:12). The Message translation of this same verse reads, "Don't be so naive and self-confident. You're not exempt. You could fall flat on your face as easily as anyone else. Forget about self-confidence; it's useless. Cultivate God-confidence." You cultivate God-confidence by doing things His way. When you operate His way, you have the confidence of His results and His blessings. However, the opposite also holds true. Your way, your results! Jeremiah 9:23–24 offers the best advice on this subject, "This is what the LORD says: 'Let not the wise man boast in his wisdom, nor the strong man in his strength, nor the wealthy man in his riches. But let him who boasts boast in this, that he understands and knows Me, that I am the LORD, who exercises loving devotion, justice and righteousness on the earth—for I delight in these things,' declares the LORD." Self-confidence deceives you into thinking it's all about you and what you bring to the table, while God-confidence says, "It's all about the God in me and the tools He has uniquely gifted and equipped me with, so I'll consult His instruction before making any move I'm considering." Checkmate!

Reference:

Job 28:28, James 1:5, James 3:13–18, Proverbs 22:17–19, Proverbs 3:6–9

WISDOM TIP 297

Soften your head and loosen the crook in your neck in order to open yourself to a new level of growth.

"Whoever stubbornly refuses to accept criticism will suddenly be destroyed beyond recovery."

PROVERBS 29:1 (NLT)

"For people who hate discipline and only get more stubborn, There'll come a day when life tumbles in and they break, but by then it'll be too late to help them."

PROVERBS 29:1 (THE MESSAGE)

A hard head makes a soft behind! Your behind becomes soft from falling on it over and over again. In fact, the harder the head, the softer the behind. Some would like to characterize this type of stubbornness as having a "stiff neck." You have been warned, corrected, instructed, and gently advised, but your neck is so stiff with your own agenda that you refuse to turn it to the right or to the left in order to consider another viewpoint. A telltale sign of being a hardhead, stiff-necked, soft behind fool is if you have absolutely no one in your life at this very moment who speaks truth to you. Your mother does not count! We all need someone outside of our parents, who may tend to be a little biased in our favor, to speak the whole truth and nothing but the truth to us. Not to mention, your mama may not be aware of your exploits last night or that shady business deal you made last week. Your mama definitely has no clue about the emotional affair you are having with that man you connect with on Facebook Messenger every morning. The second pointer of this wisdom tip is that acceptance of criticism can be constructive. Stop viewing criticism as something that is meant to tear you down when its real purpose is to cause you to self-reflect, tweak, and possibly completely revamp the area in which the criticism is concerned. Criticism opens your eyes to other perspectives and vantage points that you may be completely unaware of. Soften your head and loosen the crook in your neck in order to open yourself to a new level of growth that occurs when you welcome constructive criticism and correction.

Reference:

2 Chronicles 36:16, Proverbs 1:24, Jeremiah 17:23

WISDOM TIP 298

Know the difference between a compliment and two-faced flattery.

"To flatter friends is to lay a trap for their feet."
PROVERBS 29:5 (NLT)

"A flattering neighbor is up to no good; he's probably planning to take advantage of you."
PROVERBS 29:5 (THE MESSAGE)

Why is flattery such a big deal in proverbs? Let's take into consideration the characteristics normally associated with flattery: dishonesty, insincerity, deceit, and fabrications of all kinds. Let's also consider that the goal of flattery is normally the advancement of some sort of underhanded agenda only truly known by the flatterer. Not to mention, the effects of long-term flattery causes the subject to think more highly of themselves than they ought to. Flattery will leave you with your head floating in the clouds as if the rest of the ink spots surrounding you, called people, are worthless. Worst of all, flattery will cause a person to be deceived within himself which leads to nothing but TROUBLE with a capital T. Let me break it down for you in everyday terms. The pastor's daughter has been flattered to believe that she can "Whitney Houston" sing all her life in the small town where her father's church is located. Sunday after Sunday for years, she has been allowed to lead songs in the church choir with praise and exaltations heaped upon her after service by all the good parishioners who desire to stay in the pastor's favor. This same girl auditions for her high school's jazz choir, selecting Whitney Houston's "Greatest Love of All" ballad as her audition piece. I smell something that starts with a capital T. Little Miss Songbird was greeted by the truth for the first time in her life. The truth of "You can hold a tune, but you cannot 'sing' like Whitney" crushes her and she flees embarrassed, heartbroken, and angry with everyone who once flattered her into believing that she really had a voice that should be featured on the next *America's Got Talent*. This is an extreme example, but I believe you get the point of the harm that can be caused by flattery. Another form of flattery that occurs all over the world to young women in just about every culture is the flattery that comes from a man whose hidden agenda is to use her body for his pleasure. You will be the most beautiful girl he has ever seen until he is allowed to partake of your forbidden fruits. Afterwards, you become the plain Jane who should be honored that he paid any attention to you whatsoever. Beware of the flattering tongue of someone whose sole desire is to get something from you. Wisdom will allow you to perceive the difference between a compliment and insincere flattery.

Reference:

Psalm 5:9; Proverbs 26:28, 28:23; Job 17:5; Psalm 5:9, 12:2; 1 Thessalonians 2:5

WISDOM TIP 299

The unifying power of love can diffuse hateful agitation.

"Mockers can get a whole town agitated, but the wise will calm anger."

PROVERBS 29:8 (NLT)

"Scoffers set a city aflame, but the wise turn away wrath."

PROVERBS 29:8 (ESV)

"A gang of cynics can upset a whole city; a group of sages can calm everyone down."

PROVERBS 29:8 (THE MESSAGE)

In recent years, we have seen an increase in speeches that are meant to arouse the passions of people in the wrong way. Small towns and big cities across America have witnessed the fanning of flames that have turned neighbor against neighbor and brother against brother, in some cases, Christian against Christian. Most of the agitation preys on the inner fears and underlying prejudices of people that once lay dormant, unchecked, and neatly tucked away until the right words ignited the sparks of hate that were believed to be buried. The root of strife and contentions that have invaded our politics, schools, churches, homes, and communities are steeped in hate. If you are not selling love, then allow me to remind you that the opposite of love is hate and there is not another way to clean it up or dress it up. Call it what it is so wisdom can instruct you on how to overcome in that area of your life. The wise person knows how to calm the hateful wrath in others. The wise person will seek to bring unity in the face of division. The wise person will be a calming voice that reminds those around them of the commonality in opposing opinions and the unity in differing perspectives. When we get to the point where we truly believe that we are "one nation, under God, indivisible, with liberty and justice for all," we will be able to stand in unity around that common cause as we humble ourselves, our need to be right, and prayerfully seek God's face for the healing of our land. Got that, "our land"!

Reference:

Proverbs 11:11, Proverbs 29:9, Isaiah 28:14

WISDOM TIP 300

Wisdom knows when to speak, but wisdom also knows when to be quiet and simply walk away.

"When a wise man has a controversy with a foolish man, The foolish man either rages or laughs, and there is no rest."

PROVERBS 29:9 (NASB)

Note to self, do not argue with a fool. A fool will either become angry and violent or will make light of the entire situation. Either way, it is a waste of time and energy on your part. A foolish person cannot be pacified with wisdom, so do not arouse yourself in the process of trying to get your point across. Wisdom knows when to speak, but wisdom also knows when to be quiet and simply walk away. Find consolation in the fact that you will save your elevated blood pressure for a worthier cause. When we argue with a fool, we become like that fool. Foolishness is so unbecoming on a wisdom seeker. Take the higher route and "walk on by" with your temperance, blood pressure, and reputation intact.

Reference:

Proverbs 17:12, 26:4, Matthew 7:6

WISDOM TIP 301

Master the art of commanding your temper, or your temper will command your life.

"A fool always loses his temper, but a wise man holds it back."
PROVERBS 29:11 (NASB)

"A fool lets it all hang out; a sage quietly mulls it over."
PROVERBS 29:11 (THE MESSAGE)

To mull something over means to pause and think about it in detail over and over again. A person of wisdom, masters the skill of mulling matters over before unleashing a flood of unfruitful emotions. A fool will go "plum off" at the drop of a hat. Literally, you accidentally drop a fool's hat and wait for it ... boom! An overpowering explosion unfit for the occasion. If you anger a fool, you will hear it, feel it, regret it, and pray that you live to tell about it all within a matter of seconds. A foolish person lacks the fruit of self-control, gentleness, patience, and kindness. Actually, a fool lacks just about every fruit of the spirit listed in Galatians 5:22–23. When we fail to master the art of commanding our temper, our temper will command our lives. Mastering your temper has a lot to do with mastering your tongue. When you master the tongue, you will have mastered the inciter of many negative emotions in yourself and in others. On the other hand, learn to hold your tongue and you will slowly sense the negative emotions that incite anger fleeing from your mind and body. Once the emotions flee, you have the opportunity to rationally think over the situation in a sensible mind frame, more conducive to providing a wise response versus an angry response. Put it to practice today and let me know how it works for you. I'm sure you will agree that the results saved bail money as well as relationships, just to name a few.

Reference:

Proverbs 12:16, 12:23, 14:33, 19:11

WISDOM TIP 302

A child left undisciplined will one day bring shame to himself and his parents.

"To discipline a child produces wisdom, but a mother is disgraced by an undisciplined child."

Proverbs 29:15 (NLT)

"Wise discipline imparts wisdom; spoiled adolescents embarrass their parents."

Proverbs 29:15 (THE MESSAGE)

Think of all the unruly people you encounter throughout your day. If you are currently raising children, ask yourself, "Would I want my child to grow into an adult who behaves in such a manner?" If the answer is no, then this wisdom tip is especially for you. If you are still hanging in the balance of excuses, hang out in your local Walmart and just sit and observe for about an hour, and I'm sure you will walk away with an enlightened sense of perspective and urgency to discipline your child promptly and often. An undisciplined child is likened to one who is "allowed to wander unchecked as the wild ass" (Job 39:5). The lack of discipline produces a lack of self-discipline and the behaviors that follow as a result; recall your recent Walmart experience. Hear me parents, when Kevin Jr. tells you no at two years old and you laugh it off as his way of becoming aware of his wants and needs, please do not think it strange when rebellion issues arise when he is twelve going on twenty-two because he now believes he does not have to listen to anyone other than his own degenerate mind. Foolishly indulging our children will ruin them. If they could rear themselves, it would not have taken two people to produce them. Discipline not only produces wisdom, but the awareness of consequences in our children. It also fosters a sense of responsibility. A child left undisciplined will eventually embarrass the liberality right out of you. Wisdom, consequences, and responsibility are all good bullet points for college admission essays and work resumes that will get your children out of your house and into the pool of contributing, taxpaying adults.

Reference:

Proverbs 10:1, 13:24, 17:25, 19:18, 22:15, 29:17

WISDOM TIP 303

Lead with your ears, follow up with your tongue.

"There is more hope for a fool than for someone who speaks without thinking."

PROVERBS 29:20 (NLT)

"Observe the people who always talk before they think—even simpletons are better off than they are."

PROVERBS 29:20 (THE MESSAGE)

The old King James translation of this verse possess this question, "Seest thou a man that is hasty in his words?" Have you seen someone with a mouth almighty, tongue-everlasting that speaks the first thing that comes to his mind in any and every situation without tact? James 1:19 warns us to "Let every man be swift to hear, slow to speak." The Message translation puts it this way, "Post this at all the intersections, dear friends: Lead with your ears, follow up with your tongue, and let anger straggle along in the rear." A hasty speaker is often an ill-advised speaker who speaks without consultation or advice, and takes no thought of the words he will speak or how they will affect those who hear them. A "talk before I think about my words" type of individual has the task of taming the tongue, which also involves taming the heart. Unfortunately, not many have conquered either on their own terms because they will not close their mouths long enough to seek the help required to assist them. James 3:5 puts it this way, "But no one has ever been able to tame the tongue. It is evil and uncontrollable, full of deadly poison." Meaning, no one can tame the tongue alone, it requires accountability and a heart submitted to God and others. If this is you, seek God for the wisdom you need to set your heart and tongue in the right direction. Afterwards, seek a trusted accountability partner to meet with regularly, preferably someone in close proximity with access to your day-to-day life who will offer godly counsel as well as pull your collar when needed.

Reference:

James 1:19; Proverbs 19:2, 26:12, 29:11; Ecclesiastes 5:2

WISDOM TIP 304

Pride makes "yourself great" while humility allows you to be "made great."

"Pride ends in humiliation, while humility brings honor."
PROVERBS 29:23 (NLT)

"Pride lands you flat on your face; humility prepares you for honors."
PROVERBS 29:23 (THE MESSAGE)

Luke 14:11 (GNT) reads, "For those who make themselves great will be humbled, and those who humble themselves will be made great." We are given two options. The first is to "make yourself great." The other is to be "made great." I personally struggle with pride, so I've learned to do the opposite of my first reaction. When we learn to allow our day-to-day actions to attain the honor we are seeking, then pride will be put at bay because the mundanity of our daily tasks often come without glory or honor. For instance, when I separated from the Air Force to stay home with my firstborn, I constantly struggled with changing diapers, washing clothes, and feeding a newborn all day. If my husband were to ask me to do something for him, I would quickly remind him that had a degree in business and was once heralded as the Millennial Airman. Those poopy diapers, soiled laundry, and dirty dishes could care less who I proclaimed to be. If I looked at my resume in pride, my current tasks would humiliate me over and over again as I drifted into the "woe is me," "what have I done with my life" verbiage. However, when I learned to humbly accomplish those tasks for the sake of my daughter, my husband, and what I believed to be the best for our family, then I slowly began to enjoy my seemingly simple daily tasks. The honor came later when others outside of my home began to take note of my organization and how well I maintained the cleanliness of my home. I was not seeking to "make myself great." I had to learn to humbly accept my new position as a stay-at-home mother and others brought the honorable words and accolades as I humbly fulfilled my daily tasks and acts without an audience. You may go years of being unaware of those who have taken notice of your daily actions, but trust me, they have taken notice, and one day, honor will be bestowed upon you for the consistency in which you have humbled yourself for the sake of others. Further, God has taken notice and He will see to it that your faithfulness in the little things will bring you to a position of being "made great" in larger matters.

Reference:

Matthew 23:12; Luke 14:11; James 4:6, 10; Proverbs 15:33, 16:18, 25:6, 11:6; Isaiah 57:15

WISDOM TIP 305

If you are not assisting the outcome of justice, then you are concealing justice as an accomplice to the crime.

"The accomplices of thieves are their own enemies; they are put under oath and dare not testify."

PROVERBS 29:24 (NIV)

"If you assist a thief, you only hurt yourself. You are sworn to tell the truth, but you dare not testify."

PROVERBS 29:24 (NLT)

If you have ever found yourself in the middle of a situation that if you were to tell the truth about it, you would incriminate yourself in a court of law, then nine times out of ten you are most likely an accomplice. Most people will think about the big things like accomplice to a robbery, or accomplice to a home invasion. But what about the seemingly innocent things like downloading a movie, music, or book without reproduction rights. To make matters worse, we don't just download a copy for ourselves, we download copies for various people and share it on social media. In this information age in which we reside, most people never stop to think about who owns the rights to the intellectual property they share. Now that I have your attention, let's dive into weightier matters. If you have important information about a crime, but refuse to come forward with it, even if you were an innocent bystander who witnessed the account, then you, my friend, have just become an accomplice. Withholding truthful information is the same as practicing deceit; if it interferes with the path of justice and judgment, then you have aligned yourself with the person who committed the act. I know it's a hard pill to swallow, but the truth will help the pill go down a little smoother. How about this one. Someone approaches you to purchase equipment you believe may be stolen, but it is such a good price that you shrug off your instinct and purchase it anyway. You are now an accomplice. A five-, four-, or three-finger discount is not worth being implicated in a sting operation! Consider the outcome before you purchase stolen goods, help hide or conceal stolen goods, assist a crime in action, or later remain silent about what you know. Remember, if you are not assisting justice or the outcome of a proper judgment, then you are concealing justice as an accomplice. Choose wisely, you never know when Big Brother may be watching.

Reference:

Leviticus 5:1, Proverbs 1:11–19, Psalm 50:18–22

WISDOM TIP 306

Don't allow the shifting opinions of others to lure you into the trap of being liked over being truly loved.

"The fear of human opinion disables; trusting in God protects you from that."

PROVERBS 29:25 (THE MESSAGE)

"Fearing people is a dangerous trap, but trusting the LORD means safety."

PROVERBS 29:25 (NLT)

The opinions of others are noted with every like, share, and comment on social media. While our technological advancements are great tools to connect us with others, they have also made us more aware of the opinions of others, often making us slaves to those opinions. Caring about what others think is a dangerous trap when it controls what you do, say, or how you value yourself. A person who betrays their moral compass and offends God over offending the person on the other side of their smart phone is in danger and headed toward a life-altering trap of losing their own identity. Don't allow the shifting opinions of others to lure you into the trap of being liked over being truly loved, or being tolerated instead of being respected. False acceptance will ultimately lead to a pitfall of rejection. Seek to please an audience of one and God's love will be a shield of identity protection for you.

Reference:

Luke 12:4, John 12:43, 1 Samuel 15:24

WISDOM TIP 307

Workplace etiquette will take you further than you can imagine.

"Never slander a worker to the employer, or the person will curse you, and you will pay for it."

PROVERBS 30:10 (NLT)

"Don't blow the whistle on your fellow workers behind their backs; they'll accuse you of being underhanded, and then you'll be the guilty one!"

PROVERBS 30:10 (THE MESSAGE)

A little workplace etiquette will take you further than you can imagine. The busy bodies who are always stirring up chaos and suspiciously accusing others of not working, taking too many breaks, or having an office romance are being called out. Again, that small piece of your body called a mouth will get you into more trouble than you can dig out of whether at home, at work, or at play. I am in no way advocating not speaking up against something that is truly wrong, but casting suspension, slandering, or accusing without a justifiable or truthful basis is the warning given in this wisdom tip. Bottom line, don't be the busybody at work who stays in everyone's business. Manage your own projects and workload and you will not have time to be concerned about what your coworkers may or may not be doing. Further, don't get caught up with the current office busybody. We all have them and everyone knows who they are. Find a way to gently inform them that you are not interested in hearing the latest gossip or remove yourself from the circle when the gossip begins. Some other ways to avoid participation is to wear headphones, pretend you didn't hear what they said, or change the subject to the project you are currently working on. For the bold, like myself, just tell them, "I don't have time to listen to all of this I'm too busy focusing on my own work, maybe you should try it out." The workplace etiquette of tending to your own business and working your own desk is a sure strategy of advancement guaranteed to further your career goals.

Reference:

Deuteronomy 23:15, Proverbs 26:2, 1 Samuel 22:9, Romans 14:4

WISDOM TIP 308

Self-righteousness smells like a pile of funk!

"Don't imagine yourself to be quite presentable when you haven't had a bath in weeks."

PROVERBS 30:12 (THE MESSAGE)

Go take a bath and wash off your own funk before you start to comment on how bad you believe I smell. Once you start to smell like the scent of fresh Ivory soap, then maybe your aroma will override mine. This wisdom tip seeks to have you examine the condition of your heart. Are the funky smells of judgment, criticism, and self-righteousness hitting you in the face so hard that you are knocked backwards by the odor? If yes, then it's time for a trip to the original Bath & Body Works. I recommend the scents of self-examination, grace, mercy, humility, and good old-fashioned worry about yourself while leaving other people's business alone. Once you understand the state of your own body odor, compassion for others will cause you to share that pure, crisp scent of forgiveness and love. Freely you have received a sweet aroma, now freely give that same aroma of love to others.

Reference:

Luke 18:11; Titus 1:15–16; Proverbs 16:2, 21:2; Psalm 36:2; Proverbs 20:9; Isaiah 4:4; Job 9:30; Jeremiah 2:22

WISDOM TIP 309

Arrogance is a lofty goal that cannot sustain.

"Don't be stuck-up and think you're better than everyone else."

PROVERBS 30:13 (THE MESSAGE)

Arrogant, stuck-up, high-mindedness will prove to be a snare. Money, possessions, knowledge, and everything else that fits into the pedigree of the arrogant are all fleeting. Not to mention the relationships you will forfeit along the way since most people will not rise to the level of your lofty expectations. When we look upon others with scorn and contempt instead of compassion because our circumstances are more favorable than theirs, then arrogance has begun to creep into the crevices of our hearts and we must take a good hard look at ourselves. Arrogance is a form of pride and we have already foretold the future fall of those who are enamored with pride and conceit. Remember, pride comes before the fall. Let not the arching of your eyebrow or the coiling of your upper lip be in contempt of another person. Instead, make this your declaration, "If not for the Grace of God; there go I." We are who we are and we stand where we stand as a symbol of God's undeserving favor, and as a result of others who have toiled on our behalf. Reach out a helpful hand instead of a judgmental grip.

Reference:

Psalm 131:1; Isaiah 2:11, 5:15; Proverbs 6:17, 21:4

WISDOM TIP 310

Check your circle for the "Gimme" and "Gimme more" twins, then sever their attachment.

"The leech has two daughters: Give and Give. There things are never satisfied, four never say, 'Enough!': Sheol, the barren womb, the and never satisfied with water, and the fire that never says, 'Enough!'"

PROVERBS 30:15–16 (ESV)

"A leech has twin daughters named 'Gimme' and 'Gimme more.' Three things are never satisfied, no, there are four that never say, 'That's enough, thank you!'—hell, a barren womb, a parched land, a forest fire."

PROVERBS 30:15–16 (THE MESSAGE)

A leech is compared to forces of nature that are never satisfied: hell, a woman's womb that has not birthed a child, especially if she posseses a deep desire for children; land yearning for the taste of water during a drought; and a forest fire that will ravage and consume everything in its path until it is completely demolished. A leech's consumption is just as consuming as these four acts of nature because a leech will continue to take and take without ever drawing the conclusion that he has taken too much from his source of charity. A leech will "neva" fix his mouth to say, "Not this time, you've given enough," or something simple as "Let me handle the check this time." What is wisdom attempting to relay to our consciousness with this firm warning about a freeloading, bloodsucking, sponging leech? First, they will in fact take you for everything you have to offer. Secondly, they will never stop unless you take the initiative to stop them. Lastly, kick the leech out as soon as you notice the leechy behavior patterns, or you will live to regret their consumption of your time, your money, your emotions, your talent, and maybe even your last nerve. Another thing, do not try to rehabilitate a leech—it will never be enough. Trust me on this one, many before you have declared bankruptcy on countless levels trying. Make a firm decision to cut ties with the leeches in your life today.

Reference:

Isaiah 56:11–12

WISDOM TIP 311

The safety of exclusivity will save you from the muddled bath of infidelity.

"An adulterous woman consumes a man, then wipes her mouth and says, 'What's wrong with that?'"

PROVERBS 30:20 (NLT)

"Here's how a prostitute operates: she has sex with her client, takes a bath, then asks, 'Who's next?'"

PROVERBS 30:20 (THE MESSAGE)

Ladies, if you are anything like me you are wondering why women are singled out in this proverb. We all know that adultery takes two to tango. Both men and women have prostituted their bodies, lustfully consumed sexual and emotional pleasures with the spouse of another, then wiped their mouths in an attempt to cover up the act by declaring, "I've done nothing wrong." Further, when exposed, some simply move on to the next person as if this lifestyle has become a mode of pursuing and operating in relationships. I've even heard of some men and women who prefer to be in adulterous relationships with married people because of the upfront expectations of no attachments and assumed freedom. Simply put, the decision comes down to what you desire to personally reap in life. If you desire to live a lie, be continuously haunted by the guilt of covering up, or destroy your legacy with a person who will simply move on when they are "found out" or "done with you," then take your bath in deception until the cover up is exposed. However, if the opposite holds true and you desire an honest relationship that is blessed over the years to produce fruit beyond what you and your spouse could ever imagine inclusive of a legacy that will speak for generations to come, then steer clear of adultery and those who may entice you to follow that road. I cannot give you the strategy that will work for you and your spouse, but I can tell you that after more than two decades of marriage, I have followed the simple mantra of "If I wouldn't say it or do it in front of my husband, then I will not say it or do it in his absence." This mantra leaves no room for secrets. From now on, bathe in the exclusivity that you share with your spouse and enjoy the pleasure of knowing that you have both saved your most intimate moments for one another.

Reference:

Proverbs 5:6, 7:13–23

WISDOM TIP 312

Check yourself before the results of foolish living wrecks your life.

"Three things are too much for even the earth to bear, yes, four things shake its foundations—when the janitor becomes the boss, when a fool gets rich, when a whore is voted 'woman of the year,' when a 'girlfriend' replaces a faithful wife."

PROVERBS 30:21–23 (THE MESSAGE)

I'm all for elevating your socioeconomic status, but when it constitutes becoming a tyrant in the process of going from humble beginnings to CEO, then my advice is best expressed in the words of the great poet, Ice Cube, "Check yourself before you wreck yourself!" Likewise, for a woman who has been waiting most of her life for Mr. Right and finally he comes along and puts a ring on it, but you make it your sole mission in life to grudgingly flaunt that ring and your new "wifey" status in the face of all those who said it would never happen instead of placing your time and attention on Mr. Right, check yourself, Boo-Boo! A person with a poverty mentality who comes into a large sum of money with no plan to preserve the money flow beyond the end of the year, chickity … check yourself and your cashflow before you end up broke, busted, and disgusted with your poor spending habits. When a girlfriend replaces a "faithful wife," we all stand in unison, put our hands over our hearts, and yell out with Fred from *Sanford and Son*, "Elizabeth, I'm coming to join you!" because of the shockwaves that reverberate through our entire being.

How can this be? The answer is simple—foolishness! Guard against the results of foolishness being acted out on the stage play of your life. It's all fun and games to read about, may be even laugh about the foolishness you witness in the lives of others, but when you become entrapped by it without recognizing the traumatic results in your own life, then foolishness has successfully wrecked your life in more ways than one. Take a deep, long, hard look at the crazy situations in your life and "Check yourself before you wreck yourself!"

Reference:

Proverbs 19:10

WISDOM TIP 313

Tenacious activity, preparation, accuracy, precision, and unified teamwork are acts that produce success.

> "There are four small creatures, wisest of the wise they are—ants—frail as they are, get plenty of food in for the winter; marmots—vulnerable as they are, manage to arrange for rock-solid homes; locusts—leaderless insects, yet they strip the field like an army regiment; lizards—easy enough to catch, but they sneak past vigilant palace guards."
>
> PROVERBS 30:24–28 (THE MESSAGE)

> "There are four things on earth that are small but unusually wise: Ants—they aren't strong, but they store up food all summer. Hyraxes—they aren't powerful, but they make their homes among the rocks. Locusts—they have no king, but they march in formation. Lizards—they are easy to catch, but they are found even in kings' palaces."
>
> PROVERBS 30:24–28 (NLT)

The four creatures mentioned in these verses are small and seemingly insignificant, yet they show an exceeding amount of wisdom in how they maneuver amongst us humanly "gods" of the earth. Take time to observe and learn from the seemingly "least of them" who, by divine direction and intuitiveness, have grasped the concepts of living wisely. First, the success of these insignificant beings can be attributed to tenacious activity and teamwork, as each one fulfills the job mandated by creation. Likewise, we each have a unique purpose that has been "mandated" upon our creation. A stamp that was designed specifically for us. However, not all have bought into the concept that teamwork really does make the dream work. Another concept is that of preparation. Preparation time is never wasted time. If you stay ready, you don't have to get ready. Think of how much smoother your day would begin if you simply took the time to prepare for it the day before. Now think in grander terms, how much better would your community be with targeted collective preparation? How about your family? Finally, the art of precision can be identified amongst these exceedingly wise creatures. They are precisely accurate with their efforts. I believe this is a direct result of preparation harmonizing with specific mandate. Our efforts should be aimed at a direct target. Again, generating a plan that will allow you to prepare for the mandate you have in life will allow you to precisely and wisely direct your efforts toward the right mark. Finally, observe the unity amongst these creatures. They are unified around a common goal and they precisely attack that goal in unison. If we, human beings, could learn a portion of the art of unifying around a common goal, we could end world hunger, poverty, racism and bigotry, sexism, and every other -ism known to man. Now that you have been inspired to purchase an ant farm for purposes of wisdom observations, go forth with these concepts and determine how their application can transform your focus and your efforts in life.

WISDOM TIP 314

Just as churned milk turns into butter; irked emotions turn into fist fights. That's Bible!

> "If you're dumb enough to call attention to yourself by offending people and making rude gestures, don't be surprised if someone bloodies your nose. Churned milk turns into butter; riled emotions turn into fist fights."
>
> PROVERBS 30:32–33 (THE MESSAGE)

> "If you have been foolish enough to be arrogant and plan evil, stop and think! If you churn milk, you get butter. If you hit someone's nose, it bleeds. If you stir up anger, you get into trouble."
>
> PROVERBS 30:32–33 (GNT)

Like oil and water, some things just don't mix. Evil plans and peace don't mix. Offending people and making friends don't mix. Scheming against your boss and employment don't mix. I think you get the picture. When you churn milk long enough, you will inevitably make butter. Likewise, when you stir up trouble, some type of a dispute will break out. When you stir up trouble against someone in a position of authority over you, you are sure to be left standing with your tail between your legs. That's an old school way of saying you will be caught slipping! A fool doesn't even understand the notion that if you attempt to bite someone's hand, you will likely get bitten back ten times as hard. Stop and think about the consequences before you move forward with words or actions that are designed to rile the emotions of others, eventually leading to a reaction that may not end well for you. Remember these words, "Don't start none, won't be none." Time to put those words into action before a violent dispute breaks out. **Don't push me cause I'm close to the edge, I'm trying not to lose my head.**

Reference:

Proverbs 10:12, 29:22

WISDOM TIP 315

Prepare a premeditated response before the lure of sex and sensuality show up at your front door.

"Don't spend all your energy on sex and all your money on women; they have destroyed kings."

PROVERBS 31:3 (GNT)

"Don't dissipate your virility on fortune-hunting women, promiscuous women who shipwreck leaders."

PROVERBS 31:3 (THE MESSAGE)

The task of conquering the state of temporary insanity that the power of sex and sensuality seems to lure its victims into is a battle of the ages. Many powerful people from the beginning of time have lost it all as a result of this all-consuming predator. The key to not falling prey is to simply heed the voice of wisdom. It has been laid out for you, but you must act on this knowledge that has been presented and come up with your own premeditation plan. Premeditate your response, premeditate your escape route, and premeditate how not to find yourself in a compromising position with someone you are attracted to. While this proverb focuses on men, countless women have also fallen prey to the power of sex and sensuality and found themselves left with the humpty-dumpty broken pieces of life, attempting to put it all together again in the end. All the king's horses and all the king's men couldn't help Humpty because they too had fallen and couldn't get back up again. The good news is that Lady Wisdom is not only a guider but a restrainer as well. Rely on her and submit your most urging desires for assistance and wisdom will empower you with the restraint required to quickly respond with your premeditated plan of action.

Reference:

Proverbs 5:8–11, 7:25–27

WISDOM TIP 316

Be the change you wish to see in the world around you.

"Speak up for those who cannot speak for themselves; ensure justice for those being crushed. Yes, speak up for the poor and helpless, and see that they get justice."

PROVERBS 31:8–9 (NLT)

"Speak up for the people who have no voice, for the rights of all the down-and-outers. Speak out for justice! Stand up for the poor and destitute!"

PROVERBS 31:8–9 (THE MESSAGE)

In the age of cyberbullying, Black Lives Matter, immigration issues, the #MeToo movement, and a politically toxic environment that has somehow spilled over into our neighborhoods, schools, and churches, we, the citizens of humanity, are called to stand up for righteous causes and be the voice for those who are unable to stand up for themselves. Some are physically and mentally impaired, while others are simply paralyzed by fear. Some are stumped by lack of funds or education, while others are simply lacking in courage. While wisdom does not lend itself to speaking up for every matter that appears before you, wisdom will direct you into the specific area where you are designed to speak up, as well as the action in which your assistance will be of the greatest use. The key is to be open in the direction in which wisdom guides you and courageously proceed with the power of heaven backing your efforts. Look around your community, you may only need to look as far as your own address. What situation do you see that could be radically changed if the wisdom of God were made known and applied? If it tugs your heart past the moment of empathy into a decision to act, then you will wisely know that your call for justice has chosen you. Now go and make a difference by being the difference and speak up for righteous causes—not politically correct, not comfortable for your circle of friends, but righteous causes that provoke the heart of God.

Reference:

Proverbs 29:7, Psalm 82:3–4

WISDOM TIP 317

A wife is the crown representing her husband's empire.

> "Her husband has full confidence in her and lacks nothing of value. She brings him good, not harm, all the days of her life."
>
> PROVERBS 31:11–12 (NIV)

> "Her husband trusts her without reserve, and never has reason to regret it. Never spiteful, she treats him generously all her life long."
>
> PROVERBS 31:11–12 (THE MESSAGE)

Before we dive into what constitutes a good woman, let's evaluate the need for a man and a woman to both make a wise choice in who they will "have and hold until death do them part." Men, please read Proverbs 31:10–31 and ask yourself this honest question, "Does my premarital choice represent anything that I just read?" Women, do the same thing. I know it's coined the Proverbs 31 woman, but if you have a man who doesn't measure up to what this phenomenal woman does for her family, then you may want to reevaluate your decision. Now that we understand the importance of making a wise choice in the beginning, it should be very easy for a husband to trust his wise choice without reserve by giving her his full confidence. And ladies, it should be easy to align your actions and motives with the good of your husband, understanding that he has given you an honor that no other woman in his life has been given—his name! You must be careful to honor his name, his reputation, and his well-being if you in fact made a wise choice in the premarital stage. I know this may seem a bit traditional in this millennial generation, but it is the truth of God's Word that does not change. Your husband is your covering and you are his crown. Keep the crown shiny and bright, a representation of your husband for the world to look at and admire him even before having the privilege of meeting him. You are the representation and reputation that precedes him.

Reference:

1 Samuel 25:18–22, 26–27; Proverbs 12:4; Proverbs 31:23

WISDOM TIP 318

For the ladies only: Act like a lady, dress like a lady!

"She is clothed with strength and dignity, and she laughs without fear of the future."
PROVERBS 31:25 (NLT)

You attract what you present! Ladies, please know that this is coming from a good place in my heart. Go cover up with some strength and dignity before you put that outfit on! As a matter of fact, I wish Dillards, Saks, and Nordstrom had a new section entitled the strength and dignity apparel. The anything goes ensembles I see loosely draped across some bodies just should not be displayed in public. What image are you desiring to present to the world? Strength and dignity or an all-you-can-eat buffet of human flesh? The choice is yours but recall my expression, "You will attract what you present!" Strength and dignity does not mean putting your sexy on a shelf to shrivel up and fade away. Strength and dignity are first an inner working that shows in your attitude, your behavior, and ultimately your attire. Not to mention, strength and dignity will attract a man who also represents those same qualities. If you want to continue to run into the men who believe in the "all-you-can-eat" buffet of human flesh selections, then continue to present that mentality in your attire. Any time you decide to switch lanes and come over to the fine dining, a'la carte, one per selection type of man—meaning he selects one and sticks to that choice—then you may want to inbox me about the strength and dignity section coming to a department store near you!

Reference:
1 Timothy 2:9–10

WISDOM TIP 319

The Proverbs 31 mouth has something of value to speak.

"When she speaks, her words are wise, and she gives instructions with kindness."
PROVERBS 31:26 (NTL)

"When she speaks she has something worthwhile to say, and she always says it kindly."
Proverbs 31:26 (THE MESSAGE)

A mouth that speaks wisdom with kindness is gender neutral so try not to get lost in translation with this particular wisdom tip. Do your words minister, care for, look after, or administer to the people who hear them? The Proverbs 31 mouth speaks gracefully with the sole purpose of building up the person on the receiving end. Think about how well-thought-out your words will have to be in order to effectively minister to the person with whom you are speaking. Gossip, slander, idle, and vile talk should find no place on any taste bud of a Proverbs 31 mouth. This will necessitate a retraining of your word palate to acquire the taste for words of the English diction that represent love, joy, peace, patience, kindness, gentleness, goodness, and self-control (Galatians 5:22–23). Yes, the Fruit of the Spirit is necessary to complete this transformation process. Find an accountability partner to keep you in check with this one and let your remodeled Proverbs 31 mouth flow with kind words of wisdom.

Reference:

Proverbs 10:31, 12:18, 16:24

WISDOM TIP 320

You are responsible for what you know.

We are all works in progress. No one will become the epitome of wisdom in this lifetime; however, we are responsible for applying what we know. We are accountable to ourselves, God, and our loved ones to pursue the wisest version of ourselves possible. The good news is that we are not required to pursue this journey alone. My prayer is that this book will simply serve as a guide. I had you, the reader, in mind as I crafted each word. My purpose for each selection is to give Iman, Jayda, Robert, my godchildren, my numerous nieces and nephews, and each of you a tried and true pathway to assist your personal journey. I consider each wisdom tip gifts that will keep on giving when they are taken seriously, reflected upon, and applied to your everyday life. Now that you've read them, go and grow all the wiser!

CPSIA information can be obtained
at www.ICGtesting.com
Printed in the USA
LVHW101058270919
632476LV00009B/11/P